END-TIMES SUPER TRENDS

RON RHODES

HARVEST HOUSE PUBLISHERS
EUGENE, OREGON

Cover by Bryce Williamson, Eugene, OR

Cover Image © Studio-Pro / iStock

END-TIMES SUPER TRENDS

Copyright © 2017 Ron Rhodes
Published by Harvest House Publishers
Eugene, Oregon 97402
www.harvesthousepublishers.com

ISBN 978-0-7369-7025-9 (pbk.)
ISBN 978-0-7369-7026-6 (eBook)

Printed in the United States of America

17 18 19 20 21 22 23 24 25 / VP- SK / 10 9 8 7 6 5 4 3 2 1

*In appreciation for three of my former
mentors at Dallas Theological Seminary, now absent
from the body but at home with the Lord—*

*John F. Walvoord
J. Dwight Pentecost
Charles C. Ryrie*

ACKNOWLEDGMENTS

This book is dedicated to three of my former mentors at Dallas Theological Seminary in the 1980s—Dr. John F. Walvoord, Dr. J. Dwight Pentecost, and Dr. Charles C. Ryrie. All three have now entered into heavenly glory. The insightful teachings of each of these men played a significant role in shaping my views on biblical prophecy. Only eternity will reveal how many people these men spiritually blessed through their many years of teaching.

I continue to overflow with gratitude for Kerri, not only for the blessing she is as my wife, but also as the mother of our two grown children, David and Kylie. Words are inadequate to describe the blessing she has been to each one of us. She is a "virtuous and capable wife" who is "more precious than rubies" (Proverbs 31:10). She has consistently and faithfully stood by me and my work, and I could not have engaged in this life of ministry without her.

Most of all, I express profound thanks and appreciation to our Lord Jesus Christ, who Himself is the heart and center of biblical prophecy. May He be glorified and exalted in this book.

Come soon, Lord!

CONTENTS

END-TIMES SUPER TRENDS

Many trends we see today are disturbing. The Barna Group, after an extensive 2016 study, concluded: "From the most hardened social critic to the most optimistic church lady, Americans recognize that they are living in dangerous and bewildering times. The evidence is everywhere, and it is undeniable."[1] Following is a brief sampling of the typical American experience today:

> The possibility of terrorism striking near home has created substantial—and increasing—anxiety. Fewer American parents than at any time since scientific polling began believe their children will have a better life than they did. Violent crimes have become commonplace, while confidence in the police has plummeted. Distrust of government, social institutions, and businesses is at record-setting levels. People's sense of victimization, powerlessness, and social detachment is unprecedented. Climate change and other environmental challenges baffle people and add to their impression that the world is out of control. The nuclear armament of America-hating nations like Iran, Russia, and North Korea adds to the public's sense of fear. Religion has shifted from providing a sense of peace, purpose, and order to becoming a source of division and confusion.[2]

My friends, the more I understand about Bible prophecy, the clearer it becomes to me that we are living in the end times. The prophetic "signs of the times"—signs accompanied by current prophetic trends—lead me to this conclusion.

A "sign of the times" is an event of prophetic significance that points to the end times. We might say that the signs of the times found in the pages of Scripture constitute God's "intel in advance" regarding what the world will look like as we enter into the end times.

If these are truly the "last days," then we would expect to see certain developments in the world—developments that relate specifically to the end times as prophesied in Scripture. These developments include a falling away from the truth, the widespread embracing of doctrinal error, a significant moral decline, a growing tolerance for all things evil, a widespread outbreak of a variety of sexual sins and perversions, the steady diminishing of religious freedom, the global persecution of God's people, Israel being a sore spot in the world, ever-escalating conflict in the Middle East, efforts being made to rebuild the Jewish temple, the stage being set for a massive invasion of Muslim nations into Israel, the steady rise of globalism, political and economic steps toward the establishment of a revived Roman Empire (a United States of Europe), the emergence of a cashless world in preparation for the antichrist's control of the world economy during the tribulation, and much more. It is sobering—*even a bit frightening*—to recognize that all of these are trending in our present day. I'll prove it in this book.

Trends Are Important

Trends are important. They often help us understand things in our world more clearly, and they help us make important decisions.

- Economic trends help both the government and the business community make financial decisions about the future.

- Investment trends enable investors to pick the most lucrative stocks and mutual funds for their portfolio.

- Consumer trends help marketers profit from the biggest selling products.

- Fashion trends help clothes designers put together their new lines of clothing.

- Disease trends help the Centers for Disease Control respond quickly to prevent or at least minimize outbreaks.

- Crime trends help local police departments make important decisions about patrolling their communities.

- Weather trends help climatologists warn us when bad storms are approaching.

- Trends on Twitter help us to get a feel for hot topics of discussion among the general populace.

End-time trends—*trends that relate to the prophetic signs of the times in the Bible*—help us to understand that we are indeed living in the end times. They also give us a sense of what we might reasonably expect in the near-term prophetic future.

I'll talk a lot about these signs in this book. At the outset, however, I need to emphasize that from a biblical perspective, many of these signs are specifically said to emerge during the seven-year tribulation period that precedes the second coming of Christ. How do we know this? In Matthew 24:3, the disciples asked Jesus: "Tell us, when will all this happen? What sign will signal your return and the end of the world?" In verses 4 and following, Jesus speaks of a number of signs that will predominate during this seven-year period prior to the second coming.

Jesus then instructs: "Now learn a lesson from the fig tree. When its branches bud and its leaves begin to sprout, you know that summer is near. In the same way, when you see all these things, you can know his return is very near, right at the door" (Matthew 24:32-33). In other words, Jesus says His followers ought to be watchful of prophetic signs.

The question for you and me today is this: *Are the prophetic signs that will emerge during the seven-year tribulation period also relevant to us today, even before the tribulation period?* My answer: *Most certainly!* Look at it this way: Just as tremors (or foreshocks) often occur before major earthquakes, so preliminary manifestations of some of these tribulation "signs of the times" are now emerging in our own day. Someone said that prophecies cast their shadows before them. I think this is true. Prophecies that relate specifically to the tribulation period are presently casting their shadows before them. We can logically infer that the stage is now being set for the future tribulation period and the second coming of Christ that follows it.

Dr. John F. Walvoord, one of my mentors at Dallas Theological Seminary, gave a great illustration on anticipating the rapture, an event that could occur at any time. He compared the rapture to Thanksgiving and the second coming of Jesus Christ to Christmas (keeping in mind that the rapture precedes the tribulation period, while the second coming follows it). There are all kinds of signs— TV ads, radio ads, newspaper ads, manger scenes, Christmas lights and decorations—indicating that Christmas is drawing near. The signs are everywhere. But Thanksgiving can sneak up on us. We really don't see obvious signs that Thanksgiving is approaching. But one thing is sure. If Thanksgiving has not yet taken place, and yet we're seeing clear signs for the soon arrival of Christmas, we know that Thanksgiving is all the nearer. By analogy, as we witness the stage being set today for events that will transpire during the tribulation period in anticipation of the second coming of Christ, we can logically infer that the rapture is drawing all the nearer.

The "Super Sign" that Makes Current Prophetic Trends So Significant

While I will mainly address the present and near-term future in this book ("end-times super trends"), I must digress to the 1940s for a moment, for this decade holds a key to the prophetic future. The date Israel became a nation again and declared her independence was May 14, 1948. And what a phenomenally important event this was from the perspective of biblical prophecy (Ezekiel 37:1-14)! Indeed, we might call this a "super sign" of the end times. After all, Israel's rebirth sets the stage for a number of other biblical prophecies—including the return of Jews to the Holy Land from all over the world (Ezekiel 36:24), the rebuilding of the Jewish temple (Daniel 9:27; Matthew 24:15-16), the signing of a covenant with Israel by a world leader who is yet to emerge, the antichrist (Daniel 9:27), and more. Without the rebirth of Israel, these and many other biblical prophecies would make no sense. We might also say that without the rebirth of Israel we shouldn't be wasting our time watching for end-times trends. But because Israel has indeed become a state again, end-time trends take on powerful relevance. Because the super sign has now been fulfilled, the individual signs of the times serve to inform the kinds of trends we should be watching for as we move deeper into the end times.

So that this critically important point is not lost, I want to be sure you understand the biblical basis for Israel being born again as a nation. In Ezekiel 36:10 God specifically promised: "I will greatly increase the population of Israel, and the ruined cities will be rebuilt and filled with people." He then promised: "I will gather you up from all the nations and bring you home again to your land" (36:24).

This reference to a gathering "from all the nations" is highly significant. In biblical times, Israel had been in bondage to single nations, the Babylonians being a great example. After 70 years, God delivered the Jews from Babylon and brought them back to the Holy Land. But never before in biblical history have the Jews been brought back to the Holy Land "from all the nations." It wasn't until Israel became a state again in 1948 that we witnessed the beginnings of this prophecy being fulfilled.

Israel's rebirth is also clearly prophesied in the vision of the valley of dry bones in Ezekiel 37. In this passage, the Lord miraculously brings the bones back together into a skeleton, and the skeleton becomes wrapped in muscles and tendons and flesh, and God then breathes life into the body. There is no doubt that this chapter is speaking about Israel, for we read that "these bones represent the people of Israel" (37:11). Hence, this chapter portrays Israel as becoming a living, breathing nation, brought back from the dead, as it were.

"Dead" is a good way to describe Israel prior to its rebirth. In AD 70, Titus and his Roman warriors trampled on and destroyed Jerusalem and its temple, definitively and thoroughly ending Israel as a political entity (see Luke 21:20-24). Since then, the Jews have been dispersed worldwide for many centuries. In the year 1940, no one could have guessed that within a decade Israel would be a nation again. And yet, it happened. Israel achieved statehood in 1948, and the Jews have been returning to their homeland ever since.

Notice that Ezekiel's vision of the dry bones points to *a process*. The bones come back together, form a skeleton, following which the skeleton becomes wrapped in muscles and tendons and flesh, and then God breathes life into the body. The process begins with Israel's rebirth. The process continues with the Jews progressively streaming back to the Holy Land. The process will culminate when Israel becomes spiritually regenerated toward the end of the tribulation period. At that time, the Jewish remnant will finally recognize that Jesus truly is the divine Messiah, and Israel will become spiritually born again (see Ezekiel 37:5,14; Zechariah 12:10; Romans 9–11).

I can't stress it enough. Israel's new statehood in 1948 was an incredible miracle. God's fingerprints were all over it. Only divine intervention could have brought it about. I love the way prophecy scholar Randall Price describes it:

> The modern return of the Jewish people to the Land of Israel has been called the "Miracle on the Mediterranean." Such a return by a people group that had been scattered among the nations is unprecedented in history. Indeed, the Jewish people are the only exiled people to remain a distinct people despite being dispersed to more than 70 different countries for more than 20 centuries. The mighty empires of Egypt, Assyria, Babylon, Persia, Greece, and Rome all ravaged their land, took their people captive, and scattered them throughout the earth. Even after this, they suffered persecution, pogrom, and Holocaust in the lands to which they were exiled. Yet, all of these ancient kingdoms have turned to dust and their former glories remain only as museum relics and many of the nations that opposed the Jews have suffered economic, political, or religious decline. But the Jewish people whom they enslaved and tried to eradicate live free and have again become a strong nation![3]

Amazing! Just amazing!

Not only was Israel reborn as a nation in 1948, but—as prophesied—the Jews have been streaming back to the Holy Land "from all the nations" ever since. One is reminded of this Jewish return to the land every time someone flies into Israel and lands at the Ben Gurion Airport. Here's a firsthand account of the welcome sign people encounter when arriving at this airport:

> People are greeted by a huge and colorful tapestry welcoming them to the Land. On it is depicted masses of

people streaming into the gates of the City of Jerusalem. On the tapestry, in Hebrew, is a prophetic text from Jeremiah that speaks about the ingathering of the exiles: "So there is hope for your future," declares the LORD. "Your children will return to their own land" (Jeremiah 3:17 NIV). Whether or not the incoming Jewish people can yet read the words, the lesson is understood, for they who are coming home are part of God's present purpose in regathering His people for the fulfillment of His promise.[4]

As we look to the future, I believe Jews will continue to flow to Israel from the United States, from European nations, and indeed, from all the nations of the world, just as prophesied. Meanwhile, my main point remains: *Israel's rebirth is a "super sign" that makes relevant all the prophetic signs of the times that follow.* And it is these signs of the times that inform the prophetic trends we are to watch for in the end times.

I will focus attention on these signs and trends throughout the rest of the book. In the process, I will set forth...

- a *political forecast*—relating to, for example, the Middle East conflict, the nations that will participate in the Ezekiel invasion against Israel, the emergence of a revived Roman Empire, cyber relations among the nations of the world, and the move toward globalism

- an *economic forecast*—relating to, for example, our world becoming cashless, the move toward a one-world monetary unit, and the antichrist's eventual control of the world economy

- a *cultural forecast*—relating to, for example, religion, morality, sexuality, tolerance, and the family unit

Rejoice—God Is in Control!

As is true with all my writings, I pray that this book would not only inform your mind but also touch your heart. I pray that you not only become knowledgeable about the relevance of prophecy for our day, but that this also serves to stimulate your heart with joyful anticipation of the future. Our Lord reigns—*and He is actively at work in our world today.*

Our God is an awesome God whose sovereign plan is unfolding in human history. God asserts, "Everything I plan will come to pass, for I do whatever I wish" (Isaiah 46:10). God assures us, "It will all happen as I have planned. It will be as I have decided" (14:24). In view of such scriptural facts, theologian Robert Lightner advises us:

> When viewed from the perspective of Scripture, history is more than the recording of the events of the past. Rather, what has happened in the past, what is happening now, and what will happen in the future is all evidence of the unfolding of the purposeful plan devised by the personal God of the Bible. All the circumstances of life—past, present, and future—fit into the sovereign plan like pieces of a puzzle.[5]

In like manner, well-known author C.S. Lewis, once a professor at Oxford University, commented: "History is a story written by the finger of God." His point was that God controls nations (Job 12:23-24; Psalm 22:28; Jeremiah 27:5-6; Daniel 4:17), sets up kings and deposes them (Daniel 2:21), and does all according to His sovereign divine plan (Acts 4:27-28). Our God is an awesome God, and He is in ultimate control. That is good cause to rejoice!

The Benefits of Recognizing End-Time Trends

As I close this introduction, allow me to touch on the benefits that come with recognizing end-time trends:

1. This recognition helps us to see that we are indeed living in the end times. That being the case, we ought to follow the biblical injunction to live righteously as we await the coming of the Lord (see Romans 13:11-14; 2 Peter 3:10-14; 1 John 3:2-3). I'll talk more about this in the postscript of this book.

2. Recognizing end-time trends helps us to avoid the prophetic agnosticism that has become so prevalent in our day. The word *agnosticism* comes from two Greek words: *a*, meaning "no" or "without," and *gnosis*, meaning "knowledge." *Agnosticism* literally means "no knowledge" or "without knowledge." More specifically, an agnostic is a person who claims he is unsure—*having no knowledge*—about the existence of God.

Many today have succumbed to *prophetic agnosticism*, claiming that they are unsure (have "no knowledge") about the specifics of prophecy. They typically say that because there are so many views of the rapture (pretribulationism, midtribulationism, posttribulationism, the partial rapture theory, and the pre-wrath view), one cannot be sure about the timing of the rapture. Likewise, because there are different views of the millennium (premillennialism, amillennialism, and postmillennialism*), one cannot be sure about the nature of the millennium. And because we can't be sure about such matters, perhaps we shouldn't spend much time studying prophecy.

Such a viewpoint is tragic given how much of the Bible is prophetic in nature. Out of the 23,210 verses in the Old Testament, 6641 are prophetic. (That's 28.6 percent.) Out of the 7914 verses in the New Testament, 1711 are prophetic. (That's 21.6 percent.) Merging the Old and New Testaments together, 26.8 percent of the Bible—over one fourth—is prophecy. *That's too much to ignore.*

The antidote to prophetic agnosticism is a literal approach to interpreting biblical prophecy. Just as all the prophecies relating to the first

---

* If you are unfamiliar with these "Christianese" terms, don't worry. I will clearly define every term you need to know as we progress through the book.

coming of Christ were literally fulfilled, so the prophecies relating to the second coming of Christ—and all the events that lead up to the second coming of Christ—will be literally fulfilled. As we will see in this book, the end-time trends addressed in Scripture are seemingly finding their initial fulfillments—or the stage is being set for their fulfillment—in our own day. These are exciting times to be alive.

3. *Studying end-time trends helps us to answer scoffers.* Christians are warned in 2 Peter 3:3-4 of the unbelief that will predominate on planet earth in proximity to the second coming of Jesus Christ. We are told that "in the last days scoffers will come, mocking the truth and following their own desires" (verse 3). They will scoff by saying, "What happened to the promise that Jesus is coming again? From before the times of our ancestors, everything has remained the same since the world was first created" (verse 4; compare with John 14:1-3; Acts 1:11; 1 Corinthians 15:23; 2 Corinthians 1:14; Philippians 1:6; 1 Thessalonians 3:13; 4:14-18; 2 Thessalonians 1:10; 2:1; 1 Timothy 6:14; 2 Timothy 4:8; Titus 2:12-13; Hebrews 9:27-28; James 5:7). Jude 18 likewise warns that "in the last times" there will be "scoffers whose purpose in life is to satisfy their ungodly desires."

Christians are increasingly being mocked and ridiculed for their beliefs—especially by a new and more vitriolic breed of atheists, agnostics, and skeptics. Such attacks are easy to answer, however, by pointing to what prophetic Scripture says about end-time trends, and how the initial fulfillment of these prophecies are either taking place in our day or the stage is being set for their fulfillment. One thing among many we might say to the atheist is this: "All I know is that Israel became born again as a nation, just as the prophets foretold; and after that, the Jews have been streaming back to the Holy Land, year by year, just as the prophets foretold. Check out Ezekiel

36 and 37. I don't know about you, but I can't possibly ignore something that the prophets so obviously nailed."

4. A final benefit of understanding end-time trends relates to the scriptural teaching on the imminence of the rapture of the church. The term *imminent* literally means "ready to take place" or "impending." The New Testament teaches that the rapture is imminent—that is, there is nothing that must be prophetically fulfilled before the rapture occurs (see 1 Corinthians 1:7; 16:22; Philippians 3:20; 4:5; 1 Thessalonians 1:10; Titus 2:12-13; Hebrews 9:27-28; James 5:7-9; 1 Peter 1:13; Jude 21). The rapture is a signless event that can occur at any moment. This is in contrast to the second coming of Christ, which is preceded by many events in the seven-year tribulation period (see Revelation 4–18). The fact that we are now witnessing the initial stages of the fulfillment of what prophetic Scripture says about end-time trends indicates that the rapture must be all the nearer.

In view of this exciting reality, let us delay no further. Let us now begin our journey through the prophetic Scriptures and focus our attention on end-times super trends.

> *Lord, by the power of Your Spirit, please enable my reader to understand the prophetic verses we will study throughout this book. Please excite him or her with Your Word, and instill a sense of awe for the person of our Lord Jesus Christ— who is Himself the heart and center of biblical prophecy. I thank You in His awesome name. Amen.*

1

A DEPARTURE FROM THE FAITH: END-TIMES APOSTASY

I once visited a liberal church. The head pastor told me that the Bible is inspired just like Shakespeare is inspired—that is, it's inspiring to read. He also said human beings are not really sinners; they just make mistakes from time to time.

I spoke with the associate pastor at the same church. He told me that it was never God's intention for Jesus to die on the cross. The Jewish leaders simply got angry at Jesus and had Him executed.

Yet another pastor at the church informed me that the "second coming" occurs whenever a person finds God again in his or her heart. There is no literal, future second coming of Christ. This church was obviously in the firm grip of apostasy.

Apostasy comes from a similar-sounding Greek word, *apostasia*, which means "falling away." In the context of this chapter, the word refers to a falling away from the truth. It pictures a determined, willful "defection from the faith" or an "abandonment of the faith."

We find many examples of such apostasy in the Bible. In the New Testament, Judas Iscariot and his betrayal of Jesus for 30 pieces of silver is a classic example of apostasy and its dire effects (see Matthew 26:14-25,47-57; 27:3-10). He defected from following Christ for monetary purposes. Later, in remorse, he hanged himself (Matthew

27:5), after which his body fell headlong and "his body split open, spilling out all his intestines" (Acts 1:18).

We can also point to Hymenaeus and Alexander, who experienced a virtual shipwreck of their faith, having apparently engaged in blasphemy against God (1 Timothy 1:19-20). Yet another example is Demas, who turned away from the apostle Paul because "he [loved] the things of this life" (2 Timothy 4:10).

Scripture warns us of the specific ways people can apostatize. These include a denial of God (2 Timothy 3:4-5), a denial of Christ (1 John 2:18-23), a denial of Christ's return (2 Peter 3:3-4), a denial of the faith (1 Timothy 4:1-2), a denial of sound doctrine (2 Timothy 4:3-4), a denial of morals (2 Timothy 3:1-8), and a denial of authority (2 Peter 2:10).

The apostle Paul, well aware of the dangers of such denials, warned church elders in Ephesus that after he departed, false teachers would rise up who would seek to lead church members into apostasy: "I know that false teachers, like vicious wolves, will come in among you after I leave, not sparing the flock" (Acts 20:29). Paul warned that "even some men from your own group will rise up and distort the truth in order to draw a following" (verse 30).

Scripture soberly warns that there will be a notable increase of apostasy in the end times. In 1 Timothy 4:1-2 Paul lamented: "The Holy Spirit tells us clearly that in the last times some will turn away from the true faith; they will follow deceptive spirits and teachings that come from demons. These people are hypocrites and liars, and their consciences are dead."

It is highly relevant that many of the cults and false religions that pepper the religious landscape today first emerged out of the Christian church. In many cases, they started when the leaders of these groups received an alleged revelation from an "angel"—which we know to be fallen angels or demonic spirits. A classic example is Mormonism, which was founded by Joseph Smith after he received an alleged revelation from the angel Moroni. Another example is Islam, which is based on alleged revelations brought to Muhammad by "the angel Gabriel" (a demonic imposter). In both cases, the revelations that came from these spirits contradict the teachings of the Bible in major ways.

Paul continued his warning about end-times apostasy in 2 Timothy 4:3-4: "A time is coming when people will no longer listen to sound and wholesome teaching. They will follow their own desires and will look for teachers who will tell them whatever their itching ears want to hear. They will reject the truth and chase after myths." My friends, who can doubt that these words describe the very days in which we live? Channel surfing on television yields multiple examples of false teachers espousing doctrines that appeal to people's passions, such as the health-and-wealth gospel.

Paul gets even more explicit in 2 Timothy 3:1-5 regarding the apostasy that will emerge in the end times:

> In the last days there will be very difficult times. For people will love only themselves and their money. They will be boastful and proud, scoffing at God, disobedient to their parents, and ungrateful. They will consider nothing sacred. They will be unloving and unforgiving; they will slander others and have no self-control. They will be cruel and hate what is good. They will betray their friends, be reckless, be puffed up with pride, and love pleasure rather than God. They will act religious, but they will reject the power that could make them godly. Stay away from people like that!

Notice that in the last days there will be *lovers of self* (we might call this humanism), *lovers of money* (materialism), and *lovers of pleasure* (hedonism). Humanism, materialism, and hedonism are three of the most prominent philosophies in our world today, and they often go together in a complementary fashion. These philosophies grow more popular with each passing day.

Of course, prophetic Scripture affirms that apostasy will rise to a fever pitch during the future seven-year tribulation period. Jesus Himself warned: "Many will turn away from me and betray and hate each other. And many false prophets will appear and will deceive many people" (Matthew 24:10-11). Jesus also warned, "False messiahs and false prophets will rise up and perform great signs and wonders so as to deceive, if possible, even God's chosen ones" (24:24). It goes without saying that a counterfeit prophet or a counterfeit Jesus who preaches a counterfeit gospel will always yield a counterfeit salvation, which, in reality, is no salvation at all (see Galatians 1:6-9). That's what makes apostasy so incredibly dangerous.

Apostasy and the American Religious Landscape

There are manifold evidences that apostasy is solidly entrenched in America today. The religious landscape has changed dramatically over the past few decades. One alarming finding is that the unchurched in America (over 150 million Americans) are better categorized as "de-churched." I say this because, according to reliable polls, the unchurched used to be church attenders, but they've now departed from the faith community altogether.[1] In fact, between the ages of 15 and 29, some 59 percent of Americans disconnect from church life.[2] That, my friends, is a departure from the faith!

It is not just that people today are departing from the church. It is also that religious activities, including participating in any kind of religious small group, reading the Bible, and even praying, have declined significantly over the past decade. Many Americans seem to have muscle memory of once being a "Christian," but Christianity no longer plays a role in their priorities or their lifestyle. Christians and Christianity are now background noise to many.

Such individuals are not shy about telling us their reasons for the exodus. They find the Christian church to be restrictive, overprotective, judgmental regarding sexual issues, unfriendly to doubters, antagonistic to science—and they are emphatic in saying that the exclusive claims of Christians are a real turn-off.[3]

Another alarming finding is the powerful and growing resistance to all things Christian among our younger people. In their book *Good Faith: Being a Christian When Society Thinks You're Irrelevant and Extreme*, David Kinnaman and Gabe Lyons observe: "When one-third of college-aged adults want nothing to do with religion, and 59 percent of Christian young adults drop out of church at some point in their twenties, it's the new reality on the ground."[4]

Meanwhile, millennials—people who reached young adulthood around the year 2000—"appear poised to wholeheartedly support the shift away from biblical Christianity and toward new belief patterns." They have little interest in attending Christian church services. They tend to view spirituality as "a private matter to be pursued on one's own terms, in one's own timing."[5] Such individuals often claim to be spiritual without being religious. They obtain much of their spiritual input from social media, the Internet, and other forms of technology. Their "religion" essentially involves a privatized digital religious experience.

In keeping with all this, a 2016 *Newsweek* article titled "Are Americans Becoming as Godless as Europeans?" reports that "American religiosity has been declining for decades." Indeed, "religious affiliation, church attendance and belief in God have all fallen in the US…The overall level of belief is being eroded as people born early in the 20th century are replaced by members of subsequent generations with weaker religious convictions." The article suggests that "children are raised by parents who are less religious than their parents were, and the culture is reshaped with the passing of each generation."[6]

Increasing Skepticism About the Bible

As a person who loves reading the Bible, I find the growing skepticism people have about the Bible especially disturbing. In the past, the Bible played a significant role in shaping American culture, especially its moral values. Today, the Bible has been so marginalized in American society that it plays little if any role.

The Barna Group recently published a book titled *The Bible in America: The Changing Landscape of Bible Perceptions and Engagement*. Their polling results are alarming:

> The steady rise of skepticism is creating a cultural atmosphere that is becoming unfriendly—sometimes even hostile—to claims of faith. In a society that venerates science and rationalism, it is an increasingly hard pill to swallow that an eclectic assortment of ancient stories, poems, sermons, prophecies and letters, written and compiled over the course of three thousand years, is somehow the sacred "Word of God."…The data is trending toward Bible skepticism. With each passing year, the percent of Christians who believe that the Bible is "just another book written by men" increases. So too does the perception that the Bible is actually harmful and that people who live by its principles are religious extremists.[7]

The polls also indicate that many Americans no longer view the Bible as a guide for living a meaningful life.[8] Non-Christian millennials see nothing divine within its pages. The descriptors they use for the Bible—they typically use more than one—are highly revealing: 50 percent say the Bible is a "story"; 38 percent say it is "mythology"; 36 percent say it is "symbolic"; 30 percent say it is a "fairytale"; 27 percent say it is "a dangerous book of religious dogma."[9]

In view of such dismal statistics, can anyone doubt why there is such a high level of biblical illiteracy in America today? Not even half the American public can name the four Gospels. Half of Americans believe a key teaching of the Bible is that God helps those who help themselves. (The truth is that God helps the helpless.) Millions of Americans believe Joan of Arc was Noah's wife. One out of every seven Americans believes Sodom and Gomorrah were people who were married.[10]

Though almost everyone owns a Bible today, it has now become one of the least-read books in America. In his book *The Invisible Bestseller: Searching for the Bible in America*, Kenneth Briggs says: "While it is everywhere in America…and is a standard item in public places from libraries to court houses, it is also famously unlikely to be noticed, let alone picked up and read. It has increasingly become the most revered, invisible feature of our surroundings. It is everywhere and nowhere."[11] He says that "for more and more Americans, the Bible has become a museum exhibit, hallowed as a treasure but enigmatic and untouched."[12]

Tragically, even many churches have reduced the Bible's place in worship and congregational life. In keeping with this reduced use of the Bible, the majority of church-attenders are not involved in any form of evangelism. The majority of Christians—65 percent—no longer share the gospel with unbelievers. Many have acquiesced to keeping their personal religious beliefs private. Less than one in five "are totally committed to investing themselves in spiritual development." Only one in five say that the most important decision they've made is to trust in Jesus Christ for salvation.[13]

Pastoral Defections from the Faith

An increasing number of pastors are defecting from the faith these days. One of many examples is Jerry DeWitt, who has been widely featured in newspapers across the country. DeWitt had been a pastor in the Bible Belt. But the problem of evil in the world tormented him. He couldn't make sense of it. He eventually came to believe that there must be no God. He promptly wrote a book titled *Hope after Faith: An Ex-Pastor's Journey from Belief to Atheism*.

Today there are Internet websites designed to help pastors and Christian leaders adjust to their new lives after defecting from the faith. The *Clergy Project* website claims to be a confidential online community for active and former clergy who no longer hold supernatural beliefs. The website seeks to help members move beyond their former faith. The website also assists members in "coming out"—that is, assisting them in telling their loved ones that they no longer believe.

Another website is *Recovering from Religion*, which affirms: "If you are one of the many people who have determined that religion no longer has a place in your life, but are still dealing with the aftereffects in some way or another, *Recovering from Religion* may be just the right spot for you." The primary focus of *Recovering from Religion* is "to provide ongoing and personal support to individuals as they let go of their religious beliefs."[14]

Some defectors from the faith stay in "ministry." An example is a "dynamic, activist minister" with a loyal following at a Protestant congregation who is now an outspoken atheist. The Reverend Gretta Vosper says, "We don't talk about God," and says it's time the church gave up on "the idolatry of a theistic god." Her church is said to be a haven for nonbelievers "looking for a community that will help them create meaningful lives without God."[15]

This is in keeping with the bizarre claim of some that one can be both spiritual and an atheist. Dr. Anthony Pinn, a professor at Rice University, notes that "there's a growing population of folks in the United States who claim no religious affiliation, and within that category are people who identify as agnostic, humanist, or atheist." He says "there are some millennials who claim they are atheist *and* spiritual. We tend to think of those two things as distinct: an atheist doesn't believe that any of this is real—it's all fictitious—and folks who claim to be spiritual tend to understand that there is something beyond us informing and influencing us, but they just can't deal within institutionalized stuff. So you have this population that's kind of blending these ideas that used to be much more rigid." Pinn suggests, "I think what's taking place is stronger than a trend—this will be the 'new normal.'"[16]

Apostasy and Hybrid Religions

Meanwhile, hybrid religious movements are forming before our very eyes, and these represent yet another form of apostasy that has penetrated the Christian church. One example is the emergence of "Christian Wicca"—or Christian witchcraft. This involves mixing the pagan principles of Wicca with a commitment to Jesus Christ. Christian Wiccans define the Trinity as God, the Wiccan Goddess, and Jesus, all subsumed within "the one." Some even claim Jesus had His own coven with His male disciples. This has become a popular belief system among many teenagers and college students. (If you haven't heard of it, keep in mind that one of their rules is to never tell parents about their involvement.)

Chrislam is another recent movement that advocates that Christianity and Islam are compatible with each other. It is claimed that Christianity and Islam worship the same God, have similar ethical principles, and that both the Bible and the Quran are holy books.[17]

Somewhat surprisingly, Christian psychics have also popped up on the religious landscape. The late Sylvia Brown, who sounded very Christian, was heavily involved in occultism. She often referred to God and Christ and the Holy Spirit during her television appearances. While she was still alive, her website claimed that the Holy Spirit worked through Sylvia, enabling her to contact the dead on behalf of living humans. We were assured that God Himself had given her psychic abilities. At the same time, she mixed in a variety of pagan concepts, such as how both Father-God and Mother-God are infinitely loving, with virtually no wrath.

Sylvia tragically discovered the error of her ways immediately following her death—too late to believe in the true Jesus and the true gospel.[18]

Mysticism, Inclusivism, and the Emerging Church

Today's church has plummeted into various forms of mysticism. The big emphasis is on feelings and affections, not on rational thought. People have rejected an evidential and facts-based faith in favor of an experience-based faith. Within the church, we are now witnessing such things as deep breathing and proper posture, yoga, chanting (like Benedictine monks), the use of mantras (holy words repeated over and over to help one go into a deep meditative state), and contemplative prayer (a mystical form of prayer whereby one experiences a sense of union with God). Such mysticism is a veritable fast-track to apostasy.

Meanwhile, emerging church leaders are busy "reimagining" Christianity. One such leader is Brian McLaren, dubbed by *Time* magazine as one of the 25 most influential evangelicals. Phyllis Tickle, late editor at *Publisher's Weekly*, said McLaren is the Martin Luther for the twenty-first century. McLaren urges that we cannot be certain about a lot of theological matters today. We cannot be certain about biblical inerrancy, divine sovereignty, eternal punishment, exclusive religious claims, any doctrinal distinctive, and any teaching that would exclude other religions. He even states: "If I seem to show too little respect for your opinions or thought, be assured I have equal doubts about my own, and I don't mind if you think I'm wrong. I'm sure I am wrong about many things, although I'm not sure exactly which things I'm wrong about. I'm even sure I'm wrong about what I think I'm right about in at least some cases. So wherever you think I'm wrong, you could be right."[19] This is the Martin Luther of the twenty-first century? I. Don't. Think. So.

McLaren doubts that Jesus is the only way of salvation. He says: "It bothers me to use exclusive and Jesus in the same sentence."[20] He suggests that maybe God's plan of salvation is an *opt-out* plan, not an *opt-in* one. If you want to stay out of the party, you can. Otherwise, you're automatically saved—regardless of whether you're a Christian, a Hindu, a Muslim, a Buddhist, or a member of any other religion or cult.

McLaren then expresses agreement with those who claim that the death of Christ on the cross was nothing less than cosmic child abuse on the Father's part. Alan Jones—whose book *Reimagining Christianity* is endorsed by McLaren—says the cross of Jesus is a vile doctrine: "The Church's fixation on the death of Jesus as the universal saving act must end, and the place of the cross must be reimagined in Christian faith. Why? Because of...the vindictive God behind it." Jones states: "Implicit in the cross [is the idea] that Jesus' sacrifice was to appease an angry god. Penal substitution was the name of this vile doctrine."[21]

I could provide many more examples. Suffice it to say that apostasy has become like a giant octopus whose massive tentacles have attached to all things religious.

Looking to the Future

The various forms of apostasy that have been growing worse through recent years will continue to escalate in the years ahead. The *present* helps us predict the *future*. I think there are six primary battlegrounds where apostasy will show its ugly head more and more:

1. The Bible will increasingly be undermined by liberal critics. The Bible will be portrayed as a human book

with human mistakes. Critics will continue to claim that differences in the manuscripts prove the Bible is not truly the Word of God.

2. Colleges will continue to provide our young with all the ammo they need to reject the Bible, Christianity, and "extremist" Christian morality. The Bible, in particular, will be targeted as being mere myth, legend, and lore.

3. Especially among the young, the Bible will increasingly be viewed as an irrelevant book, meaningless in providing any real help to people living in modern America. Accordingly, increasing numbers of people will continue to disconnect from church life.

4. Mysticism and subjectivism will increasingly be the means by which people discover religious truth. The idea is: *If it feels right, it must be true.* All experiences will be viewed as valid, including those in different religions. This being so, Bible-based and fact-based spirituality will continue to wane.

5. The uniqueness of Christianity will continue to be undermined. The claim will be that there is truth in all religions and there are many holy books—the Bible, the Hindu Vedas, the Muslim Quran, the New Age *Aquarian Gospel of Jesus the Christ*, and many others.

6. Along with the rejection of the Bible, the gospel that saves will continue to be attacked and undermined. The idea that Jesus is the only way of salvation will be anathema to many. *Inclusivism* will be the word of the hour.

I've noted in a number of my books that apostasy will escalate geometrically once the rapture of the church occurs—an event that precedes the seven-year tribulation period. This is an important observation, for at present the Holy Spirit restrains evil and restrains the emergence of the antichrist (2 Thessalonians 2:3-7). Since the Holy Spirit indwells all believers (John 3:16; 14:16-17; 1 Corinthians 3:16-17), He will essentially be "removed" from earth when the church is raptured, thus making possible an explosion of ever-worsening apostasy throughout the world. The antichrist will find it easy to fan apostasy into a flame.

Sobering days lie ahead!

2

ALTERNATIVE RELIGIONS IN THE END TIMES

I've been studying the kingdom of the cults and false religions for decades. I've also written over a dozen books on the subject.[1] I believe the prophetic Scriptures that warn us about the rise of false Christs and false prophets point to the rapid escalation of the cults and false religions in these end times. These cults and false religions are ultimately helping to set the stage for the deceptions that will unfold during the seven-year tribulation period. (More on this a bit later.)

In His Olivet discourse, Jesus warned that "many will come in my name, claiming, 'I am the Messiah.' They will deceive many" (Matthew 24:5). He also warned that "many false prophets will appear and will deceive many people" (Matthew 24:11). He urged:

> "Then if anyone tells you, 'Look, here is the Messiah,' or 'There he is,' don't believe it. For false messiahs and false prophets will rise up and perform great signs and wonders so as to deceive, if possible, even God's chosen ones. See, I have warned you about this ahead of time.
>
> "So if someone tells you, 'Look, the Messiah is out in the desert,' don't bother to go and look. Or, 'Look, he is hiding here,' don't believe it!" (Matthew 24:23-26).

The apostle Paul likewise warned that "in the last times some will turn away from the true faith; they will follow deceptive spirits and teachings that come from demons" (1 Timothy 4:1). Moreover, "a time is coming when people will no longer listen to sound and wholesome teaching. They will follow their own desires and will look for teachers who will tell them whatever their itching ears want to hear. They will reject the truth and chase after myths" (2 Timothy 4:3-4). Scripture also issues strong warnings about those who teach a different Jesus, a different Spirit, and a different gospel (2 Corinthians 11:4; Galatians 1:8; 1 John 4:1).

My friends, these words aptly describe not only the apostasy addressed in the previous chapter, but also the false religions and cults that are so pervasive. There's never been a time in human history when there have been more religious options than there are today. More than ever before, ours is a pluralistic society in which Christianity is just another option in a whole cafeteria of religious choices. We can no longer imagine or pretend that America is a Christian country in which the Christian faith is the only real option. A multiplicity of false religions and cults now pepper our religious landscape.

Let's consider some details.

The term *religion* is somewhat difficult to define. At its most basic level, it embraces a set of strongly held beliefs and values to live by. Most religions have common characteristics, including:

- answers to ultimate questions—such as *Who am I? Why am I here?*

- sacred writings—whether one or many

- religious beliefs and practices (rituals)

- individual (home) and community experiences (churches, temples, mosques)

- ethical principles to live by
- belief in a spirit world beyond the physical world
- belief in some form of an afterlife

Aside from Christianity, the world religions include Islam, Hinduism, Buddhism, Zoroastrianism, Jainism, Sikhism, Taoism, Confucianism, Shintoism, and Judaism. Each of these sets forth false ideas about God, how to be saved, and other important matters.

What about the term *cult*? When I use this word, I do not intend it as a pejorative, inflammatory, or injurious word but simply as a means of categorizing certain religious or semireligious groups. Theologically, a cult is a religious group that emerges out of a parent religion (such as Christianity), but departs from that parent religion by denying—explicitly or implicitly—one or more of the essential doctrines of that religion. Cults include such groups as Jehovah's Witnesses, the Mormons, the Unification Church (now called the Family Federation for World Peace and Unification), the Mind Sciences, Satanism, Spiritism, Baha'ism, the Way International, Wiccans, and the Unitarian Universalists. All of these set forth false ideas on Scripture, God, Jesus, the gospel of salvation, and more.

Many Christians today seem unconcerned about false religions and cults. However, the explosive and relentless growth of such religions and cults is one among a number of indicators that we are living in the end times.

The Numbers Don't Lie

Statistics prove beyond any doubt that false religions and cults have deceived myriads of people. And the deception grows with each passing day.

Islam, for example, is growing at an unprecedented pace. This religion boasts well over 1.3 billion adherents, encompassing over

20 percent of earth's population. Out of the 1.3 billion adherents, between 130 million and 260 million are radical extremists. There are thousands of Muslim mosques in the United States alone, with a new one being built each week. Over 65 nations in the world are Islamic. There is currently a massive Muslim presence in the United Kingdom and France. There seems to be no stopping this religion.

Other world religions are also deceiving vast numbers of people. Hinduism has 851 million followers, Buddhism 375 million, Sikhism 25 million, Confucianism 6.4 million, Jainism 4.5 million, and Shintoism has 2.8 million followers.

The cults used to be on the outer fringes of our society, but today they've gone mainstream. Each year that passes, more people are engulfed in the kingdom of the cults.

For example, there are today some 8 million Jehovah's Witnesses, and over 750,000 of them regularly commit 50 hours or more per month spreading Watchtower doctrines door-to-door. The *Watchtower* magazine, published by the Jehovah's Witnesses, has an average print run of 42 million copies. Jehovah's Witness books are published in more than 300 languages. More than 50 new Jehovah's Witness congregations emerge each week worldwide, and more than 5 million Bible studies are conducted each month with prospective converts.

One of the most significant findings in my research is that a huge segment of the American public believes in spiritistic phenomena. A Gallup poll revealed that 32 percent of Americans—that's more than 100 million Americans—believe in some sort of paranormal activity.[2] Moreover, 38 percent of Americans believe that ghosts or spirits can come back in certain situations. As well, 28 percent think that people can communicate with or mentally talk to the dead.[3]

No longer can Spiritism (spirit contact) be confined to the periphery of our society as a fringe phenomenon. Brooks Alexander, a cofounder of the Spiritual Counterfeits Project, suggests that "Spiritism has moved beyond the weird and the supernatural into the normal and the mundane."[4]

Another poll conducted by the Barna Group found that 7 million teenagers in the United States say they have personally encountered a spirit entity, and 2 million of them claim to have psychic powers.[5] They have no idea of the spiritual danger they are flirting with.

Meanwhile, Wicca (witchcraft) is growing at an astounding pace in the United States. Some estimate that the number of Americans that are Wiccans doubles every 30 months. Every major city in the United States has networks of Wiccans. Today there are more than 200,000 registered witches and approximately 8 million unregistered practitioners of Wicca. Bookstore shelves are loaded with popular books on the subject.

I could allocate another 25 pages to statistics alone. But this brief sampling is sufficient to indicate that we are witnessing an explosion of cults and false religions—and it's a *worldwide* explosion. The deception is enormous. People are being deceived away from the true Jesus and the true gospel on a global scale. This—along with the apostasy in the church addressed in the previous chapter—spells D-I-S-A-S-T-E-R.

A Representative Sampling of False Doctrines

Since Jesus Himself warned us about end-time falsehoods from the mouths of false Christs and false prophets, and since the apostle Paul offered similar warnings, it behooves us to understand the false teachings being set forth today. This will give us a handle on Satan's end-times strategy of deception—for his ultimate goal is to keep people away from the true God, the true Jesus, and the true gospel.

Among the cults and false religions, one typically finds an

emphasis on new revelation from God, a denial of the sole authority of the Bible, a distorted view of God and Jesus, a denial of salvation by grace through faith, and other such denials. While not every cult or false religion manifests every characteristic below (nor in the same degree), these characteristics are quite common. We will see that the deception is enormous, and it is growing rapidly. The following is just a representative sampling—the proverbial "tip of the iceberg."

New Revelation

Many cult leaders and leaders of world religions claim to receive new revelations, either from God or some other spiritual entity. Mormon presidents claim to receive revelations from God. New Agers claim to receive revelations from the "Ascended Masters"— alleged highly evolved beings who seek to enlighten us. UFO cult leaders claim to receive revelations from spiritually enlightened "space brothers." Spiritists claim to receive revelations from the great beyond—such as from dead people or angels. Baha'is claim that the latest and greatest revelation from God has come through the prophet Bahaullah. Christian Scientists believe Mary Baker Eddy received revelations that are necessary for us to understand previous revelations in the Bible. Muhammad claims to have received revelations from the angel Gabriel, which eventually gave rise to the publication of the Quran.

As is typical of cults and false religions, if there is a conflict between the Bible and the new revelation, the new revelation supersedes the Bible. Moreover, if the teachings of the cult or false religion change over time (which often happens), then new revelations supersede the earlier revelations. We see this often in Islam.

Denial of the Sole Authority of the Bible

Many cults and false religions deny the sole authority of the Bible. Christian Scientists, for example, elevate Mary Baker Eddy's book, *Science and Health with Key to the Scriptures*, to supreme authority. Unification Church members elevate Reverend Moon's *Divine Principle* to supreme authority. New Agers place faith in such holy books as *The Aquarian Gospel of Jesus the Christ* and *A Course in Miracles*. The Mormons say there are translation errors in the Bible, and believe *The Book of Mormon, Doctrine and Covenants*, and *The Pearl of Great Price* are more reliable Scripture. The Jehovah's Witnesses are unique, for even though they do argue for the authority of the Bible, you can use only *their version* of the Bible—the New World Translation—and it can be understood only when reading it alongside Watchtower publications, such as *Studies in the Scriptures*.

Meanwhile, Muslims typically claim that the original Bible contained revelations from God, but that the Jews altered the Old Testament and Christians altered the New Testament such that the Christian Scriptures can no longer be trusted. The Quran is considered the superior holy book. Hindus ascribe authority to the Vedas, the Upanishads, and the Bhagavad-Gita. The Buddhist scripture is the Pali Tripitaka. The most important scripture for Zoroastrianism is the Avesta. The sacred texts of Jainism are found in six groupings: Angas, Upangas, Pakinnakas, Chedas, Mulasutras, and Sutras. The scripture of Sikhism is the Granth Sahib. The scripture of Taoism is Tao Te Ching.

We live in a world permeated by many false scriptures.

A Distorted View of God

Many cults and false religions espouse a distorted view of God. The Jehovah's Witnesses are an example, claiming that the doctrine of the Trinity is rooted in paganism and is inspired by the devil. The Way International likewise says the "false doctrine of the Trinity" is rooted in ancient pagan religions. New Agers believe that all in the universe is God (pantheism). Mormons believe human beings can become gods, and therefore there are many gods in the universe (polytheism). They also redefine the Trinity in terms of tritheism (belief in three separate gods). Witches and Wiccans believe in a mother goddess (paganism). Oneness Pentecostals believe Jesus is the one God, and that He Himself is the Father, the Son, and the Holy Spirit (modalism). The Unitarian Universalists deny the doctrine of the Trinity (they are Uni-tarians).

Meanwhile, Muslims hold to a form of radical monotheism, staunchly denying that God is a Trinity. Muslims also staunchly deny Christ's deity, arguing that there is no such thing as a "son of God."

Early Hinduism was polytheistic. Eventually, three gods became preeminent: Brahma (the Creator), Vishnu (Preserver), and Shiva (Uniter/Destroyer). Behind the many gods of Hinduism stands the one monistic reality of Brahman—the "Universal Soul."

In Zoroastrianism, there are two opposing forces: Ahura Mazda, the Lord of Wisdom, is the one true God and benevolent Creator of life. He is aided by good spirits or angels (ahuras). Against these good spirits is the evil and destructive Angra Mainyu, who is aided by demonic spirits (daevas).

In Jainism, there is no supreme Creator-God. Rather, there are innumerable lesser gods (tirthankaras). These lesser gods are not outside of (or above) the present cosmos but are just a little higher than humans.

In Shinto, local deities (kami) are numberless. Such gods can indwell objects in the material world. They can be helpful or harmful.

Distortions of the doctrine of God today are seemingly endless.

A Distorted View of Jesus Christ

Another common mark of cults and false religions is that they deny the full deity of Jesus Christ. The Jehovah's Witnesses hold that Jesus was created by the Father billions of years ago as the Archangel Michael, and is hence a lesser god than the Father, who is "God Almighty." The Mormons argue that Jesus was born as the first and greatest spirit child of the Heavenly Father and Heavenly Mother, and was the spirit-brother of Lucifer. Spiritists say the human Jesus became the Christ through reincarnation. Some New Agers believe the human Jesus attained Christhood by learning from gurus as a child in India. UFO cults suggest that Jesus was a hybrid being—half human and half alien (thus accounting for His miracles). Members of the Baha'i faith argue that Jesus was just one of many manifestations of God throughout history. Unitarian Universalists deny that Jesus was God, and argue that He was basically a good moral teacher. The Jesus of psychic Edgar Cayce is a being who in his first incarnation was Adam and in his thirtieth reincarnation became "the Christ" (the sinner and the Savior are found in the same person).

Meanwhile, Islam teaches that Jesus was not God and was not the Son of God, but rather was simply a prophet to Israel—lesser than the prophet Muhammad. In Hinduism, Jesus is believed to have attained God-realization and was thus an enlightened guru. He was not a Savior, nor the Son of God, nor did He rise from the dead. In Buddhism, Jesus is considered an enlightened master.

There is no shortage of false ideas about Jesus Christ today.

A Distorted View of Christ's Work at the Cross

Cults and false religions not only deny the full deity of Jesus Christ, they also have a wildly distorted view of His salvific work at the cross. Jehovah's Witnesses say Jesus died on a stake (not a cross) as a mere man (not the God-man), and He died for the sins of Adam. The Mormons claim the work of Christ on the cross provided for the ultimate resurrection of all people, but did not provide individual salvation from sin's guilt and condemnation. Many New Agers say Jesus died to balance world karma. Reverend Moon of the Unification Church believed Jesus did not complete the work of redemption, and hence the Lord of the Second Advent (Reverend Moon) came to complete the job. Meanwhile, Islam denies that Jesus was crucified or died for the sins of humankind. Rather, He was simply caught up to Allah's presence without experiencing death.

The cross is truly in the crosshairs today.

A Distorted View of the Holy Spirit

Cults are well known for their distorted views of the Holy Spirit. The Jehovah's Witnesses deny the Holy Spirit's personality and deity, and argue that the Spirit is simply God's impersonal "active force" for accomplishing His will and purpose in the world. The Way International also interprets the Holy Spirit as the force of God. The Children of God believe the Holy Spirit is the feminine aspect of God, and is often depicted as a sensuous woman. Some New Agers equate the Holy Spirit with the Chi force—an impersonal energy often associated with Taoism. Oneness Pentecostals argue that the Holy Spirit is simply one of the modes in which Jesus Christ manifests Himself. In the Mind Sciences, the Holy Spirit is interpreted not to be the third person of the Trinity but rather is Divine Science itself.

Such confusion!

A Distorted View of Humankind

Not surprisingly, many cults and false religions espouse a distorted view of humankind. New Agers believe human beings are a part of God and hence can create their own realities. Mind Science enthusiasts believe the same. Mormons believe that through a long process of eternal progression, human beings may become exalted to godhood, just as the heavenly Father was. Scientology teaches that every human being in his true identity is a thetan (pronounced "thay'-tn")—an immortal god-like spirit. The Raelians, a UFO cult, teach that human beings were long ago planted on planet earth by advanced aliens.

Madness!

Denial of Salvation by Grace

Of great concern is the fact that cults and false religions typically deny salvation by grace, thus distorting the purity of the gospel. The Mormons emphasize the necessity of becoming increasingly perfect in this life. Justification by faith alone is said to be a "pernicious doctrine." The Jehovah's Witnesses emphasize the importance of distributing Watchtower literature door-to-door as a part of "working out" their salvation. They must dedicate their lives to Jehovah and remain faithful to Him to the end for fear of losing salvation. Oneness Pentecostals say that to be saved, one must have faith in Christ, repent of all sins, be baptized in water in the name of Jesus only, be baptized in the Holy Spirit as evidenced by speaking in tongues, and obey the holiness code throughout life.

Meanwhile, Muslims believe that only those who submit to Allah may be saved. In the end, good deeds and bad deeds will be weighed, and those found worthy by Allah *may* go on to paradise—but it's not a sure thing.

In Hinduism salvation comes when one realizes that one's individual soul (atman) is identical with the Universal Soul (Brahman). Through numerous deaths and rebirths (reincarnation), one finally comes to this realization, after which one is freed from the bondage of life and achieves absolute unity with Brahman.

In Buddhism, salvation comes through following the "eight-fold path": (1) right worldview; (2) right intention; (3) right speech;

(4) right action; (5) right livelihood; (6) right effort; (7) right mindfulness; and (8) right contemplative absorption.

In Zoroastrianism, a person's ultimate fate hinges on whether he or she sides with the benevolent Ahura Mazda or the evil Angra Mainyu. In deciding for the good, each person must resist the influence of the daevas and focus on holiness, pure thoughts, good words, and good deeds. If one's good deeds outweigh one's bad deeds at the future judgment, one can be saved.

Those who believe in Jainism base their view of salvation on reincarnation. The soul is believed to be liberated—released from matter—when it becomes unfettered from the effects of karma. To attain this state, one must engage in asceticism to eliminate all previous karma and live in moral sobriety to prevent accumulating new karma.

In Sikhism, sins are removed by repeating and meditating on Sat Nam ("True Name"). Each person must become God-focused, live selflessly, engage in charity, and live morally.

I could cite many further examples. Suffice it to say that in the cults and world religions, salvation is all about *works, works, works.* The deception is enormous—staggering beyond belief.

The Ultimate Source of the Deception

Immense doctrinal deception exists in the false world religions and the kingdom of the cults. But I want to pause a moment and ask you a question: *Who do you think is ultimately behind all these false teachings?*

I believe it is Satan. Jesus said in John 8:44: "He has always hated the truth, because there is no truth in him. When he lies, it is consistent with his character; for he is a liar and the father of lies." In keeping with his role as the father of lies, Satan is also continuously involved in blinding people from the truth: "Satan, who is the god of this world, has blinded the minds of those who don't believe. They are unable to see the glorious light of the Good News" (2 Corinthians 4:4).

Satan's deviousness is evident in all the counterfeits he has inspired through the centuries. It was Augustine who called the devil *Simius Dei*—"the ape of God." Satan is the great counterfeiter. He deceptively mimics God in many ways. He loves to masquerade as an "angel of light" (2 Corinthians 11:14). Consider his deceptions:

- Satan has his own *church*—a "synagogue" that "belongs to Satan" (Revelation 2:9).
- Satan has his own *ministers*—ministers of darkness who bring false sermons (2 Corinthians 11:4-5).
- Satan has formulated his own *system of theology*, which are "teachings that come from demons" (1 Timothy 4:1; see also Revelation 2:24).
- His ministers proclaim his *gospel*—"a different kind of Good News than the one we preached to you" (Galatians 1:7-8).
- Satan has his own *throne* (Revelation 13:2) and his own *worshippers* (13:4).
- Satan inspires false *Christs* and self-constituted *messiahs* (Matthew 24:4-5).
- Satan employs false *teachers* who bring in "destructive heresies" (2 Peter 2:1).
- Satan sends out false *prophets* (Matthew 24:11).
- Satan sponsors false *apostles* who imitate the true (2 Corinthians 11:13).

Satan—A Master Niche Marketer of False Ideas

Satan has become a master niche marketer of false ideas in these last days. There's virtually something for everyone in the kingdom of the cults as well as the various false religions. Satan provides a variety of deceptive options to satisfy peoples' varied desires. Those who find appeal in being their own gods might look to the New Age movement or to Mormonism. If personal empowerment and creating your own reality appeals to you, then (again) the New Age movement might be for you. If you like health and wealth, then the Word-Faith movement might be just for you. If you don't like the ideas of pain, suffering, and death, then Christian Science might be your ticket (since pain, suffering, and death are denied in this cult). If you're more interested in contacting dead loved ones, then perhaps Spiritism is your ticket. Do you like the idea of living many lives through reincarnation? Then maybe Hinduism is for you.

As I said, Satan is a master niche marketer of false ideas. With each cultic group and false religion, he seeks to keep people away from the true God, the true Jesus, and the true gospel. It is no wonder that Scripture exhorts Christians to beware of Satan's "evil schemes" (2 Corinthians 2:11).

A Central Role in the Fulfillment of Prophecy?

One of the oddities about the cults is that they often see themselves as playing a central role—if not *the* central role—in the fulfillment of end-times biblical prophecy. Just a few examples will suffice:

Joseph Smith, the founder of Mormonism, edited the King James Version of the Bible, deleting certain parts and adding others. He called his Bible the "Inspired Version." He inserted a prophecy of himself in Genesis 50. Thus, when Smith came on the scene in the 1800s, he was seen as a fulfillment of prophetic Scripture. The Mormons are also called Latter-Day Saints, pointing to their identity as God's end-times people.

The Jehovah's Witnesses have often portrayed themselves as God's only end-time witnesses, bearing testimony prior to the unleashing of Armageddon, which is allegedly right around the corner. They believe they are the only ones on earth who will survive this worldwide catastrophe. The Watchtower Society, which governs all Jehovah's Witnesses, has made many false prophecies through the years, including that in 1914 Jehovah would overthrow all human governments and set up His own government on earth. They repeated this same prophecy in 1975.

The Unification Church (Family Federation for World Peace and Unification) often cites Revelation 7:2-4, which speaks of an angel who will come from the east with a seal of God. This allegedly means that the "second messiah" (Reverend Moon) would be born somewhere in the East. Moonies reason that Korea is the only viable country, for Japan worships pagan gods and China is a communist country. Reverend Moon, of course, was born in Korea, and he is viewed as a second messiah.

According to the Baha'i faith, the references to the second coming of Christ in the Bible were fulfilled in the coming of the great prophet Bahaullah. He is said to be the promised Messiah, and his teachings supersede those of Jesus and the New Testament. Baha'is realize that Christians continue to talk about the second coming as the personal return of Jesus, but these Christians are mistaken. The Christian Bible has purportedly been misunderstood for several millennia by Christian clergy, and the proper understanding comes through Baha'i, which is viewed as the true form of Christianity. Just as the ancient Jews misunderstood the Old Testament Scriptures and therefore opposed Jesus, so Christians today have misunderstood Scripture and are thus in opposition to Bahaullah.

These and other cults that make similar claims are misguided and have been blinded by the father of lies, Satan (John 8:44). Meanwhile, they continue to deceive the masses of humanity.

The Present and the Near-Term Future

The present deception promulgated by false religions and cults is immense, and it's going to get even worse in the coming years. What is taking place now is simply setting the stage for the ultimate deceptions that will fall during the future seven-year tribulation.

Today we often talk about false Christs. In the future tribulation period, the antichrist will emerge as the ultimate false Christ.

Today we talk about false prophets. In the future tribulation period, *the* false prophet will emerge. He will be the first lieutenant—the right-hand man—of the antichrist. He will be the ultimate false prophet.

Today we talk about distorted views of the Holy Spirit. In the future tribulation period, the antichrist will be energized by the *un*holy spirit—Satan himself.

Likewise, today we talk about distorted views of the Trinity. In the future tribulation period, we will witness the ultimate distortion of the Trinity—the antichrist, the false prophet, and Satan.

These are days for discernment.

3

ANYTHING GOES:
END-TIMES MORAL DECLINE

In the introduction of this book, I noted that prophetic Scripture provides us with specific "signs of the times." These signs help us to see that we are living in the end times. We might say that the signs constitute God's "intel in advance" regarding what the world will look like as we enter into the end times.

There are a variety of such signs in prophetic Scripture. The "super-sign" is the rebirth of Israel as a nation, an event that took place in 1948. Beyond that, there are also *national-alignment signs* (relating to, for example, the Muslim nations that will join together to invade Israel in the end times), *religious signs* (including the rise of false prophets and false Christs), *technological signs* (an example is our increasingly cashless world, which will make it easy for the antichrist to control the world economy), *earth-and-sky signs* (such as the sun darkening and the moon turning red), and *moral signs*.

The moral signs of the times, like the other signs of the times, generally relate to the future seven-year tribulation period. The apostle Paul in 2 Timothy 3:1-5 describes the kind of morality that will prevail during these years: People will love themselves, love their money (they'll be very materialistic), be full of pride, boast to others, disrespect and disobey their parents, be thoroughly ungrateful for what they have, have no concept of what it means to love and forgive others, slander other people, lack self-control in their behavior, act cruelly toward others, hate all things that are good, betray their own friends, and be intensely in love with pleasure instead of God (they'll be hooked on hedonism).

Jesus also prophesied that people will be preoccupied with partying it up in the end times:

> "When the Son of Man returns, it will be like it was in Noah's day. In those days before the flood, the people were enjoying banquets and parties and weddings right up to the time Noah entered his boat. People didn't realize what was going to happen until the flood came and swept them all away. That is the way it will be when the Son of Man comes" (Matthew 24:37-39).

While these passages specifically refer to the future tribulation period, we see preliminary manifestations of these prophecies in our own day. These prophecies indicate that people in the end times will be primarily concerned with *self* and *self-gratification*. People will have little concern for moral living.

"I Have My Own Truth"

Today moral relativism reigns supreme. The philosophy of life that many ascribe to can be summarized in one sentence: "Whatever works for you is your moral truth; whatever works for me is my moral truth." If all truth is relative, then one person's "truth" is just as good as another person's "truth." Christian apologist Elliot Miller put it this way: "It is the height of presumption to think that one knows the key truth for all people. On the other hand, it is the apex of love to 'allow' others to have their own 'truth.'"[1] Today an unspoken commandment seems to be, "Thou shalt not interfere with another person's reality."

David Kinnaman and Gabe Lyons, in their book *Good Faith:*

Being a Christian When Society Thinks You're Irrelevant and Extreme, suggest that today, "the greatest sin you can commit is saying someone else is wrong. No matter how nicely you disagree, it is a real possibility that you could be thrown into the proverbial furnace reserved for social outcasts and cultural traitors."[2]

Christian thinker Carl F.H. Henry lamented more than two decades ago that the West had lost its moral compass.[3] It has only gotten worse. There's no way to tell which way is north and which way is south when it comes to right and wrong. America is engulfed in a sea of moral confusion.

As we accelerate down the road where moral relativity takes us, there is no absolute truth, "no center stripe down the highway of life."[4] There are many casualties on this highway. As Christian journalist Russell Chandler put it, "The loss of objective authority and a transcendent morality has infected our national ethical foundations with a sickness nigh unto death."[5]

Me, Myself, and I

In today's world, it seems that *self* now reigns supreme. George Barna conducted a poll and concluded that "the broader culture has adopted self-fulfillment as its ultimate measure of moral good. The shift that is underway moves authority from outside ourselves (for example, the Bible) to within us."[6] What is good for the self has become the spiritual and moral compass for the vast majority of adults, while the Bible has been quietly relegated to a storage box in the closet. One report tells us: "A majority of Americans, including three-quarters of Millennials,* say that morality is based solely on their personal feelings. In a poll of 1,237 people, 57 percent agreed that 'whatever is right for your life or works best for you is the only truth you can know,' while 74 percent of Millennials affirmed the statement."[7]

---

* A "Millennial" is a person reaching young adulthood around the year 2000.

Researcher and cultural analyst David Kinnaman concludes that "the highest good, according to our society, is 'finding yourself' and then living by 'what's right for you.'" Even church members reflect this view. Kinnaman laments that "while we wring our hands about secularism spreading through culture, a majority of churchgoing Christians have embraced corrupt, *me-centered* theology." Indeed, "the morality of self-fulfillment is everywhere, like the air we breathe." We are told that "if something or someone stands in the way of my fulfillment, that obstacle must be removed. That person represents the enemy, the embodiment of evil."[8]

I find myself reflecting on how all this is not unlike the attitude of the Israelites during the time of the judges: "In those days Israel had no king; *all the people did whatever seemed right in their own eyes*" (Judges 21:25, emphasis added). Everyone made up their own rules. Each person was a law unto himself or herself. We see the same kind of attitude today. It seems that anything can be true for the individual, but nothing can be true for everyone. In other words, *there are no absolute moral truths*.

"Anything Goes"

Because people are now making moral decisions based not on the Bible but rather on *self*, they have a much more liberal attitude on a variety of ethical issues. For example[9]:

- 71 percent of Americans now believe that divorce is morally acceptable. Ignored is the fact that God Himself created marriage, and He intended it to be permanent (Genesis 2:18-25; Matthew 19:4-6). God hates divorce (Malachi 2:16). Marriage in the Bible was intended to be dissolved only when one of the marriage partners dies (Romans 7:1-4; 1 Corinthians 7:8-11; 1 Timothy 5:14).

- 68 percent of Americans now believe that sex between an unmarried man and unmarried woman is okay. Ignored is the fact that Scripture affirms that the body is not for fornication and that a person should flee it (1 Corinthians 6:13-18). Fornication should not even be named or spoken of among those who call themselves Christians (Ephesians 5:3 ESV).

- 63 percent of Americans now believe that cohabitation—living together outside of the bonds of marriage—is okay. Ignored is the fact that God Himself instituted marriage, and Scripture instructs that if a man and woman are sexually attracted to each other, "they should go ahead and marry" (1 Corinthians 7:9).

- 63 percent of Americans believe it is okay to enjoy sexual thoughts or fantasies about someone other than one's spouse. Ignored is Jesus' injunction to maintain purity in one's thought life: "You have heard the commandment that says, 'You must not commit adultery.' But I say, anyone who even looks at a woman with lust has already committed adultery with her in his heart" (Matthew 5:27-28).

- 63 percent of Americans believe that gay or lesbian relations are okay. Ignored is the fact that Scripture consistently calls homosexuality a sin (Leviticus 18:22; Romans 1:26-27; 1 Corinthians 6:9-10).

- 61 percent of Americans believe it is fine to have a baby out of wedlock. Ignored is the biblical emphasis that childbearing should take place within the marriage relationship (Genesis 1:28; 1 Timothy 5:14; Titus 2:3-5).

- 69 percent of Americans believe "euthanasia is

acceptable, and more than half of them support doctor-assisted suicide…Fifty-one percent of Americans say they would consider ending their own lives if diagnosed with terminal illness."[10] As well, 40 percent of Christians agree with the practice.[11] Ignored is the fact that issues of life and death properly lie in the sovereign hands of God alone (Job 14:5; Psalm 139:16). Euthanasia and suicide violate the sixth of the Ten Commandments: "You must not murder" (Exodus 20:13).

• 53 percent of Americans agree that it's okay to have a sexual relationship with someone of the opposite sex to whom you are not married. Ignored is the fact that adultery is consistently condemned in Scripture (Exodus 20:14; Leviticus 20:10; Matthew 5:27-28; Hebrews 13:4).

We also find God's Word consistently ignored when it comes to pornography. At present, 34 percent of Americans believe that viewing pornography is morally acceptable. There is, however, a significant gender gap: "Almost twice as many men (43%) approve of pornography as do women (25%)."[12]

Of greater concern is that the Gallup organization has noticed over a five-year period "a consistent gradual shift toward more people accepting the practice and fewer disapproving."[13] We are witnessing a definite uptrend on the acceptability of pornography.

Related to all this is "revenge porn," a somewhat recent phenomenon. This involves the disseminating of sexual images without consent by one person in a partnership that has gone sour. Here's the typical scenario: When a couple breaks up, one of them may post intimate pictures of the other person on the Internet to get even. This means that "the Internet and social media are increasingly being used to control, terrorize, and humiliate." And according to one analysis, "it is well-nigh impossible to police, prevent, or stop online perpetrators."[14] This vicious practice is also trending upward.

Any use of porn is off-limits for the Christian. The apostles urged all Christians to abstain from any form of sexual immorality (Acts 15:20). Paul said that the body is not for sexual immorality and that a person should flee it (1 Corinthians 6:12-20). Jesus indicated that we must guard our minds in this regard (Matthew 5:27-28). (I will address sex and gender issues in more detail in chapter 7.)

The Moral Crisis We Face

In view of such facts, it is not surprising that many people see America as now facing a moral crisis. The polls prove it. Barna says, "In general, Americans are aware that the nation's moral values are abysmal...Only one out of five adults (19 percent) has a positive evaluation of the nation's values, while four out of five (79 percent) have a negative view...By more than a three-to-one margin, adults contend that people's morals are getting worse (72 percent) rather than improving (22 percent)."[15] A Gallup poll likewise concludes that "over a 15-year trend, solid majorities have consistently viewed the direction of the country's values negatively."[16]

One could reasonably argue that the gutter-level morality of Americans seems much more akin to Sodom and Gomorrah than to the kingdom of God. A little compare and contrast is highly revealing. Americans say we can find moral guidance by looking to *self*, while the kingdom of God instructs us to look outside of *self* for moral guidance—that is, look to Scripture and the life of Christ. Americans say it is unloving to criticize someone else's lifestyle, while the kingdom of God instructs that we speak up *precisely because* we love people, and that being loving does not mean being silent. Americans say we find our greatest joy in pursuing the things we desire, while the kingdom of God instructs that joy is found in giving to and blessing other people. Americans say our big goal in life should be personal enjoyment, while the kingdom of God instructs that we find our highest joy in glorifying God. Americans say that any kind of sexual relationship between consenting adults is fine, while the kingdom of God instructs that sexual joy is reserved for the marital relationship, and that sex outside of marriage leads only to spiritual and emotional injury.[17]

Oh, how America has turned from the kingdom of God. As one analyst put it, "Christian morality is being ushered out of American social structures and off the cultural main stage, leaving a vacuum in its place—and the broader culture is attempting to fill the void."[18]

While the world does not want to hear it, the truth is that absolute morals—such as "You must not murder" (Exodus 20:13)—are grounded in the absolutely moral God of the Bible. Scripture tells us: "You are to be perfect, even as your Father in heaven is perfect" (Matthew 5:48). Moral law flows from the moral Lawgiver of the universe—God. And God stands against moral relativists whose behavior is based on "whatever seemed right in their own eyes" (Judges 17:6; 21:25; Deuteronomy 12:8; Proverbs 21:2). Since there is an absolutely moral Creator-God (Isaiah 44:24) who has communicated precisely what moral behavior He expects (Exodus 20:1-17), then we as His creatures are responsible to render obedience (Deuteronomy 11:26-28).

But alas—such truths do not resonate with today's culture. Such ideas are relegated to the ancient past. Today, people are far more interested in *happiness* than in *holiness*. They yearn more for *pleasure* than for *pursuing God*. It's a recipe for national disaster.

Will the USA Morally Implode?

Because of the ever-escalating moral and spiritual degeneration in this country, it is entirely possible that God may bring judgment upon it. I hate saying it. Christian leaders have been warning about this for decades, and their warnings are typically met with deaf ears, much like prophets were often ignored during Old Testament times.

Scripture reveals that God is absolutely sovereign (Psalm 50:1; 66:7; 93:1; Proverbs 19:21; Isaiah 14:24; 46:10), and in His sovereignty He blesses nations that submit to Him and brings down nations that rebel against Him. In the book of Job we read, "He builds up nations, and he destroys them. He expands nations, and he abandons them" (Job 12:23). Daniel 2:21 tells us that God "controls the course of world events; he removes kings and sets up other kings."

In view of such scriptural facts, one must wonder if America is ripe for judgment. Let's review the pertinent facts:

- God is absolutely sovereign over the nations.
- Both the Old and New Testaments affirm that God is a God of judgment.
- America is presently in a free fall, plummeting morally and spiritually, with no repentance in sight.
- It is therefore reasonable to expect that God may sovereignly judge America in the end times for turning away from Him.

Those who doubt the possibility of God's judgment against America should consult what the apostle Paul affirmed in Romans 1:18-21,24-28 (it's long, but well worth the read):

> God shows his anger from heaven against all sinful, wicked people who suppress the truth by their wickedness. They know the truth about God because he has made it obvious to them. For ever since the world was created, people have seen the earth and sky. Through everything God made, they can clearly see his invisible

qualities—his eternal power and divine nature. So they have no excuse for not knowing God.

Yes, they knew God, but they wouldn't worship him as God or even give him thanks. And they began to think up foolish ideas of what God was like. As a result, their minds became dark and confused...

So God abandoned them to do whatever shameful things their hearts desired. As a result, they did vile and degrading things with each other's bodies. They traded the truth about God for a lie. So they worshiped and served the things God created instead of the Creator himself, who is worthy of eternal praise! Amen. That is why God abandoned them to their shameful desires. Even the women turned against the natural way to have sex and instead indulged in sex with each other. And the men, instead of having normal sexual relations with women, burned with lust for each other. Men did shameful things with other men, and as a result of this sin, they suffered within themselves the penalty they deserved.

Since they thought it foolish to acknowledge God, he abandoned them to their foolish thinking and let them do things that should never be done.

If this passage tells us anything, it is that when a nation willfully rejects God and His Word, turning its back on His moral requirements, God eventually reveals His wrath against that nation. God has a long track record of wrath against ungodly nations. This passage reveals that one way God reveals His wrath is by allowing the people of that nation to experience the full brunt of the ravaging consequences of their sin.

It is sobering that many great nations and civilizations have risen and fallen throughout human history. In each case, the nation had no expectation of its impending demise. Indeed, the mentality of those who lived within these nations was that their nation could never fall. As one researcher put it, "Anthropology tells us that many of the fallen civilizations in history also thought they were superior to their neighbors and forebears. Few of their citizens could have imagined their society would suddenly collapse."[19] But the harsh reality is that great nations do fall—*and they fall hard*.

The Babylonians never thought Babylon would fall, but its demise came in less than a century. The Persians never thought the Persian Empire would fall, but it finally capitulated after about two centuries. The Greeks never thought Greece would fall, but it waned in less than three centuries. No one thought the mighty Roman Empire would ever decline, but it too waned after holding out for nine centuries. In each of these cases, the fall of these nations was preceded by a gross moral decline, and God rendered appropriate judgment.

Here, then, is a question to ponder: If what we are witnessing in America today—pornography, premarital sex, extramarital sex, widespread homosexuality, same-sex marriages, abortions, drunkenness, drugs, divorce, the disintegration of the family, an ever-escalating crime rate—were taking place in ancient Babylon, would you think that Babylon was ripe for judgment? I think so! The problem today is that many in our country have become so desensitized to biblical morality that they're not even aware of how bad things really are. That is a dangerous state to be in, for God's patience will not last forever.

Looking to the Future

The various indications of moral decline that have been growing worse will *continue* to grow worse in the years that lie ahead of us.

I don't like saying it, but I think it's true. The *present* helps us predict the *future*.

The way I assess things, the current moral decline will even get worse in the following areas:

1. Increasing numbers of people will become me-focused instead of God-focused.

2. Increasing numbers of people will live their lives based on the vile dictum, "You can have your truth and I can have my truth."

3. The pursuit of pleasure-seeking will continue to escalate at the expense of righteousness.

4. People will continue to manifest little or no concern for immoral living in the face of a future judgment by God.

5. Many will continue to grow in their love for money and material things over love for God.

6. Heterosexual sin—premarital, extramarital, and porn-based fornication—will continue to escalate.

7. Homosexual sin will continue to escalate, and same-sex marriages will continue to spread globally.

8. There will continue to be relentless murders of the unborn.

Paul was right: "In the last days there will be very difficult times" (2 Timothy 3:1).

Such times are now upon us.

4

TOLERANCE FOR ALL: THE NEW GOLDEN RULE

Do you believe Jesus is the only way to heaven? *Extremist.* Prayed for someone you don't know? *Extremist.* Believe marriage is meant to be between one man and one woman? *Extremist.* Would you give up a good-paying job to do mission work? *Extremist.* Do you believe Christians have a responsibility to talk about Jesus with nonbelievers, even with strangers? *Extremist.*[1]

My friends, we live in an age of radical tolerance. One risks being accused of *in*tolerance—and even *extremism*—if one should say anything negative about someone else's beliefs or act in a way contrary to their beliefs. Today a growing population of people are convinced that "a life lived with religious conviction is not just countercultural or counterintuitive but dangerous, even damaging. In their view, if you raise your children to embrace the same convictions, you are beyond extreme; you may be criminal."[2]

The apostle Paul once asked, "Have I now become your enemy because I am telling you the truth?" (Galatians 4:16). Speaking the truth these days can get you into big trouble!

I've always been a big believer in the Golden Rule. In Matthew 7:12, Jesus put it this way: "Do to others whatever you would like them to do to you. This is the essence of all that is taught in the law and the prophets."

Today, however, many are following a different—indeed, a *perverted*—version of the Golden Rule. It goes something like this: "Be tolerant of others (their beliefs, actions, and lifestyle) as you would have them to be tolerant of you (your beliefs, actions, and lifestyle)—*for all beliefs, actions, and lifestyles are equally valid.*"

Redefining Tolerance

The meaning of *tolerance* has changed somewhat over the past 50 or 60 years. Back in the fifties and sixties (yes, I was around back then), being tolerant meant putting up with the neighbor who played the radio a little too loud while lying out by the backyard pool. Being tolerant meant not overreacting to someone who cut into your lane on the highway. Being tolerant meant allowing your teenage son to wear pants and a shirt that did not match—and allowing him to wear his hair longer than you like. However, as Christian author William D. Watkins points out,

> Being tolerant never meant condoning immoral behavior, letting harmful beliefs go unchallenged, or permitting a person's dangerous lifestyle to influence, much less be taught, to others. In those days we may have disagreed about what is true, but few challenged the bedrock conviction that "true" is the opposite of "false," and that truth does not tolerate untruth. We believed then that some beliefs and lifestyles promoted the common good while others undermined it.[3]

Today, the "tolerant" person is wide open to other belief systems, truth claims, moral convictions, and lifestyle choices. He or she believes that "whatever works for me is my truth" just as "whatever

Tolerance for All: The New Golden Rule • 63

works for you is your truth." We should all just live and let live. This means that being tolerant today means not merely that we recognize another person's right to have a belief different from our own, but it means we agree that *all views are equally valid and all lifestyles equally appropriate.* D.A. Carson, in his insightful book *The Intolerance of Tolerance*, suggests that the shift from accepting the existence of different views to believing that all views are equally valid is "subtle in form, but massive in substance."[4] It is massive in substance because virtually all belief systems, truth claims, moral convictions, and lifestyle choices are now deemed acceptable.

The new tolerance is grounded in relativism (see the previous chapter).[5] Relativism involves the idea that anything can be true for the individual, but nothing can be true for everyone. It is considered presumptuous to think one knows the truth for all people. The truly loving thing to do is to unquestioningly allow everyone to hold their own truth without challenge. *That's* tolerance!

In this chapter, I will demonstrate that this new version of tolerance affects one's attitude toward other religions, other lifestyles, and controversial choices. Tolerance has become the de facto mindset of Western culture.

Tolerance Toward Other Religions

I came across some interesting words when doing research for this chapter: "Christians are seen as the pit bulls of culture wars—small brains, big teeth, strong jaws, and no interest in compromise."[6] In other words, they are viewed as closed-minded and intolerant. I know what it is like to be viewed in this way.

I once spent almost an entire hour on the national *Bible Answer Man* radio broadcast talking to a Jewish man who expressed openness to the possibility that Jesus might be the Messiah, but he was not quite ready to make the commitment. I talked to him because I cared for him—*and he came so close to believing.* But then the broadcast ended. A while after the broadcast, I received an extremely hostile phone call from a person in New York. He said, "How dare you inflict your beliefs on this person. You are disgusting. You are wicked and evil. I am so sick of intolerant, narrow-minded people like you." (He added some colorful metaphors, which will go unmentioned.)

During the entire broadcast I had been kind and gentle, and I deliberately made every effort to avoid sounding pushy. The entire discussion was polite and friendly. And yet this New Yorker perceived me as some kind of intolerant and narrow-minded beast from the pit of hell. Truth be told, *he* was the one being intolerant—*of yours truly!*

In chapter 1, I spoke about a liberal church I visited. At that church, I attended a class for young adults taught by the head of the education department at the church. This person taught that Jesus is one of many ways to salvation and that all religions are like spokes on a wheel—they all lead to God.

With a friendly smile on my face, I politely raised my hand and respectfully said, "Have you considered Jesus' words in John 14:6: 'I am the way, the truth, and the life. No one can come to the Father except through me.' Peter in Acts 4:12 likewise said, 'There is salvation in no one else! God has given no other name under heaven by which we must be saved.' And the apostle Paul said in 1 Timothy 2:5, 'There is one God and one Mediator who can reconcile God and humanity—the man Christ Jesus.'"

The teacher shook his head and with a sour look said, "That's just really sad. I feel sorry for you going through life so incredibly narrow-minded."

The "tolerant" mindset of today views members of all religions—Buddhists, Hindus, Muslims, Jains, Sikhs, Confucians, Taoists, Zoroastrians, Baha'is, Theosophists, Rastafarians, witches, goddess worshippers, and whoever else—as being on equally valid paths to God, with no one path higher or more virtuous than another. Another "equally valid" path is not believing in any deity at all. In this line of thinking, we ought never evangelize those outside our personal faith (as I had tried to do). I had committed a cardinal sin.

Tolerance Toward Other Lifestyles

The "tolerant" person of today is also open to any sexual relationships, including heterosexual, homosexual, bisexual, pansexual, and whatever else. Regardless of our various sexual preferences, "whatever works for me is my truth" just as "whatever works for you is your truth." We should all just live and let live. Those who do not go along with this view experience a head-on collision.

For a time during 2016, the California state legislature considered legislation for Christian colleges and universities that would enforce the following policy: *Embrace transgender rights or lose funding for students.* More specifically, if the legislation had passed, Christian colleges and universities would have been disqualified from receiving state-funded student financial aid if they denied students based on sexual orientation, gender identity, or gender expression.

Advocates for Faith and Freedom responded to this proposed legislation by stating: "It is clear that the agenda of California's progressive legislature, including the openly gay authors of [the legislation], goes well beyond their original mantra of seeking equality. Their sights are now firmly set on destroying and dismantling all faith-based entities that disagree with their lifestyle."[7]

I'm thankful that the legislative proposal was dropped in the latter part of 2016. Nevertheless, the very attempt reveals the extent to which some people will go to marginalize, victimize, and ostracize Christians who hold to their biblical convictions. Clearly, we are in the midst of a major culture clash.

It bothers me that Christians are often made out to be the bad guys in situations like this. This was illustrated in a subtle way when Ellen DeGeneres gave an acceptance speech for an Emmy for co-writing the "coming out" episode of *Ellen*. DeGeneres said: "I accept this on behalf of all people, and the teenagers out there especially, who think there is something wrong with them because they are gay. There's nothing wrong with you. *Don't ever let anybody make you feel ashamed of who you are*" (emphasis added).

Understandably, many perceived DeGeneres as being an open, fair, tolerant person who wanted to render help to young people in understanding their sexuality. The problem is, DeGeneres subtly implied that those of us who reject her view—namely, traditional Christians—are not only stupid but harmful. If you're not picking up on this, consider how Christian apologist Francis Beckwith explains it:

> Imagine if a conservative Christian Emmy-award winner had said, "I accept this on behalf of all people, and the teenagers out there especially, who think there is something wrong with them because they believe that human beings are made for a purpose and that purpose includes the building of community with its foundation being heterosexual monogamy. There's nothing wrong with you. Don't ever let anybody, especially television script writers, make you feel ashamed because what you believe is true about reality." Clearly this would imply that those who affirm liberal views on sexuality are wrong. An award winner who made this speech would be denounced as narrow, bigoted, and intolerant. That person could expect never again to work in Hollywood... Ellen's Emmy speech does the same to those with whom she disagrees. By encouraging people to believe there is nothing wrong with their homosexuality, she is saying

there *is* something wrong with those—that is, Christians and other social conservatives—who don't agree with this prescription.[8]

While Ellen's words were viewed by most people as good, true, and beautiful, they nevertheless strongly imply that those who hold a different view are bad, false, and ugly. It's not that I'm trying to pick a fight. But the truth is that Ellen is every bit as much intolerant and narrow as her so-called detractors.

Tolerance on Controversial Choices

The "tolerant" person of today is also open-minded on controversial choices, embracing them as perfectly valid. Consider Jack Kevorkian, known by many as Dr. Death. Before he died in 2011, Kevorkian assisted in the suicides of dozens of people, many of whom were not even seriously ill. Kevorkian claimed: "The highest principle in medical ethics—in any kind of ethics—is personal autonomy, self-determination. What counts is what the patient wants and judges to be a benefit or a value in his or her own life."[9] In other words, "whatever works for me is my truth" just as "whatever works for you is your truth." We should all just live and let live— even if it involves the purposeful termination of human life.

We see the same mindset regarding abortion. I recently heard a politician say that while he personally does not go along with abortion in his family, he nevertheless embraces abortion as a valid and acceptable practice for any who choose that option. We should all just live and let live (or in this case, perhaps "live and let die").

One of the underlying justifications many give for abortion is that women ought to have the right to control their own bodies. The truth is, however, that the baby in the womb is *not part of the woman's body*. The baby has his or her own body within the womb of the mother's body. It is true that the mother's body sustains the baby's body with nutrients and a protective environment, but it is nevertheless a distinct body from her own. For her to have an abortion is not just an operation on her own body but amounts to killing another human being whose body is within her body.

When I make statements such as this, I am condemned as being a narrow-minded and intolerant extremist—a religious nut, an intellectual Neanderthal. (Believe me, I've experienced this firsthand.)

Fuzzy Thinking

Many of those promoting the new "tolerance" in our culture seem oblivious to their fuzzy thinking. Consider the claim that "all views are equally valid." If it is really true that all views are equally valid, then proponents of tolerance have no choice but to admit that the Christian view must be equally valid to their view. But wait a minute. The Christian view says that all views *are not* equally valid (see, for example, John 14:6; Acts 4:12; 1 Timothy 2:5). Of course, modern advocates of tolerance are blind to this logical problem.[10]

It is hard to avoid the conclusion that those making accusations of intolerance are the true intolerant ones in our midst. They claim to be tolerant of the beliefs of all people, but they are unbendingly *intolerant* of Christians who believe in God and who love Jesus. Hence, today many are attempting to silence Christians. As Daniel Taylor put it, "At the core of tolerance is a kind of intolerance...The intolerant person is the one thing that cannot be tolerated, the one person who must be shamed or silenced."[11]

Elliot Miller is spot-on in affirming that "the fundamentalism of tolerance is just as dogmatic as any other fundamentalism, only it is deceptive in its profession of tolerance...It may actually prove to be less tolerant, since it does not seem to recognize the right of others to reject its relativistic view."[12] Beckwith in like manner concludes that "liberal tolerance is a sham. Although portrayed by its advocates as an open, tolerant, and neutral perspective, it is a dogma whose proponents tolerate no rivals."[13]

Relevance for the Present and the Future

At the beginning of this chapter I quoted the apostle Paul: "Have I now become your enemy because I am telling you the truth?" (Galatians 4:16). In a very real way, Christians often are viewed as an enemy for telling the truth about Christ and Christian values. It seems that just about everyone and everything on planet earth is tolerated *except for* Bible-believing Christians. Christians are increasingly the bad guys in a relativistic world.

I believe the ever-escalating tolerance we witness today relates directly to end-time Bible prophecies. Such tolerance lies at the heart of Jesus' words about the end times being like the days of Noah:

> When the Son of Man returns, it will be like it was in Noah's day. In those days before the flood, the people were enjoying banquets and parties and weddings right up to the time Noah entered his boat. People didn't realize what was going to happen until the flood came and swept them all away. That is the way it will be when the Son of Man comes (Matthew 24:37-39).

While this passage refers specifically to the future seven-year tribulation, I cannot help but notice that the attitude Jesus described is evident even in our day. People are merrily going about their way, unconcerned for the things of God. People seem to be tolerant of just about anything.

Tolerance certainly relates to the end-times apostasy discussed in chapter 1. Recall that 1 Timothy 4:1 warns us: "The Holy Spirit tells us clearly that in the last times some will turn away from the true faith; they will follow deceptive spirits and teachings that come from demons." We might loosely paraphrase this passage: "The Holy Spirit tells us clearly that in the last times some will not tolerate the true faith; but they will tolerate deceptive spirits and teachings that come from demons."

Likewise, 2 Timothy 4:3 warns us: "A time is coming when people will no longer listen to sound and wholesome teaching. They will follow their own desires and will look for teachers who will tell them whatever their itching ears want to hear." We might loosely paraphrase this passage: "A time is coming when people will no longer tolerate sound and wholesome teaching, but they will tolerate teachers who tell them whatever they want to hear."

Scripture also warns us that in the future seven-year tribulation, there will emerge a one-world government and a one-world false religious system (see Daniel 2 and 7, and Revelation 13). I believe the current rise in tolerance is setting the stage for all this. People are increasingly open to anything—and in the future they will be open to a one-world government and a one-world false religion. Many will also be open to receiving the mark of the beast, which shows allegiance to the antichrist and his purposes (Revelation 13:16-17).

Meanwhile, Christians who stand for the truth will continue to be marginalized, victimized, and ostracized. Those who advocate tolerance will not tolerate Christians who hold to the absolute truth of God's Word. We may therefore expect the persecution of Christians in these end times to continue to escalate (see chapter 6).

In view of this sobering reality, I close this chapter with a call to stand strong for Christian truth in these difficult times. We should not give in to the agenda of toleration proponents, for their desire is to intimidate us into utter silence. Their desire is to shut us down. They'll tolerate nothing less.

One only need consider Christ's words to the seven churches of Revelation 2 and 3 to see that God wants us to stand for the truth instead of being intimidated into silence. In Revelation 2, we see that the church at Ephesus would not tolerate false apostles. Jesus said to them, "I know you don't tolerate evil people. You have examined the claims of those who say they are apostles but are not. You have discovered they are liars" (Revelation 2:2). These Ephesian believers tested false apostles against the clear teachings of Scripture (compare with Acts 17:11; 1 Thessalonians 5:19-22), and held fast to the Scriptures. One might recall that decades before the book of Revelation was written, the apostle Paul warned the Ephesian elders that false teachers would seek to lead them astray (Acts 20:28-31; see also 2 Corinthians 11:12-13). The discerning believers at Ephesus remembered this and rejected the teachings of the false apostles. They would not tolerate false teachings.

Jesus also commended the Ephesians: "You hate the evil deeds of the Nicolaitans, just as I do" (Revelation 2:6). The Nicolaitans were open to license in Christian conduct (including "free love"), ate food sacrificed to idols, and engaged in idolatry. The Ephesians would not tolerate such things, and Jesus essentially gave them two thumbs-up for their strong stance.

To the church at Pergamum, Jesus said: "I know that you live in the city where Satan has his throne, yet you have remained loyal to me. You refused to deny me even when Antipas, my faithful witness, was martyred among you there in Satan's city" (Revelation 2:13). Antipas—perhaps a church leader—was a faithful defender of the truth who was burned to death inside a brass bull positioned over burning flames. He refused to go along with emperor worship and false doctrine. *He wouldn't tolerate it.*

Sadly, not everyone in the church at Pergamum was as faithful as Antipas. Jesus said to the church: "I have a few complaints against you. You tolerate some among you whose teaching is like that of Balaam, who showed Balak how to trip up the people of Israel. He

taught them to sin by eating food offered to idols and by committing sexual sin. In a similar way, you have some Nicolaitans among
you who follow the same teaching. Repent of your sin…" (Revelation 2:14-16). In Jesus' thinking, toleration of such things is not
acceptable for His people.

One further passage that comes to mind is Revelation 2:20-21,
where Jesus said to the church at Thyatira: "I have this complaint
against you. You are permitting that woman—that Jezebel who calls
herself a prophet—to lead my servants astray. She teaches them to
commit sexual sin and to eat food offered to idols. I gave her time
to repent, but she does not want to turn away from her immorality."
This woman apparently promoted the idea that people could engage
in sins of the outer body (like sexual immorality) without doing
injury to their inner spirit. *Jesus indicated that Christians should never
tolerate such things.*

My friends, Scripture urges all Christians: "Keep a close watch
on how you live and on your teaching. Stay true to what is right for
the sake of your own salvation and the salvation of those who hear
you" (1 Timothy 4:16). "Defend the faith that God has entrusted
once for all time to his holy people" (Jude 3). Any who teach false
ideas within the church are to be corrected: "Reprimand them
sternly to make them strong in the faith. They must stop listening to Jewish myths and the commands of people who have turned
away from the truth" (Titus 1:13-14). There is no tolerance here for
false ideas or false doctrine.

Of course, our refusal to tolerate false ideas must be communicated in a way that is honoring to Jesus Christ. James 1:19-20 tells
us, "Understand this, my dear brothers and sisters: You must all be
quick to listen, slow to speak, and slow to get angry. Human anger
does not produce the righteousness God desires."

Likewise, we are exhorted in 1 Peter 3:15-16: "If someone asks about your hope as a believer, always be ready to explain it. But do this in a gentle and respectful way." The word *gentle* carries the idea of meekness and humility. There is not to be even the slightest hint of arrogance as we speak (1 Peter 3:4). This does not mean the Christian defender is to seem weak or hesitant, but rather he or she is to communicate strong truth from the Bible in a gentle and humble way. The Christian should certainly not try to ram truth down the throat of others, nor speak patronizingly, nor act condescendingly, nor have a critical countenance. Let us not forget that gentle answers have a positive benefit—they deflect anger (Proverbs 15:1). A gentle answer is easy to swallow.

The word *respect* has two important nuances. On the one hand, we are to maintain a reverential awe of God (1 Peter 1:17; 2:17; 3:2). On the other hand, we are to treat the people with whom we are speaking with respect (Colossians 4:6).

I urge you to let the words *gentle* and *respect* burn into your heart. No matter how strong your theological arguments may be, they will have very little effect on our relativistic and "tolerant" culture if they are not communicated with gentleness and respect.

THE STEADY DETERIORATION
OF RELIGIOUS FREEDOM

eligion in America. Even for the nonacademic, this is one of the
most fascinating topics a person could ever pursue. One historian said that the religious history of the American people is "one of
the grandest epics in the history of mankind. The stage is continental in size, and the cast is produced by the largest transoceanic migra-
tion and the most rapid transcontinental dispersion of people the
world has ever seen."[1] And underlying America's religious history is
one fundamental concept: FREEDOM.

Every American is guaranteed the free exercise of religion. This
is one of the things that makes America so great. The First Amend-
ment, ratified in 1791, affirms that "Congress shall make no law
respecting an establishment of religion or prohibiting the free exercise thereof."[2]

In keeping with this, James Madison, who became the fourth
president of the United States (1809–1817), wrote, "The religion...
of every man must be left to the conviction and conscience of every
man...We maintain, therefore, that in matters of religion no man's
right is [to be] abridged by the institution of civil society."[3] Such religious freedom is cherished by most Americans.

While Americans still enjoy the constitutional right of freedom of religion, there has been a massive societal shift toward a new cultural policy: "Tolerate everyone and everything except for Christians and Christian morality." This has led to a growing infringement on Christian freedoms. The USA has now become less faith-friendly.[4] In the crosshairs are Christian holidays, Christian nativity scenes, Christian morality, the Christian Bible, and public displays of the Christian cross. Many today also seek to marginalize Christian influence in schools and education, in government, in public policy, and in the media. Religious freedom doesn't seem so *free* today.

I read about a Christian apartment owner who refused to rent an apartment to an unmarried couple. He didn't want fornication taking place in his building. He was promptly brought to court and forced to allow the couple to move in.

A sixth-grade schoolgirl gave an oral book report on the Bible. Students had been told they could give a report on the book of their choice. Following her presentation, she gave printed copies of her report to any friends who requested it. Shortly thereafter, a teacher at the school escorted the girl to the principal's office. She was interrogated by school administrators, during which time she was denied the right to even call her mother.

A similar thing happened to a six-year-old boy. The children were told to bring their favorite books to school for show-and-tell. This boy brought his Bible. But then he was told to take it home because it was "against the law." I'm sure he'll remember that moment for the rest of his life.

I read about a graduating senior in high school—the valedictorian of her class—who was denied the right to give her graduation address. The denial was rooted in her refusal to withdraw a remark about how Jesus had brought meaning to her throughout her life. Religious freedom doesn't seem so *free* anymore.

More recently, I read about a Christian family who owns a local pharmacy in Olympia, Washington. They, along with a few other pharmacists, sued the state for forcing them to sell abortifacient drugs. As Christians, they wanted no part of killing babies in the womb. A federal court ruled in their favor and said they could not be forced by the state to violate their religious convictions. However, a federal appeals court reversed the decision. They then took it to the Supreme Court—but the Supreme Court decided against hearing the case thus letting stand the ruling from the federal appeals court. They were forced to either sell abortion-inducing drugs or go out of business.

Though outvoted, conservative justice Samuel Alito at the Supreme Court thought the case should have been heard. In his dissent, Alito penned a sober warning against the eroding of religious freedom in America. "If this is a sign of how religious liberty claims will be treated in the years ahead, those who value religious freedom have cause for great concern."[5]

I also read about a major of the United States Air Force who removed a Bible from his workspace after a complaint by the Military Religious Freedom Foundation. It was claimed that this major's open Bible on his desk was an "outrageous display of callous and bold Christian primacy." It was recommended that the major be "swiftly, visibly and aggressively punished." After all, the major's display of an open Bible violated Air Force Instruction 1-1, Section 2.11 and 2.12. These state that leaders "must avoid the actual or apparent use of their position to promote their personal religious beliefs to their subordinates," and that their personal faith should not "degrade morale, good order, and discipline."[6] Religious freedom doesn't seem so *free* anymore.

We see this same type of thing with a fire chief in Atlanta who was fired because the city took offense at a book he wrote on his personal time that promoted biblical marriage and a biblical view of sex (he was against homosexuality). He now laments, "There is an ever-increasing attack on religious freedom and expressive freedom" in the country, and the government is "its biggest threat."[7]

Meanwhile, there remains a strong anti-Christian bias in Hollywood films and television. Christians continue to be demonized in the popular media. A favorite media tactic is to use the pejorative term *religious right* to describe Christian conservatives. The intent is to portray Christians as intolerant backwoods fanatics who do not use their brains. At the same time, humanist secularists are portrayed as enlightened intellectuals. Christians are truly in the crosshairs today.

As a result of the onslaught, many Christians are feeling the heat in regard to their Christian faith. One study reveals:

> When we look at the broadest segment of practicing Christians…a majority says they feel "misunderstood" (54 percent) and "persecuted" (52 percent), while millions of others use terms like "marginalized" (44 percent), "sidelined" (40 percent), "silenced" (38 percent), "afraid to speak up" (31 percent), and "afraid to look stupid" (23 percent) to describe living their faith in society today. Evangelicals are even more likely to perceive their experience of faith in culture in these negative terms.[8]

The Potent Influence of Secular Humanism in Western Society

While religion is oppressed, secular humanism continues to be on an upward trend, especially in Western societies. In this worldview, religion of any kind is viewed as damaging to human beings. In the secular humanistic worldview there is no such thing as the supernatural. As stated in Humanist Manifesto II (signed by such luminaries as author Isaac Asimov, psychologist B.F. Skinner, and ethicist Joseph Fletcher), "We find insufficient evidence for belief in the existence of a supernatural; it is either meaningless or irrelevant to the question of the survival and fulfillment of the human race. As nontheists, we begin with humans not God, nature not deity."[9]

This view is unwavering in claiming there is no God. In his book, *What Is Secular Humanism?* Dr. James Hitchcock states:

> Groups like the American Humanist Association are not humanists just in the sense that they have an interest in the humanities or that they value man over nature… In their self-definition, God does not exist…They promote a way of life that systematically excludes God and all religion in the traditional sense. Man, for better or worse, is on his own in the universe. He marks the highest point to which nature has yet evolved, and he must rely entirely on his own resources.[10]

The late Isaac Asimov, one of the most prolific authors and science writers of all time, was bluntly honest regarding his disbelief in God: "Emotionally I am an atheist. I don't have the evidence to prove that God doesn't exist, but I so strongly suspect he doesn't that I don't want to waste my time."[11] Likewise, the late scientist Carl Sagan asserted at the beginning of his *Cosmos* television series, "The Cosmos is all that is or ever was or ever will be."[12] In other words, *there is no deity with whom we need concern ourselves.*

Since there is no supernatural and no God, secular humanists staunchly emphasize that there is no Creator. Asimov said that the "universe can be explained by evidence obtained from the Universe alone…no supernatural agency need be called upon."[13] The typical explanation of human origins is the theory of evolution.

Frederick Edwords explains human origins this way:

> Human beings are neither entirely unique from other forms of life nor are they the final product of some

planned scheme of development...All life forms are constructed from the same basic elements, the same sorts of atoms, as are nonliving substances...Humans are the current result of a long series of natural evolutionary changes, but not the only result or the final one. Continuous change can be expected to affect ourselves, other life forms, and the cosmos as a whole. There appears to be no ultimate beginning or end to this process.[14]

In view of all this, secular humanists argue—often with vitriol—that there is no divine purpose for humanity. The Humanist Manifesto II asserts: "We can discover no divine purpose or providence for the human species. While there is much that we do not know, humans are responsible for what we are or will become. No deity will save us; we must save ourselves." In other words, we are all alone in this great big universe, with no ultimate purpose or destiny.

Secular humanists are also sure there is no afterlife. In his book *Forbidden Fruit: The Ethics of Humanism*, Paul Kurtz said that "the theist's world is only a dream world; it is a feeble escape into a future that will never come."[15] Kurtz also stated: "Promises of immortal salvation or fear of eternal damnation are both illusory and harmful. They distract humans from present concerns, from self-actualization, and from rectifying social injustices...There is no credible evidence that life survives the death of the body. We continue to exist in our progeny and in the way that our lives have influenced others in our culture."[16]

In 2012 I was speaking at a church about current attacks against Christianity by humanists and atheists. During my message, I noted that Paul Kurtz was getting so old that his time to repent and turn to the Lord was rapidly running out. Four hours later, I received news that Kurtz had just died. *Too late.*

Secular humanists are making militant efforts to squash out all religion—especially Christianity—wherever it may be found. They are not only launching academic attacks against Christianity and other religions, but are also seeking to remove religious "myth" from all textbooks used to train our children at school. *A culture war has been declared!* And secular humanists aim to win it. Part of their strategy is to squash—or at least greatly impede—the religious freedom of Christians.

Religious Oppression—A Global Phenomenon

It would be wrong to conclude that religious freedom is waning only in the United States. *The International Religious Freedom Report*, put out by the U.S. State Department, indicates that one-in-four countries in the world oppress religious freedom, affecting roughly 75 percent of the world's population. These countries have laws—some are anti-blasphemy laws, others are simply harsh statutes—that directly impede religious freedom.[17]

The report indicates that "the existence of these laws has been used by governments in too many cases to intimidate [and] repress religious minorities, and governments have too often failed to take appropriate steps to prevent societal violence sparked by accusations of blasphemy and apostasy." We are told that "no one region, country, or religion is immune to the pernicious effects of such legislation." Tragically, "in countries where religious minorities have long contributed to their national societies in relative comity for decades, centuries, even millennia, we continue to witness violent upheavals, some of historic proportions, in which entire communities are in danger of being driven out of their homelands based solely on their religious or ethnic identities."[18]

Among the countries with the greatest religious restrictions against Christians are China, Russia, Egypt, Indonesia, Pakistan, and Turkey. "In these countries, both the government and society at large have imposed numerous limits on religious beliefs and practices."[19] Pakistan, the sixth-largest country by population, has the highest level of religion-related hostilities. One report tells us that "in Punjab province, a mob of 1,500 villagers accused a Christian couple of blasphemy—burning them alive in a brick kiln."[20] (In the next chapter, I will provide many similar examples of lethal persecution against Christians.)

China: A World Leader in Repressing Religious Freedom

It seems not a week passes before I see yet another report on the stifling of religious freedom in China. One analysis of world oppression of religious freedom concluded: "When we analyzed religious restrictions imposed by government, China, the world's largest country by population, has the highest level."[21]

It appears that all religion—including Christianity—is being removed from every nook and cranny in China. An extract from the Bible in a school textbook in Beijing was recently removed because it was "propagating 'western' values."[22] Hospitals in an eastern province of China "have banned all kinds of religious activity, including receiving pastors, praying for the sick, and preaching, in the latest crackdown on Christianity."[23] All hospital personnel have been informed that "all forms of religious activity are banned."[24]

Meanwhile, Christian crucifixes have been ordered removed from any and all buildings. Two Christian pastors protested this action and are now serving twelve and fourteen years of imprisonment respectively.[25] Crosses have also been removed from the rooftops of churches in several Chinese provinces. The goal is reportedly to "stem the growth of Christianity in the world's most populous nation."[26] Meanwhile, students attending a house church in the central Guizhou province were told they would not be allowed to go to college unless they stopped going to church.

Christian seminary students in China are also being forced to live under "absolute obedience" to the Communist Party. They are instructed to put the state ahead of God. A persecution watchdog group in China reports that "video has emerged of students at a graduation ceremony at Zhejiang Theological Seminary singing the Chinese anthem, which…is only one of the signs of the ongoing government crackdown on Christianity in the country." The seminary has now reportedly become a "Communist Party school dressed in the cloak of Christianity."[27]

How all this must grieve the heart of God.

The New Russian Repression of Religion

Russia has enacted new laws that, among other things, restrict Christians from engaging in evangelism outside of their churches. The law now "requires missionaries to have permits, makes house churches illegal, and limits religious activity to registered church buildings, among other restrictions. Individuals who disobey could be fined up to $780, while organizations could be fined more than $15,000."[28]

Russia's Baptist Council of Churches issued an open letter that warned that the new laws will "create conditions for the repression of all Christians." Indeed, "any person who mentions their religious view or reflections out loud or puts them in writing, without the relevant documents, could be accused of 'illegal missionary activity.'"[29]

The Protestant Churches of Russia also issued an open letter that stated that requiring a permit to evangelize is "not only absurd and offensive, but also creates the basis for mass persecution of believers for violating these provisions." The new law is "the most draconian anti-religion bill to be proposed in Russia since Nikita Khrushchev promised to eliminate Christianity in the Soviet Union."[30]

Many outside of Russia have also expressed concern about the new law. The European Evangelical Alliance said it was greatly concerned about how the law "greatly restricts religious freedom," and urged Christians to "pray that this new law unites Christians in new ways," and "pray that this time of trial will be used by the Lord to strengthen and grow his church." The U.S. Commission on International Religious Freedom said it "strongly condemns" this law that will ultimately "make it easier for Russian authorities to repress religious communities, stifle peaceful dissent, and detain and imprison people."[31]

The Rising Threat from Islam

Some Islamic leaders teach that jihad is a foreign policy option that can expand Islamic authority all over the world. Many Shiite Muslims believe that at the apocalyptic end of days, a great, armed jihad will result in the subjugation of the entire world to Islam.

Many Shiite Muslims have long believed in the eventual return of the Twelfth Imam, believed to be a direct (bloodline) descendant of Muhammad's son-in-law, Ali, whose family, it is believed, constitutes the only legitimate successors to Muhammad. The Twelfth Imam—who allegedly disappeared as a child in AD 941—will allegedly return as the Mahdi ("the rightly guided One"). He will create a messianic-like era of global order and justice for Shiites in which Islam will be triumphant.

In this line of thought, the appearance of the Twelfth Imam can be hastened through apocalyptic chaos and violence—that is, by unleashing an apocalyptic holy war against Christians and Jews. It is thus believed that it is within the power of modern Muslims to influence the divine timetable and bring about the end of days. Interestingly, a number of Shiite leaders in Iran say they have witnessed physical sightings of the Twelfth Imam, and claim he will reveal himself to the world soon, presumably following the imminent eruption in chaos and violence.

The radical Muslim goal is to attain "a world without America and Zionism," and once this goal is reached, the Twelfth Imam can be expected to return. It is claimed that humanity will soon know what it is like to live in a Jew-free and USA-free world. The United States and the Zionist regime of Israel will soon come to the end of their days. "Death to America" is a common slogan among such radical Muslims.

One must keep in mind that in the radical Muslim mindset, an attack against Americans is an attack against Christianity. Their reasoning is that America is a Christian nation, and America is a corrupt nation. Hence, Christianity is a corrupt religion. It must be destroyed.

Of course, radical Muslims target American Christians not just on American soil but overseas as well. One example will suffice. The Pew Research Center reports that in Egypt, "a Christian woman was attacked by a group of Muslim Brotherhood supporters when they saw a crucifix in her car…the woman was pulled by her hair into the street, beaten and killed."[32] This is not uncommon in parts of the world controlled by radical Islam. Even Christian children—young girls holding dolls in their hands—have been executed. (More on such martyrdom in the next chapter.)

Lifeway Research conducted a poll of a thousand Americans regarding Islam's threat to religious freedom. The statistics reveal that "Americans view Islam as a threat to their own nation's religious liberty almost as strongly as they consider it a danger to religious freedom internationally."[33] And because Islam is growing so rapidly around the world, the ever-escalating reduction of Christian liberty seems to be a given.

Not unexpectedly, attacks on the religious freedom of Christians is heaviest in those Muslim countries with Sharia law. Raymond Ibrahim, in his recent book *Crucified Again: Exposing Islam's New War on Christians*, writes:

The precarious status of churches and other forms of Christian expression under Sharia law is emblematic of Islam's innate hostility to Christianity. But Islamic law goes further, denying freedom of speech to all Christians and even freedom of conscience and conviction to Christian converts. Sharia curtails these freedoms by means of three laws that, though separate, often overlap: the laws against apostasy, blasphemy, and proselytism. For example, the Muslim who converts to Christianity is guilty of apostasy. But he can also be seen as a blasphemer, whose very existence is an affront to Islam. And when he speaks about Christianity—as enthusiastic new converts often do—around Muslims, he exposes himself to charges of proselytism. These three Islamic laws effectively ban freedom of speech, freedom of religion, and even freedom of thought.[34]

Some Muslim leaders have gone on record as saying that Sharia law will one day rule in the United States. That is the Islamic endgame for Western culture.

Religious Oppression in the End Times

End-time prophecies reveal that religious freedom will steadily wane in the end times. In Matthew 24:9 Jesus affirmed, "You will be arrested, persecuted, and killed. You will be hated all over the world because you are my followers." This verse addresses the future seven-year tribulation. As is often the case, however, this prophecy casts its shadow ahead of itself. Even today we are witnessing Christians being arrested, persecuted, and killed.

Religious oppression even occurs within families. Jesus said, "A brother will betray his brother to death, a father will betray his own child, and children will rebel against their parents and cause them to be killed. And everyone will hate you because you are my followers"

(Mark 13:12-13). Again, this passage is dealing with the future tribulation period. But even today we are witnessing "honor killings" in which, for example, a father might kill his son or a brother might kill his sister for departing from Islam to become a Christian.

Jesus also warned, "You will be dragged into synagogues and prisons, and you will stand trial before kings and governors because you are my followers" (Luke 21:12). Yet again, we are witnessing this very type of thing in countries like China, Russia, Egypt, Indonesia, Pakistan, and Turkey.

I don't like contemplating it, but the future looks bleak. Current trends indicate that religious oppression will not only continue, but escalate as we draw deeper into the end times.

We need to be mentally and spiritually prepared for this. I believe that during these tough days when religious freedom is waning—and persecution and martyrdom of Christians is escalating—Christ is calling His church to a deeper commitment.

Jesus instructed, "If any of you wants to be my follower, you must give up your own way, take up your cross, and follow me" (Mark 8:34). What does it mean to take up our cross and follow Jesus? Jesus' primary point is about living a life of self-denial and submitting instead to Him in all things. Jesus is calling for a total commitment. The idea is this: *If you really want to follow Me, do not do so in word only, but put your life on the line and follow Me on the path of the cross—a path that will involve sacrifice, self-denial, and possibly even suffering and death for My sake.*

6

THE RISING PERSECUTION AND MARTYRDOM OF CHRISTIANS

The previous chapter dealt with the waning of religious freedom. This chapter builds on that chapter, for the natural outcome of reducing or impeding religious freedom is the persecution of religious people. We are now witnessing the persecution of Christians worldwide. The best current estimates are that 80 percent of all acts of religious persecution around the world today are directed specifically against Christians.[1]

The prophetic Scriptures indicate that the persecution and martyrdom of believers will increase greatly during the future seven-year tribulation. To clarify, I believe that Christians on earth will be raptured prior to the tribulation (1 Thessalonians 1:10; 4:13-17; 5:9; Revelation 3:10). But many people will become believers *after* the rapture, *during* the tribulation period (Matthew 25:31-46; Revelation 7:9-10).

Perhaps some become convinced of the truth of Christianity after witnessing millions of Christians supernaturally vanish off the planet at the rapture. Or perhaps they become believers as a result of the ministry of the 144,000 Jewish evangelists introduced in Revelation 7, who themselves come to faith in Christ after the rapture. It may also be that many become believers as a result of the miraculous ministry of the two witnesses of Revelation 11, prophets who apparently have the same powers as Moses and Elijah. As well, Christian books and videos will be left behind after the rapture, and many may come to faith because of these.

These people will become targets for persecution and martyrdom during the tribulation period. Not all will be martyred, for there will be many still alive at the time of the second coming of Christ (Matthew 25:31-46). But there will be many casualties during this seven-year period.

Apparently, there will be significant martyrdom in association with the fifth seal judgment in Revelation 6:9-11:

> When the Lamb broke the fifth seal, I saw under the altar the souls of all who had been martyred for the word of God and for being faithful in their testimony. They shouted to the Lord and said, "O Sovereign Lord, holy and true, how long before you judge the people who belong to this world and avenge our blood for what they have done to us?" Then a white robe was given to each of them. And they were told to rest a little longer until the full number of their brothers and sisters—their fellow servants of Jesus who were to be martyred—had joined them.

This passage indicates that martyrdom will be an ongoing reality during the tribulation. Some of the martyred "fellow servants" are part of the "vast crowd" mentioned in Revelation 7:9-17—"the ones who died in the great tribulation" who "have washed their robes in the blood of the Lamb and made them white" (verse 14).

Revelation 13:7 tells us that the antichrist, who is energized by Satan, will be the primary instigator of persecution against God's people during the tribulation period: "The beast [the antichrist] was allowed to wage war against God's holy people and to conquer them.

And he was given authority to rule over every tribe and people and language and nation."

A parallel passage is Daniel 7:21, which tells us that the antichrist "was waging war against God's holy people and was defeating them." So, just as Revelation tells us that the antichrist will *conquer them*, so Daniel tells us that he will *defeat them*. There will apparently be many martyrs during the future tribulation period.

The Present and the Near-Term Future

While certain prophecies have particular relevance to the future seven-year tribulation, we are now witnessing initial fulfillments of these prophecies. Just as foreshocks often occur before major earthquakes, so preliminary manifestations of some of the prophecies emerge prior to the actual tribulation period. Prophecies that relate specifically to the tribulation—such as the persecution of God's people—are presently casting their shadows before them.

A recent report on religious freedom in the world shows a global increase in persecution against Christians. "A horrific catalogue of human rights abuses of Christians and other believers is listed in the latest freedom of religion or belief report from the European Union…It finds 'significant restrictions' exist on religion worldwide, including the near extinction of Christians in Syria and Iraq."[2]

Following is a brief sampling of persecution against Christians in specific parts of the world.

Persecution in Pakistan

Pakistani law is explicit: "Whoever by words, either spoken or written or by visible representation, or by any imputation, innuendo, or insinuation, directly or indirectly, defiles the sacred name of the Holy Prophet Muhammad (PBUH) shall be punished with death, or imprisonment for life, and shall also be liable to fine."[3] Laws such as this make Christians in Pakistan an endangered species.

The persecution of Christians in Pakistan has risen to epidemic levels. As one of many examples, a man in Pakistan shot his sister in the head because she married a man who had been a Christian, thereby bringing dishonor to the Muslim family. A Muslim man close to the family commented: "I am proud of this man that he has done the right thing, to kill her. We cannot allow anyone to marry outside our religion. He did the right thing."[4]

A Christian man in Pakistan had both of his arms chopped off because he refused to convert to Islam. The local police authorities did not arrest any suspects because similar dismemberments occur so regularly in Pakistan that it's impossible to keep up.[5]

The treatment of young Christian girls is atrocious. One report speaks of a nine-year-old girl who was "abducted by Muslims, gang-raped, murdered by repeated blows to her head, and then dumped into a canal." Another report documents a twelve-year-old Christian girl who was kidnapped, gang-raped, and murdered by a group of Muslims.[6]

On Easter Sunday in 2016, Christians gathered to celebrate the resurrection of the Lord at a public park in Pakistan. Widely reported in newspapers across the United States, a Muslim suicide-bomber detonated a bomb and killed 74 Christians—mostly women and children. An additional 400 Christians were injured. They were bothering no one, but because celebrating Easter is anathema to Muslims, a Taliban-affiliated group attacked and massacred them.

Meanwhile, other Christians in Pakistan, including children, remain at continual risk of kidnapping, forced marriages, and forced conversion to Islam. Those accused of blasphemy suffer the death penalty. Reports indicate that "there are regular violent assaults on Christian families, homes, shops, and churches."[7]

Muslim schoolchildren in Pakistan are being taught in their textbooks to hate Christians. "Pakistani school textbooks are full of information that incites hatred and intolerance against Christians and other non-Muslims...As a result, Christian students, as well as their elders, have been continually subjected to attacks in Pakistan." [8] There are reports of Christian students being kidnapped and beaten by unidentified assailants. Meanwhile, Christian students are forced to recite Islamic prayers in school.

Even the Pakistani government has gotten in on the act. "The government of Pakistan has announced plans to force Islam on young people by making Quranic study compulsory for all school and college students." [9] This is just one more indication of the incredible bias against Christianity in Pakistan.

Persecution of Christians in India

There is likewise rising persecution of Christians in India. One report warns: "Hundreds of thousands of Christians across India are faced with a sobering ultimatum: hide their faith, or risk harassment, intimidation, and even death...Threats against churches, arson attacks on Christian property, and the harassment and violent abuse of new converts to Christianity are all on the rise in India." [10] Christians who refuse to recant their faith are especially targeted: "If Christians refuse to recant their faith, they are chased out of their villages and beaten up." [11] There is a great effort to make India a completely Christian-free nation.

In one case, Muslims stormed and terrorized a house church in India where a prayer meeting was being held. They beat the Christians, including a 65-year-old widow. Children were screaming and running in fear. A crowd of 500 Muslims gathered to watch the 90-minute spectacle as a form of entertainment.

Persecution of Christians in China

Meanwhile, religious freedom in China is waning by the minute. The Chinese government has imposed severe restrictions on

Christians, and it appears that things are going to get much worse in the coming years. Bible verses are being removed from textbooks, religious activities are being forbidden at public establishments (such as hospitals), and crucifixes have been ordered removed from all public buildings—including churches. Meanwhile, church attenders are told that they'll lose certain personal rights if they continue going to church. The government is even trying to prohibit the spread of God's Word online. Christian seminaries are being bullied into submission to the state.

The Persecution of Christians in Laos

Laos is largely Buddhist. Government authorities in Laos are intolerant toward "non-Buddhist religions"—namely, Christians. One report indicates that "church leaders have been arrested and killed, and threatened if they did not stop preaching the gospel. Numerous Christians have been pressured to recant their faith under threats from local authorities."[12]

The Persecution of Christians in the Middle East

The persecution of Christians by Muslims is particularly vicious today. Raymond Ibrahim, in his book *Crucified Again: Exposing Islam's New War on Christians*, writes:

> At this moment, from one end of the Muslim world to the other, Christians are being persecuted. A January 2012 Reuters report cited an estimated "100 million Christians persecuted worldwide." A few years earlier the British Secret Service, M16, had put the number of Christians being persecuted around the world at twice as high, 200 million. A human rights representative for the Organization for Security and Cooperation on Europe estimates that a Christian is killed for his faith "every five

minutes." The vast majority of those martyrs are being killed in the Islamic world. Eight of the top nine offending countries—Saudi Arabia, Afghanistan, Iraq, Somalia, Maldives, Mali, Iran, and Yemen—have a majority of Muslims (the ninth, Eritrea, is roughly half-Muslim). Of the top fifty countries documented for their persecution of Christians, forty-two either are Muslim-majority nations or have a sizable Muslim population that is attempting to subjugate or eliminate surrounding Christians (Nigeria being the primary example of the latter pattern).[13]

A great deal of Muslim persecution against Christians is based on Quran 9:29, where Allah commands Muslims: "Fight those among the People of the Book who do not believe in Allah nor the Last Day, nor forbid what Allah and His Messenger have forbidden, nor embrace the religion of truth, until they pay the jizya with willing submission and feel themselves subdued." The phrase "People of the Book" refers specifically to Christians and Jews. "Jizya" refers to a per capita yearly tax historically levied by Islamic states. But the most important phrase in this verse is "feel themselves *subdued*." The word for "subdued" in Arabic is *saghirun*. This word means "to be lowly, submissive, servile, humble"; "contemptible, servile," to "fawn, cringe, grovel"; "low, lowly, despised, contemptible; humiliated, meek, dejected; submissive, servile, subject." As Ibrahim notes, "to treat people as *saghirun* is 'to belittle, deride, ridicule, debase, demean' them."[14] This is how Muslims seek to make Christians feel.

There are many examples of the persecution of Christians in the Middle East. Former United States Secretary of State John Kerry widely publicized how the terror group Islamic State (ISIS) committed mass genocide against countless Middle Eastern Christians.[15]

In areas of Syria and Iraq that are under the control of ISIS, churches have been seized, crucifixes destroyed, and paintings depicting scenes from the Bible have been obliterated—they are considered "idolatrous" by ISIS members. Countless Christians are being massacred by having their throats slit in the name of Allah.[16]

Meanwhile, the persecution of Christians has never been higher than it is today in Egypt. One report details an angry Muslim mob dragging a 70-year-old Christian woman naked through the streets.[17] *The New York Times* also reports:

> Christians continue to suffer from violence and humiliation in Muslim-dominated Egypt, where only 10 percent of the population believe in the teachings of Jesus Christ.
>
> For Christians living in Egypt, there is a constant threat that their houses and other properties will be burned down, and that they will be mugged while walking on the streets. Even churches are not being spared as they are desecrated, with hate graffiti written on their walls.[18]

One case involved some 3000 Muslims who fired guns and rifles and hurled Molotov cocktails at Coptic churches, killing many and wounding hundreds. Churches were set aflame to cries of "Allahu Akbar." Coptic homes were looted and then torched.

The Persecution of Christians in the Democratic Republic of Congo

Jihadist groups continue to gain strength in the Democratic Republic of Congo (DRC), committing atrocities against Christians. One recent report says: "At least 36 people were killed in the North Kivu region…The victims were tied up and hacked to death and some reports suggest the total casualties may be nearer 50, according to World Watch Monitor (WWM)."[19] There are multiple similar reports of death-by-hacking.

The Persecution of Christians in Nigeria

There are countless reports of persecution of Christians in Nigeria. Here is just one example: "A Christian mother of seven was hacked to death by suspected Muslim radicals in Nigeria and her mutilated body was discovered in a pool of blood along with a Bible and megaphone she used to preach every morning." She had been evangelizing near Nigeria's capital of Abuja when she was seized and hacked to death.[20] I wish this were an isolated event, but it is not.

The Persecution of Christians in Uganda

I read about a Muslim father who warned his children "not to attend church or listen to the gospel message." He threatened them with a sharp knife that he promised to use to kill them in broad daylight if they converted to Christianity. The man's daughter indeed converted and she refused to recant. He promptly "locked her up in a room for six months without seeing sunlight" and she "was not given any food." Her brother slipped her small morsels of food and sips of water whenever he could, but she grew to be extremely malnourished. She was finally rescued, and "was bony, very weak, and not able to talk or walk...Her hair had turned yellow, she had long fingernails and sunken eyes, and she looked very slim, less than 44 pounds."[21]

The Persecution of Christians in Europe

I could write an entire chapter on the persecution of Christians in Europe, but one notable example will suffice to make my point:

> The latest in a steady stream of Islamic terrorist attacks in Europe...was the killing of an elderly priest after two armed attackers claiming allegiance to Islamic State stormed into a church in Normandy during mass. Father Hamel was forced to kneel and then had his throat slit.

It later emerged that the church was on a list of targets found on an Islamic State suspect last year, which included several places of worship. Up to now, Islamic terrorism in Europe has been directed against civilians in crowds, shopping centers, or public transport. Muslims targeting worshippers in a church is a new departure for Europeans, but not for Christians in countries where Islam has a stronger presence.[22]

Another report reveals how young Muslim children are being indoctrinated with hatred toward Christians. One boy walked through the streets in Belgium shouting: "Oh Allah, destroy the terrible Christians. Oh Allah, kill them all. Do not let a single one survive."[23]

The Persecution of Christians in America

While things are not as bad for Christians in America as in other parts of the world, make no mistake: *The tide is turning against Christians in the United States.*

In Houston, where I used to live, the (gay) mayor subpoenaed the sermons of five Protestant ministers to determine if their words from the pulpit about sexuality violated a new city ordinance. While her efforts were ultimately unsuccessful, her action represents a much larger group of individuals who are now taking a militant stand against Bible-believing Christians.

Meanwhile, we witness all kinds of other examples of Christians being persecuted for believing the Bible. A military chaplain was transferred out of his present assignment because of his faithfulness to biblical values. A Christian employee at a day-care center was fired because she refused to address a six-year-old boy as a girl. And a new breed of atheists has arisen in our culture that is no longer willing to live and let live, but seeks to bury Christianity under an avalanche of attacks. The list goes on.[24]

How things have changed in America! In an insightful article, Joseph Hayes observes:

> In a day and age where everyone wants to be accepted for who they are, Christians will experience far different. As tolerance to sin grows, an intolerance for God's commands will also increase and true ambassadors of God will be faced with a stark choice…Bow to the world's demands, fit in and dishonor God. Or reject the new societal norms of the world and face intense persecution. That puts every person who believes and adheres to Jesus Christ as their Lord to have to walk in the face of persecution and pressure.[25]

The truth is that anti-Christian sentiment has been growing in the United States for many years. As one cultural analyst put it, "Christians and conservatives of all stripes are being pushed out of the public square, silenced and openly discriminated against."[26]

Princeton professor Robert George, in a speech delivered in 2014, observed:

> To be a witness to the Gospel today is to make oneself a marked man or woman. It is to expose oneself to scorn and reproach. To unashamedly proclaim the Gospel in its fullness is to place in jeopardy one's security, one's personal aspirations and ambitions, the peace and tranquility one enjoys, one's standing in polite society. One may in consequence of one's public witness be discriminated against and denied educational opportunities and the prestigious credentials they may offer; one may lose valuable opportunities for employment and professional advancement; one may be excluded from worldly recognition and honors of various sorts; one's witness may even cost one treasured friendships. It may produce

familial discord and even alienation from family members. Yes, there are costs of discipleship—heavy costs.[27]

I hate to say it, but I think we've witnessed only the beginnings of the persecution of Christians in the United States and around the world. The stage is now being set for the catastrophic persecutions that will unfold during the future seven-year tribulation.

MARRIAGE AND THE FAMILY UNIT IN A SEXUALLY DYSFUNCTIONAL SOCIETY

The rapid rise in the acceptance of homosexuality and same-sex marriages is a significant cultural phenomenon. A *homosexual* is a person who experiences erotic desires, fantasies, and attractions toward a member of the same sex. (The Greek word *homos* means "same.") *Gay* is a slang term for a homosexual of either gender. The term indicates not only one's sexual orientation, but also identifies one as being homosexual-affirming and a member of the homosexual community. A *lesbian* is a female homosexual. A *bisexual* is a person sexually responsive to both genders. The term *coming out* refers to the act of openly acknowledging and publicly revealing that one is a homosexual. *Same-sex marriage* refers to a formal marital union of two persons of the same sex. The initialism *LGBT* refers to lesbian, gay, bisexual, and transgender.

The traditional concept of the family is being challenged today like never before. A 2016 report by *CNN* noted, "The traditional concept of family has evolved over the years…Gone are the days when it was just a husband and wife and maybe some children. Now, whether it includes a single parent or maybe an LGBT couple, people are redefining what it means to be a family."[1] These days, *family* is said to be "all about giving and receiving love and affection," as well as "feeling protected and connecting with other human beings." For many people, it does not matter if that love and affection is shared between a married man and woman, an unmarried man and woman cohabiting with each other, or a same-sex couple.[2] All these are now considered "family" by the broader culture because they all involve the giving and receiving of love.

A well-known newspaper ran a photomontage on today's family unit that featured "7 stunning images." As one peruses the images, a majority of them depict same-sex couples—man and man or woman and woman—often with young children living with the couple.[3] Understandably, June 26, 2016 was a day to celebrate for same-sex couples because the Supreme Court affirmed their right to marry across the United States, agreeing with the majority of Americans who now support "marriage equality."

About a year after the Supreme Court ruling, almost half of gay and lesbian couples living together have been married. A Gallup poll tells us: "The percentage of married cohabiting same-sex couples, as opposed to couples living together but not married, rose to 49 percent from 38 percent before the ruling."[4] The Pew Research Center found that 51 percent of Americans polled now favor same-sex marriage, with 59 percent of both supporters and opposers describing it as "inevitable."[5]

Joe Dallas, a noted expert on homosexuality, addresses the current attitudes of Christians on same-sex marriage:

> Notable is the fact that resistance to the redefinition of marriage has overwhelmingly come from conservative Christians, but even in that population a generation gap seems to exist. A *Times-Picayune* survey, for example, showed 44 percent of self-identified evangelicals between the ages of eighteen and twenty-nine

supporting the rights of homosexual couples to marry…
but not necessarily indicating approval of homosexuality itself. Since the same poll found evangelical opposition to homosexuality hovering around 80 percent, the chasm between the attitudes of young and older believers is clear.[6]

So, it all comes down to this:

- Most Americans accept same-sex marriage.
- Older Christians reject it.
- Younger Christians are *tolerant* of it, even if they don't necessarily *approve* of it.

Meanwhile, the LGBT community is now flexing its collective legal muscle against any whom they perceive to be violating their rights. There are many examples, but one is sufficient to make my point. Consider ChristianMingle.com, a 16-million-member Christian dating website that has been forced to admit gay and lesbian users following an antidiscrimination lawsuit. We are told: "The country's most popular Christian dating site will offer options for same-sex matches, rather than limiting searches to 'a man seeking a woman or a woman seeking a man.'"[7] The plaintiffs in the case sued the popular website for violating a California civil rights law that requires "all business establishments of every kind whatsoever," regardless of their religious affiliation, to offer full accommodations regardless of a person's sexual orientation. I believe that Christian establishments will be increasingly targeted by the LGBT community in the years to come. Challenging times lie ahead.

God's Word Reimagined

Traditional Christians have always viewed homosexuality as a violation of God's Word. After all, the Bible explicitly warns that homosexuals will not inherit the kingdom of God (1 Corinthians 6:9-10). The Scriptures consistently condemn homosexual practices (Leviticus 18:22; Romans 1:26-27). The Bible also condemns all types of sexual immorality, which would include homosexuality (Matthew 15:19; Mark 7:21-22; Acts 15:20,29; Galatians 5:19-21; 1 Thessalonians 4:3-5; Hebrews 13:4).

Homosexuals typically respond, however, that the Bible *correctly understood* does not condemn homosexuality, but rather indicates that homosexuality is perfectly okay with God. They reinterpret—indeed, *reimagine*—all the verses in the Bible that deal with homosexuality in a way that is favorable to the LGBT lifestyle. Space does not allow me to expound on every such verse, but a look at one of the more important verses will suffice to illustrate how they spin the Scriptures to their benefit.

In Romans 1:26-27 we read: "That is why God abandoned them to their shameful desires. Even the women turned against the natural way to have sex and instead indulged in sex with each other. And the men, instead of having normal sexual relations with women, burned with lust for each other. Men did shameful things with other men."

Homosexuals typically argue that when Paul spoke against what is *unnatural,* he was not declaring that homosexuality was morally wrong for all people but simply that it was unnatural *for heterosexuals*. Homosexuality goes "against the natural way" for heterosexuals, but it does not go "against the natural way" for homosexuals. In their thinking, that which goes "against the natural way" is to be understood only in a sociological sense, not in a biological sense. Rather than condemning homosexual practices, homosexuals believe the Romans passage approves of homosexual practices *for homosexuals*.

This involves reading a meaning into the text that simply is not there (*eisegesis*). When the Bible declares that homosexual practices are "against the natural way" (Romans 1:26), it is referring to biological, not sociological, nature. Hence, this passage cannot be used to justify homosexuality.

Sexuality and sexual expression are defined biologically in Scripture from the very beginning. In Genesis 1 God created "male and female" and then told them to "be fruitful and multiply" (Genesis 1:27-28). This reproduction was possible only if he was referring to a biological male and female. Sexual orientation is understood biologically, not sociologically, when God said, "That is why a man leaves his father and mother and is united to his wife, and they become one flesh" (Genesis 2:24 NIV). Only a biological father and mother can produce children, and the reference to "one flesh" simply cannot be understood in any relationship except heterosexual physical marriage.

The latter part of Romans 1:27 affirms that the men "did shameful things with other men." The "shameful things" of which Paul speaks involve homosexual acts. What they did was not natural to them. They abandoned "normal sexual relations with women" and "burned with lust for each other" (verse 27). It is evident that God is condemning sexual sins between those of the same biological sex. Homosexual acts are contrary to human nature, not just to a heterosexual's sexual orientation.

Of course, many other Bible passages are similarly reimagined by homosexuals. Examples include Genesis 19:4-8; Leviticus 18:22; Deuteronomy 23:17; 1 Samuel 18:1-4; Isaiah 56:3; Acts 10:15; and 1 Corinthians 6:9-10. In each case, the Bible is reinterpreted in such a way that it comes out sounding like it supports the LGBT lifestyle. In truth, the LGBT community is engaging in Scripture twisting. Scripture warns: "Woe to those who call evil good and good evil, who put darkness for light and light for darkness" (Isaiah 5:20 NIV).

Increasing Openness to Premarital Sex

Meanwhile, heterosexuals are increasingly open to premarital sex. In 2016 a book was published titled *Good Christian Sex: Why Chastity Isn't the Only Option—And Other Things the Bible Says About Sex.* The book was written by the Reverend Bromleigh McCleneghan, from the Union Church of Hinsdale, Illinois. McCleneghan argues that premarital sex is okay for Christians: "We can be chaste—faithful—in unmarried sexual relationships if we exercise restraint: if we refrain from having sex that isn't mutually pleasurable and affirming, that doesn't respect the autonomy and sacred worth of ourselves and our partners."[8]

Despite the fact that McCleneghan's ideas blatantly contradict holy Scripture, her book has been praised by many reviewers. The *Washington Post* says, "McCleneghan argues against a rule-based look at biblical purity and opens up the scripture to a more holistic approach." *Publisher's Weekly* says, "McCleneghan offers ways to rethink biblical passages and find a compromise so that faith and embracing human sexuality don't have to be mutually exclusive." A rabbi commented, "*Good Christian Sex* shows what open-minded, sex-positive encounters with the holy can and should look like." An article in the *Religion News Service* says, "What you thought was naughty may actually be holy. That's the message of *Good Christian Sex*, Bromleigh McCleneghan's attempt to free Christians from shame about having premarital or extramarital sex."[9]

The truth is, McCleneghan consistently engages in *eisegesis* (reading meanings into biblical texts that are not there) instead of *exegesis* (objectively drawing the meaning out of the text of Scripture itself). She has decided in advance what she wants Scripture to say, and then she "interprets" the Scriptures to say that very thing.

Not surprisingly, premarital sex today is at an all-time high. Back in 1972, only 28 percent of Americans admitted to having sex before marriage. In 1978 the figure rose to 38 percent, and in 2004, 44 percent. In 2012 the figure rose to 58 percent. The figure is even higher today. Premarital sex is on a steady upward trend.[10]

The Barna Group found that the majority of Americans are "delinking" marriage and sex:

> Whereas practicing Christians still overwhelmingly tie sex to marriage, the move among the greater U.S. population—most evidently among younger generations—is a de-linking of marriage and sex. Sex has become less a function of procreation or an expression of intimacy and more of a personal experience. To have sex is increasingly seen as a pleasurable and important element in the journey toward self-fulfillment.[11]

Cohabitation on the Rise

In keeping with the broad acceptance of premarital sex, many heterosexual Americans are now cohabiting rather than getting married. Cohabitation is the new norm in America—and our culture considers cohabiting couples "families." A Barna poll found that "almost six in 10 (57 percent) either currently, or have previously lived with their boyfriend/girlfriend—a number very close to the 65 percent who believe it is a good idea."[12] The poll also found that 44 percent of American adults would be okay with their children cohabiting prior to marriage.

Cohabitation no longer raises eyebrows. Some Americans even consider it a virtue, believing that it enables a couple to make a discerning and well-informed decision about marrying the right person. Just as a person might test-drive a car before purchasing it, so people can cohabit to see if their partner is right for marriage. Today, two-thirds of American adults either "strongly" or "somewhat" agree that it's good to cohabit with someone—essentially forming a test family—before deciding to tie the knot in marriage.

While a growing number of people interpret this as a good thing, I see it as highly problematic. In addition to violating Scripture, cohabiting people lack the important element of permanence. At any time, as soon as one of the cohabiters feels it's time to move on—or perhaps decides it's time to cohabit with someone else— that "family" instantly changes. So-called "families" can be quickly dissolved and new ones formed when each of the partners cohabits with someone else.

Without permanence, the family no longer functions as a haven of stability, security, and dependability. And people—especially children—need stability, security, and dependability in order to be emotionally well-adjusted.

Regardless, one people group that is vocally in favor of cohabitation is today's atheists. Christian apologist Frank Turek goes so far as to say that America's fall away from God has more to do with *sex* than *unbelief in Christianity*. Whether one agrees with him, the sex factor is significant.

If a professed atheist were asked, "If Christianity were true, would you become a Christian?," Turek believes that more often than not, the atheist would say no. He believes the real reason many atheists deny God is not because of a lack of evidence that God exists, but rather they desire to pursue sexual freedom outside the confines of Christian morality.[13]

Humanist philosopher Aldous Huxley is probably the best example of this mentality. His lack of belief in God "liberated" him from morality and gave him "sexual freedom":

> I had motives for not wanting the world to have a meaning; and consequently assumed that it had none, and was able without any difficulty to find satisfying reasons for this assumption...The philosopher who finds no meaning in the world is not concerned exclusively with

a problem in pure metaphysics. He is also concerned to prove that there is no valid reason why he personally should not do as he wants to do. For myself, as no doubt for most of my friends, the philosophy of meaningless-ness was essentially an instrument of liberation from a certain system of morality. We objected to the morality because it interfered with our sexual freedom.[14]

Former atheist Lee Strobel reveals that this was a motivating fac-tor when he chose to believe in atheistic Darwinism: "I was more than happy to latch onto Darwinism as an excuse to jettison the idea of God so I could unabashedly pursue my own agenda in life with-out moral constraints."[15] He reflects:

I had a lot of motivation to find faults with Christian-ity when I was an atheist. I knew that my hard-drinking, immoral, and self-obsessed lifestyle would have to change if I ever became a follower of Jesus, and I wasn't sure I wanted to let go of that. After all, it was all I knew. Consequently, instead of trying to find the truth, I found myself attempting to fend off the truth with fab-ricated doubts and contrived objections.[16]

No wonder Christian scholar J. Budziszewski concluded that "not many people disbelieve in God and then begin to sin; most atheists adopt some favorite sin and then find reasons to disbelieve in God."[17] This brings to mind Psalm 14:1: "Only fools say in their hearts, 'There is no God.'" Notice that this verse is not saying that a person is a fool for denying the existence of God. Rather, he is called a fool for *saying in his heart* that there is no God. The implication is that he knows better. He says there is no God, despite the fact that he knows there likely is one. Such is an act of great folly. Verse 3 then tells us that such people have become corrupt. Scripture draws a very close connection between a corrupt lifestyle and a denial of God's existence (see also Romans 1:18-25).

The Ravages of Pornography

Meanwhile, more people are looking at pornography than ever before. Last year people around the world spent a whopping 4.5 billion hours looking at porn. The highest number of porn pageviews took place in the United States (accounting for 41 percent of global porn traffic), followed by the United Kingdom, India, Canada, and Germany. About 64 percent of all porn was viewed either on a cellphone or a tablet.[18] David Kinnaman and Gabe Lyons tell us:

> As an $8 billion business, porn is one of the fastest-growing segments of the entertainment industry. Porn is consumed by more than fifty million Americans. To put the size and scope of the skin business in perspective, the industry's income rivals that of iTunes digital merchandise sales and the US bottled water industry.[19]

One of the most alarming trends is how many Christian pastors are looking at porn today. The Barna Group surveyed 432 pastors and 338 youth pastors. "Most pastors (57%) and youth pastors (64%) admit they have struggled with porn, either currently or in the past," Barna reported. "Overall, 21 percent of youth pastors and 14 percent of pastors admit they currently struggle with using porn."[20] The survey also revealed that more than one in ten youth pastors (12 percent) and one in twenty pastors (5 percent) say they are addicted to porn.

Not unexpectedly, 75 percent of youth pastors and 64 percent of pastors said looking at porn has negatively impacted their ministry. As well, 87 percent of the pastors said they felt shame about their viewing habits, and 55 percent said they lived in constant fear of others finding out about it.[21]

This is tragic.

Also alarming is the rising number of females looking at porn. *Christianity Today* reports that "porn addiction is typically seen as a male problem, both in the church and society. The majority of porn addiction resources are directed at men, but awareness is growing that it isn't just a guy thing."[22] Indeed, statistics reveal that some 20 percent of Christian women admit they are addicted to pornography. Among college-age women, 18 percent admit to spending time on the Internet viewing sexual images.[23] One study found that one in three visitors to porn websites are women, and that 9.4 million women access porn monthly.[24] Understandably, 70 percent of women keep their porn use a secret.

Amazingly, viewing porn does not bother most Americans. "The moral stigma against porn and 'soft porn'—sexual images and situations on TV and in movies and video games—is loosening its hold on people. More than half of US teens and adults say, 'It really doesn't bother me' to use porn."[25]

One analysis suggests that "the Internet has become a great accelerator for pornography because it is *accessible, affordable*, and *anonymous*."[26] In other words, it's easy to obtain, at little or no cost, and no one will find out about it. *It's a recipe for disaster*.

Viewing porn can have a traumatic effect on marriage and the family unit. God designed sex to be one of the sweet and intimate joys of lifelong marriage (Genesis 2:24; Matthew 19:4-6; 1 Timothy 4:4; Hebrews 13:4; see also the Song of Solomon). Young people whose minds are regularly saturated with porn prior to getting married will find it much more difficult to experience sexual satisfaction with their spouse. Likewise, a married man or woman who feeds on porn will find it difficult to experience sexual satisfaction with his or her spouse. Counselors and sexologists tell us that porn tends to have a strong desensitizing effect. The more porn one feeds on, the more desensitized one becomes to sexual stimulation. No spouse can possibly compete with the graphic and highly stimulating sexual images and videos that are on the Internet. Marriage and the family are wounded in the world of porn.

The Lure of Sexting Among Our Youth

Sexting involves the sending and receiving of sexually explicit images or text typically through a variety of apps and social media.

Sexting has caught on in a big way among the youth of our day. A typical scenario involves a teenage boy and girl who are attracted to each other, and they end up having some sexual encounters. As their relationship progresses, they end up sending nude or partially nude pictures of themselves to each other.

While teens assume their texts and images will remain only with the person they initially sexted, the harsh reality is that sharing often takes place among such teenagers. The current statistics reveal that 17 percent of sexters share the intimate images they have received with other people, and 55 percent of those share them with more than one person.[27]

A 2014 study revealed that 54 percent of college-age students admitted to having participated in sexting before they were 18 years old. The researchers of this study admitted: "We were shocked by the prevalence and the frequency of sexting among minors."[28]

I came across one particularly disturbing news report about a 14-year-old girl who had been innocently texting with a guy she was fond of. But then the boy asked her to send him a revealing photo. She thought she was safe in doing so. Once received, he asked for an even more revealing photo. The process continued. Before long, he had some explicit photographs of this girl. She gullibly trusted that the photos would be kept confidential. But the boy shared them with his friends, who subsequently shared them with other friends.

Soon, many people had the photos on their cellphones. When the girl discovered what had happened, she was devastated beyond what words can describe.

Multiply this single episode by untold thousands of young people, and you begin to see that we've got a huge problem here. I previously mentioned that pornography is injurious to marriage and the family unit. Sexting is also injurious. There is no telling how many young people will eventually go into a marriage relationship while retaining deep emotional scars from past violations related to sexting.

Transgender Confusion

A transgender person is someone whose self-identity does not conform unambiguously to conventional notions of male or female gender. It used to be that almost everyone would have looked upon such an individual as an oddball. Not anymore! A recent poll indicates that "45 percent of Americans do not think it is morally wrong for people to self-identify as a gender different from their birth sex."[29] Moreover, "a majority of Americans reject the view of a Creator giving them a gender that shouldn't be changed."[30]

Those in favor of such an idea suggest that people often change things about themselves—including having their teeth whitened, having a facelift or a tummy tuck, dyeing one's hair, and even getting tattoos. "Many Americans view gender as one more thing on that list."[31]

One of the more controversial issues related to transgender people is *which bathroom should they use?* Former President Obama issued a directive to public schools to allow students to use the bathroom of their choosing regardless of their biological sex. He justified his position by appealing to the Golden Rule: "My reading of Scripture tells me that the Golden Rule is pretty high up there in terms of my Christian belief."[32]

Here's the problem: I don't like the idea of a teenage boy or a grown man walking into the girls' room where my little girl happens to be. Even if that boy or man says he identifies as a female, it is simply inappropriate for him to walk into a bathroom where little girls are. Such a policy leaves open the door for all kinds of abuse.

I read about a store detective at Macy's. The detective was a Christian, and after working at Macy's for over 26 years, he was fired for standing up to a man claiming to be transgender who was in the ladies' restroom.

A female customer and her daughter had informed this detective that they were afraid to use the restroom because a transgender man was in there. The detective asked the man to leave so the mother and daughter could enter. The man refused.

After a time, the man left the restroom holding the hand of his female companion—still claiming to be transgender. The man then filed a complaint with store management, and the detective was promptly fired.[33]

In the previous chapter I mentioned a Christian employee at a day-care center who was fired because she refused to address a six-year-old boy as a girl. The young boy claimed to be a girl, and because the day-care worker refused to call him a girl, the employee was shown the door.

Is it just me or does it sometimes seem like things in Western culture have taken a turn for the surreal? As a God-fearing Christian, I fear for the future of this country.

God Has Spoken

My friends, God is the one who caused the Bible to be written. And through it He speaks to us today just as He spoke to people when those words were first given. The Bible is to be received as God's words to us and revered and obeyed. As we submit to the

Bible's authority, we place ourselves under the authority of the living God. The Scriptures "are God preaching, God talking, God telling, and God instructing."[34]

From the pages of Scripture, we learn that marriage is a divinely ordered institution designed to form a permanent union between *one man* and *one woman* for the purpose of not only bringing blessing to each other but also for procreating or propagating the human race (Genesis 1:26-28; 2:24)—something that is impossible in same-sex marriages. The Lord Jesus Himself gave support for God's heterosexual design for marriage (Matthew 19:4-6).

Holy Scripture is consistent in its emphasis that a sexual relationship should be engaged in only within the confines of marriage *between a male and a female* (1 Corinthians 7:2). The apostles urged all Christians to abstain from sexual immorality (Acts 15:20). The apostle Paul said that the body was not made for sexual sin and that a person should flee it (1 Corinthians 6:12-20).

Scripture has especially strong words for those who violate their marital vows and commit adultery. Indeed, adultery is condemned (Exodus 20:14), and in the Old Testament adulterers were put to death (Leviticus 20:10). Jesus pronounced adultery wrong even in its basic motives (Matthew 5:27-28). Paul called sexual immorality, which would include adultery, an evil work of the flesh (Galatians 5:19). John envisioned in the lake of fire some of those who practiced sexual immorality (Revelation 21:8).

As we saw earlier, sex within a biblically defined marriage, however, is said to be very good in Scripture. Sex was a part of God's good creation. Indeed, God created sex and "everything God created is good" (1 Timothy 4:4). But it is good *only* within the confines of the marriage relationship, which He Himself ordained. Such words are utterly ignored by many today.

I am especially concerned for our children. I don't think a young boy or girl will learn properly about heterosexual relationships being raised by same-sex parents. I don't think a boy will learn how to become a man living with female same-sex parents, and I don't think a girl will learn how to become a woman living with male same-sex parents. I don't think a young boy or girl will come to understand and appreciate the sacredness of marriage living with cohabiting parents. And I don't think a young boy or girl will develop a healthy self-identity being raised by a transgender parent.

I know that what I'm saying is politically incorrect. I also know that my viewpoint constitutes a head-on collision with Western culture. So I humbly borrow the words of the great Martin Luther: "Here I stand, I can do no other. God help me. Amen."

Luther also once said that "family life is a school for character."[35] By this he meant that young people gain their values and indeed their moral character from their parents. But things are not as they once were. Though we cannot make a blanket statement true of all families, it is true that many families in modern America have been a dismal failure in being a "school for character."

Today many young people have become disillusioned with the values of their parents. My old friend Walter Martin (now with the Lord) explained it this way:

> Beginning with the "rock 'n roll" era of the early fifties, the youth of America have become increasingly disillusioned with their parents' values and unwilling to submit to those values. Because of a newly dominant feeling that the Self is the ultimate judge of what is right and wrong, young people have reexamined all the values passed down to them from the adult population. In their examination of these traditional values, the youth have lacked an objective ethical standard and have therefore found no reason to keep those values. Thus, many

of our youth today are valueless; truth and morality have become completely subjective.[36]

Instead of deriving values from their parents, many youth today are constructing their own values. They reject the idea that values are to be imposed from without, such as from Scripture or from parents, but must be subjectively discovered: "Whatever works for you is your truth" and "whatever works for me is my truth." The underlying assumption is that there are no absolute truths or values.

You and I know better. As Christians, we recognize that absolute morals are grounded in the absolutely moral God of the Bible (Matthew 5:48). Moreover, you and I as Christians are called to be salt and light in our society (Matthew 5:13-16). As we function as salt and light, let's heed Joe Dallas's wise words about living in a sexually dysfunctional world: "Paul's balanced approach—living peacefully with all as much as possible (Rom. 12:18) while not partaking in another person's sin (1 Tim. 5:22) nor violating one's own conscience (Rom. 14:23)—is applicable here."[37] Let's always be ready to share the truth—but let's do it with gentleness and respect (1 Peter 3:15-16).

Concerns for the Present and the Future

According to prophetic Scripture, "the Holy Spirit tells us clearly that in the last times some will turn away from the true faith; they will follow deceptive spirits and teachings that come from demons. These people are hypocrites and liars, and their consciences are dead" (1 Timothy 4:1-2). The phrase "consciences are dead" can also be translated "consciences are destroyed" (Expanded Bible).

This indicates that doctrinal apostasy in the end times will be accompanied by moral apostasy. The consciences of people in the end times will no longer be sensitive toward the things of God, for their consciences will be "dead" or "destroyed." Today, does it not seem that many people have no conscience when it comes to sexual sin?

Scripture also tells us that "in the last days there will be very difficult times" (2 Timothy 3:1). I believe this passage applies directly to the pervasive sexual sin we witness in our society. Look at it this way:

> In the last days there will be very difficult times. For people will love only themselves [including sexual self-gratification] and their money. They will be boastful and proud, scoffing at God [like humanists and atheists, who disbelieve in God precisely so they can enjoy sexual freedom], disobedient to their parents, and ungrateful. They will consider nothing sacred [not even the institution of marriage nor the marriage bed]. They will be unloving and unforgiving; they will slander others and have no self-control [but will instead engage in all varieties of sexual deviations]. They will be cruel and hate what is good. They will betray their friends, be reckless, be puffed up with pride, and love pleasure rather than God [including the lustful pleasure of deviant sex] (2 Timothy 3:1-4).

My friends, here is what I expect to see in the coming years:

- The traditional concept of marriage will continue to be marginalized.
- The traditional concept of the family unit will continue to be marginalized.
- Increasing numbers of people—including Christians—will choose to accept same-sex marriage.
- The "family" will increasingly be understood as any group of people who live together in a loving relationship.

- Scripture-twisting will continue among those seeking divine sanction for their deviant lifestyles.

- Premarital sex will increasingly be accepted as the norm.

- Cohabitation will increasingly be accepted as the norm.

- Viewing pornography will increasingly be accepted as the norm.

- Criticizing people who hold to a different view than we do will likely continue to be categorized as a "hate crime" in various countries around the world.

Lord, please embolden Your people to tell the truth—and hold fast to the truth—in these ever-darkening times. Lord have mercy.

E-MADNESS: THE ESCALATION OF CYBERATTACKS AND CYBERWARFARE

The day I started writing this chapter there was a massive cyber-attack against the United States, barring Internet access to over half the people in the country. But it's not just the country that's being attacked. Individuals are being attacked at an unprecedented pace. "More than one-third of U.S. consumers experienced a computer virus, hacking incident, or other cyberattack in the past 12 months...Young adults 18-24 were the most likely victims...The threat to cyber security for individuals and families is significant and growing."[1]

This past year, there was a hack of Democratic party records, now blamed on Russian intelligence services. Chinese hackers downloaded digital truckloads of data on more than 20 million U.S. government workers. North Korea raided Sony Pictures' computers after the movie company released a comedy movie that mocked North Korea's dictator.[2] A hacking group called "The Shadow Brokers" infiltrated NSA's computers and is now looking to sell off cyberweapons used by the agency, asking for $1 billion.[3] The United States has gotten in on the act as well. In a joint operation in 2012, the U.S. and Israel joined forces to deploy a devastating computer worm, known as Stuxnet, to damage Iran's nuclear program.

It seems strange to ponder that cyberattacks and cyberwarfare have become concerns for people planetwide. Cyberspace has now become a digital playground for countless predators—both individual and national. The problem is getting more threatening by the day. A recent report tells us that "177 million personal records were exposed in data breaches in 2015…That's double the 85.6 million records that were exposed in 2014."[4] It's difficult to assess precisely how much data has been accessed and stolen in cyberspace, for in many cases the people whose data has been stolen are unaware of the theft.

What Is Cyberspace?

Cyberspace includes the Internet where you surf the web and retrieve your email. It also includes other—often private—networks and associated infrastructures where information is stored, modified, and retrieved.[5]

Richard Clarke, in his well-received book *Cyber War: The Next Threat to National Security and What to Do About It*, puts things a bit more understandable when he says that cyberspace refers to "all of the computer networks in the world and everything they connect and control."[6] He clarifies that cyberspace includes not just the Internet, but also networks of computers that the average Joe (like you and me) are not supposed to be able to access. These may be private networks of corporations where sensitive product data or marketing strategies can be accessed. Or they may be private military networks where military personnel can access data on the latest weapon technologies. Such private networks feel very much like the Internet, but they are supposed to be separate from the Internet—at least in theory.

Other parts of cyberspace involve control systems that enable machines to communicate with other machines. For example, an electronic control panel—either nearby or far away—can communicate with water pumps, or elevators in a building, or electrical generators, or traffic lights. Still other parts of cyberspace involve the flow of data, such as data related to stock market trades and the credit card transaction at the local supermarket where you just shopped. All of this is part and parcel of cyberspace.

Accessing Private Networks

Private networks are supposed to be closed off from the Internet so that those outside the network cannot get in. A closed-off network is often referred to as an *intranet,* a network that is within (for example) a corporation, and only those inside the corporation can access it. Those outside the corporation—people who are just surfing the Internet and are not affiliated with the corporation—are not supposed to be able to access this network.

Herein lies the problem: These intranets are not always secure. Sometimes these intranets "leave a door open" so that anybody can "walk in off the street." Some people, while surfing the web, innocently and inadvertently stumble into such intranets without having tried to do anything wrong. Other people, however, are purposefully seeking to "force their way through the door" to engage in cyber espionage—spying on private secrets.

Relentless Cyberattacks

As I've already indicated, cyberattacks are increasing so fast that it is hard to keep track of it all. Many of these attacks take place through application flaws, including Microsoft Office (Microsoft Word is a popular culprit), as well as Adobe Acrobat (PDF files are a popular means of transporting electronic documents). Such software programs have security flaws that can make it easy for hackers to break in and access things they are not supposed to see at an office that uses these software programs.

Now, for an author like me, it would be no big deal if someone hacked a book I was writing with Microsoft Word. But Microsoft Word in the office of the CIA director or perhaps the secretary of state is a different matter.

Is it any wonder that computer security has become a hot field brimming with high-paying jobs? It's a lucrative field, for the government and corporations will pay big money to remain cybersecure.

An Electronic Pearl Harbor

It might surprise you to learn that the United States is highly vulnerable to severe injury via cyberweapons. Richard Clarke, an antiterrorism expert who has advised several U.S. presidents, warns that great damage could be inflicted on our country in a mere fifteen minutes. The following apocalyptic scenario is entirely possible from a single massive cyberattack:

- The unclassified Department of Defense network known as the NIPRNET collapses, with heavy-duty routers throughout the network failing and constantly rebooting.
- The Department of Defense's classified networks grind to a halt.
- Computer networks at the Pentagon collapse.
- Internet service providers go into meltdown.
- Meltdowns also take place at major financial computer centers in New York, with an incalculably large amount of financial data instantly wiped clean, such that from henceforth no one will know who owns what.
- There is a total collapse of the computer systems at the Federal Aviation Administration's national air traffic control center in Herndon, Virginia.

- Computer systems at alternate air traffic control centers go down, so they cannot see what aircraft are aloft.

- There are subsequent multiple midair collisions of jetliners.

- Infrastructure attacks cause large refinery fires and explosions in various cities.

- Chemical plants malfunction with lethal clouds of chlorine gas spewing into the air.

- Major gas pipelines explode in various suburbs.

- Subway trains crash in multiple cities.

- Traffic lights go out all over the country, resulting in thousands of casualties due to collisions.

- Freight trains derail across the country.

- Blackouts occur in major cities due to power grid failures.

- Communication, weather, and navigation satellites deviate from their orbits, disrupting all the services that depend on these satellites.

- Food and medical supplies deplete at local stores due to the disruption in transportation.

- Communication breaks down on many different levels, including between the different sectors of our government and military.[7]

Fifteen minutes, friends.

Worse comes to worst when it is realized that we may never know with certainty who was responsible for the cyberattack. Was it Russia? China? North Korea? Iran? Such ambiguity makes retaliation much more difficult. With this in mind, many anti-U.S. countries might be more tempted to engage in such an attack, knowing they may never be caught.

The Terrorist Cyberthreat to the United States

A retired director of the FBI's Computer Crime Squad once said: "You bring me a select group of hackers and within 90 days I'll bring this country to its knees."[8] I do not doubt that what this former director said is true. That being the case, here is what concerns me: Because today's Middle Eastern terrorist organizations have the financial backing of oil-rich countries such as Saudi Arabia, Iran, and Syria, they can afford not just a select group of hackers but a whole army of hackers.

Terrorism is defined by the Department of Defense as "the calculated use of unlawful violence or threat of unlawful violence to inculcate fear, intended to coerce or to intimidate governments or societies in the pursuit of goals that are generally political, religious, or ideological." Based on this, the following definition has been suggested for *cyberterrorism*:

> A computer based attack or threat of attack intended to intimidate or coerce governments or societies in pursuit of goals that are political, religious, or ideological. The attack should be sufficiently destructive or disruptive to generate fear comparable to that from physical acts of terrorism. Attacks that lead to death or bodily injury, extended power outages, plane crashes, water contamination, or major economic losses would be examples.[9]

Today, terrorists can engage in terrorist acts from the comfort of their own living rooms. It is probably true that cyberspace gives a sense of empowerment to terrorists they have never enjoyed before because they can accomplish their tasks against the United States without ever having stepped foot into the United States.[10]

Another factor that makes cyberwarfare appealing to terrorists is that it is economical. For as little as $500, one can obtain current cybertechnology suitable for engaging in a variety of terrorist acts against the United States. The potential return on investment is very appealing to terrorists.

Further, cyberspace provides easy and fast access to the entire world. From a single location in a Middle Eastern country, one could engage in terrorist activities against the United States, Britain, and Israel. There are no geographical limitations or boundaries. The same hacker, using the same computer, in the same living room in a Middle Eastern country, could engage in cyberattacks against a variety of perceived enemies.

Cyber-Jihad

Jihad comes from the Arabic word *jihadi*, which principally means "to struggle" or "to strive in the path of Allah." It seems that whenever the United States takes a stand against terrorist Muslims, a jihad or "holy war" is declared. The term is more generally taken among Muslims to refer to armed fighting and warfare in defending Islam and standing against evil.

Radical Islamic fundamentalists are well known for their use of arms and explosives in defending their version of Islam. Jihad, in their thinking, has the goal of terrorizing perceived enemies of Islam into submission and retreat.

Some Islamic terrorists consider cyberspace a means of fulfilling jihad, and cyber-jihadists are gaining momentum.[11] Among the more notable cyber-jihadist groups today are Al-Qaida, Al-Shabab (a Somalia-based militant organization with strong ties to Al-Qaida), Boko Haram (a terrorist organization that strives to establish a militant Islamic state in Nigeria), and ISIS.[12] Experts tell us that "the threat of a cyberattack is a clear and present danger to America and is more likely than a nuclear attack."[13]

Jeffrey Carr talks about this form of jihad in his book, *Inside Cyber Warfare*. He notes how some Islamic hackers speak about cyberattacks in religious terms, affirming that their attacks are tantamount to fighting jihad against Islam's enemies. One such Muslim hacker urged his comrades to engage in cyberattacks against Israel: "Use [the hacking skills] God has given you as bullets in the face of the Jewish Zionists. We cannot fight them with our bodies, but we can fight them with our minds and hands.…By God, this is Jihad."[14]

In view of all this, you can understand why so many in our government are fighting feverishly to beef up the cybersecurity of our country. The terrorists have not just a *political* motivation (thwart U.S. imperialism) but a *religious* motivation (destroy the enemies of Islam and force the entire world into submission to the Islamic faith).

With that kind of motivation, you can bet that if these terrorists *can* use a cyberattack to cripple the U.S. infrastructure (such as our electrical grid), they *will* do it. If they can use a cyberattack to cripple the U.S. economy, they will do it. If they can use a cyberattack to injure the U.S. military, they will do it. In short, these terrorists will use cyberspace to inflict whatever damage they can on the United States.

Varieties of Malware

Malware refers to malicious software that causes computers or networks to do things their owners do not want done—often injurious and disruptive things. There are a variety of kinds of malware, including viruses, worms, phishing scams, spyware, adware, and logic bombs, which I will define below. These varieties of malware constitute the essential arsenal utilized by today's computer hackers.

There are many ways malware can find its way onto your computer. You might innocently visit a website, click on a link, and without you even knowing it, malware downloads to your computer. Or you might visit a website offering what you believe to be a legitimate software program you would like to have on your computer—say, a calendar program. You have no idea that by downloading that program, you are also installing malware on your computer that either will end up damaging your computer or later be used for devious purposes, such as spying on your keystrokes.[15]

A technique that is particularly effective with teenage and twenty-something males relates to Internet pornography. A teen may seek to watch a pornographic video on his computer, but as he clicks on the link to the video, a window pops up that says a plug-in for Windows media player is needed to view the video. When he clicks on the link to the plug-in, he ends up installing malware on his computer. The particularly devious thing is that the needed plug-in is installed on his computer so the video can be viewed—but the malware is also installed behind the scenes. This teenage boy has no idea that his computer has just been infected.[16]

Yet another means of inadvertently infecting one's computer with malware is by clicking on a banner advertisement at a website. What makes this particularly deceptive is that sometimes bad guys place bad advertisements on good websites. Because it is a good website, the natural assumption is that virtually all the advertisements on the website must be produced by good guys as well. This is a false and naïve assumption. Some bad guys initially place a number of legitimate ads on a good website. Then, every once in a while, they slip in an advertisement that has malware built into the computer code.

Advertising networks and websites often do their best to keep infected ads out. Still, web advertisements contain computer code, and anything that contains computer code can also contain infected computer code. The moral of the story is: Always be cautious of advertisements, no matter where they may be found in cyberspace.

People who fail to update their system software with security patches are particularly vulnerable to being infected with malware.[17] The failure to keep system software updated amounts to "lowering your shields" so you are more vulnerable. Security patches for your system software make your computer more secure.

Yet another way that malware might find its way onto your computer relates to security flaws in Microsoft Word. For example, someone might email you a Microsoft Word document that has been infected. When you open that document, it installs malware on your computer. (I never open Microsoft Word files as attachments—not unless it is from someone I know personally and I'm convinced it's absolutely safe.)

Some malware-ridden websites you might visit might try to break into your computer by taking advantage of a security flaw in your web browser, such as Microsoft Internet Explorer. If you happen to browse such a website with a vulnerable browser and operating system configuration, there is a good chance that a piece of malware may download to your computer without you even knowing it.

I have just scratched the surface of some of the ways malware might find its way onto your computer. Cybercriminals are often very clever and are always coming up with creative ways to sneak onto your system. *Internet surfer, beware!* Following is a summary of the different kinds of malware floating around out there in cyberspace.

Computer Viruses

Viruses are essentially software programs that pass from computer user to computer user over the Internet, an intranet (for example, at your workplace), by thumb drives, or CD-ROMs. Computer viruses can disrupt the normal operation of a computer and can even render it unusable. Such viruses can also provide the hacker with a hidden access point to your system and can copy or steal information from your computer, such as banking or credit card information.

Computer Worms

Computer worms are aptly named because they do not require the computer user to do anything to spread the virus from one computer to another. Rather, computer worms can copy themselves from one computer to another by taking advantage of known vulnerabilities in other software programs. This form of malware literally worms itself through the Internet, from computer to computer, network to network. Such worms can infect hundreds of thousands of computers. In fact, they can go global within a very short time. Expanding on the virus analogy, worm viruses are very infectious and highly contagious.

Spyware

Like other forms of malware, spyware gets installed on a user's computer without that user's consent or knowledge. It typically finds its way onto a computer when the user clicks on a link in an email or opens a Microsoft Word document that has been attached to the email.

Spyware specializes in gathering information from a user's computer, including usernames and passwords. This form of spyware utilizes what is called a keystroke logger, which records everything typed into the keyboard of an infected machine. Spyware can also be used in a corporate setting to steal sensitive or proprietary documentation from an executive's computer.

Phishing Scams

Phishing scams are especially devious. You may appear to have received an email from your bank. The email displays all the same graphics and the same logo one normally sees affiliated with the bank. It appears to be a legitimate communication from the bank.

The email might request that you click on a link to go to the bank website, at which point you are requested to provide your username and password. The website itself looks like your bank website, but it is a bogus website designed by a hacker who seeks to obtain your username and password so he can have access to your money. My innocent young niece fell for a phishing scam just like this, had some money sifted from her bank account, and ended up going through a nightmare experience with her bank to unravel the cybermess and get her money back.

At present, there are over 100,000 phishing websites on the Internet, and virtually millions of phishing emails are sent out through cyberspace every day. It is one of the most effective scams out there.

Spear-Phishing Scams

Spear-phishing scams are also pervasive today. A spear-phishing scam involves an email that appears to be from someone you know (using a real name). Sometimes the names of friends, family members, or acquaintances are gathered from social networks such as Facebook and are then used in a spear-phishing attack.

The email message, seeming to be from a real friend, typically asks the recipient to click on a link or open an attachment. For example, the email might say: "Hey John, I came across this article and knew you'd love to see it. Enjoy! Love, Ginny Nelson." Once John clicks on the article link, *zap*, malware is downloaded to his computer.

Logic Bombs

A logic bomb is a nasty piece of malware. It is a software application or computer code that contains instructions that cause a computer system or network of computers to shut down or to erase all data on the network. Once a logic bomb activates on your computer or network, all of it becomes useless hardware.

Some logic bombs are particularly malicious. Let us say, for example, that a foreign hacker has tapped into the computer networks that run the electrical power grid. This hacker could infect the network that runs the power grid with a logic bomb that first initiates instructions to cause a power surge sufficient to fry the circuits of the transformers, and then issue instructions for the computer network to erase itself.[18] When all of that happens, all our electricity goes out—possibly for a very long time.

Trapdoors

Once a hacker penetrates a private network for the first time, he or she often leaves behind a "trapdoor" to permit easier and faster access in the future. This trapdoor is actually malicious software code inserted into a computer that then allows a hacker unauthorized but easy entry into a network.

These trapdoors allow hackers to gain what is known as a "root." In these days of pervasive cybercrimes, a black market of "root kits" has emerged in which hackers trade or sell these to each other—often for a good price. This gives the buyer "root access" to a network or perhaps to a software program under development. This root access allows one to poke around on the network and then erase any evidence that one was ever there. It is much like a criminal who has broken into one's house wiping his fingerprints before he leaves and unlocking a window so it will be easy to get in next time.

Botnets

A botnet is a network of robot-controlled computers that, due to a previous infection, are now forced to operate according to the commands of an unauthorized remote user (*bot* is short for "robot"; *net* is short for "network"). This usually takes place without any knowledge of the computer's owner. The only symptom that a bot is present is that your computer might slow down just a bit. A network of robot-controlled computers—involving, say, 10,000 computers—can be used by a hacker to launch an attack against a target website, typically accomplished by instructing the many bots on various computers to flood the target website with relentless Internet traffic. This causes the website to become jammed or to shut down altogether.

Antivirus Software

Many people have antivirus software on their computers that they think will keep them safe from computer viruses. Certainly, antivirus software will identify and remove some computer viruses, maybe even many viruses. But keep in mind that a new form of malware enters cyberspace every 2.2 seconds. With that statistic in mind, do you think the maker of your antivirus software has the manpower to deal with a malware onslaught that involves a new virus every 2.2 seconds? Not likely. Computer experts tell us that the major antivirus software companies find and fix about one out of every ten malware viruses that are discovered. If you are now thinking that perhaps you are not as safe as you once thought you were, *you have taken your first baby steps toward cyber wisdom.*

The Militarization of Cyberspace

Human beings initially fought all their battles on land. As the technology increased, another domain was added—the sea. Eventually humans developed the technology to engage in battle beneath the sea. Still later, after a quantum leap forward in technological advancements, a third domain for battle was added—the air. Still later, humans attained the capability of going into outer space, where they placed satellites that have military applications (such as spying on our enemies) and navigational aids (such as the global positioning system). With each new technology, human beings have discovered new ways to do battle against each other.[19]

Today, yet another domain for doing battle has emerged—only this time, it is not a physical domain. I am talking, of course, about cyberspace.[20]

Because cyberwarfare is a relatively recent phenomenon, one of the difficulties in talking about it is defining what it is. At present, the international community does not have any international agreement as to what constitutes an act of cyberwar—though our government leaders are talking about this.[21] Because no standardized definition exists, what one country considers an act of cyberwar may not necessarily be considered an act of cyberwar by another country. When one considers that countless nations today are "leveraging the Internet for political, military, and economic espionage activities,"[22] one would think that the international community might come together and hammer out some kind of agreement on the rules of engagement in cyberwarfare. But such has not yet happened. It is something to watch for in coming years.

In very broad terms, cyberwarfare involves "the art and science of fighting without fighting; of defeating an opponent without spilling their blood."[23] The focus of cyberwarfare is on using cyberspace to attack personnel, facilities, and physical equipment with the intent of degrading, neutralizing, or destroying enemy combat capability, while protecting one's own.

Richard Clarke affirms that one goal in cyberwarfare is to penetrate enemy networks and either wield control of them or crash them. If the enemy network can be controlled, that would make possible the destruction or severe injury of the enemy's infrastructure—for example, causing their electrical generators to blow up, causing their air traffic control centers to go blind, causing their trains to derail, disrupting their banks and financial institutions, sending out bogus directions to foot soldiers, and causing their missiles to blow up in the wrong place. If the enemy's network cannot be controlled but only crashed, that still would ultimately wipe all the data from their computers and networks, collapse their financial system, disrupt all their communications, and wreak general havoc.[24]

The United States is quite vulnerable in this regard. Computers and computer networks play a large role in running the infrastructure of our country—including our electrical grid, our transportation, our banking and financial institutions, and much more. The networks that control these various aspects of our infrastructure can be penetrated and exploited from overseas. It all happens in the digital world of cyberspace. That means that cyber commands given by remote control from another nation—say, China or Russia or North Korea—can do all kinds of damage in our nation.

It is not too much to say that cyberspace changes the entire nature of war, as traditionally understood. Traditional concepts of war become obsolete in a cyber-connected world. As one analyst has put it, "Now war means that any group can fight any other group, anywhere in the world, by any number of methods, instantly."[25]

Future Prophetic Wars

A U.S. security expert recently warned: "Cyberwar is a very real danger and is likely to get much worse."[26] I believe he is right. I also believe these technologies will be used in the prophetic wars of the future.

Speaking of the end times, Jesus prophesied: "You will hear of wars and threats of wars…Nation will go to war against nation, and kingdom against kingdom" (Matthew 24:6-7). We witness the eruption of war with the second horseman of the apocalypse in the book of Revelation. We read that when the second seal is opened, "another horse appeared, a red one. Its rider was given a mighty sword and the authority to take peace from the earth. And there was war and slaughter everywhere" (Revelation 6:4). The fact that the horse is red indicates bloodshed, killing with the sword, and war. Notice that peace will be taken "from the earth." Bloodshed will be global.

Of course, the ultimate war discussed in the book of Revelation is Armageddon. *Armageddon* literally means "Mount of Megiddo" and refers to a location about 60 miles north of Jerusalem. This is the location of Barak's battle with the Canaanites (Judges 4) and Gideon's battle with the Midianites (Judges 7). This will be the site for the final horrific battles of humankind just prior to the second coming of Jesus Christ (Revelation 16:16).

It is a given that cyberwarfare will play a significant role in all of this. Military generals inform us that in future wars, physical attacks against a country will always be preceded by a cyberattack against that country. The idea is to confuse and disorient the enemy by a cyberattack, and then launch the physical attack. Since wars in the end times will involve nations all around the world, it is reasonable to assume that all or most of these nations will use full cyber capabilities in standing against their enemies. Cyber technologies will also no doubt be utilized by the antichrist in maintaining global dominion as the world's leading military commander, as well as to control the world's economy.

THE GROWING NUCLEAR AND ELECTROMAGNETIC PULSE THREAT

Do the prophetic Scriptures address the issue of nuclear bombs? Although no direct reference exists, some prophecy expositors believe there may be some allusions to nuclear weaponry in prophetic Scripture.

From the perspective of the future seven-year tribulation period, Revelation 8:7 tells us that "one-third of the earth was set on fire, one-third of the trees were burned, and all the green grass was burned." In other words, a large portion of the earth will be incinerated in a very short time. Soon after, Revelation 16:2 prophesies that people worldwide will break out with "horrible, malignant sores." Some wonder whether these sores might be the result of radiation poisoning following the detonation of nuclear weapons. It is a possibility.

Others wonder whether Jesus may have been alluding to nuclear weaponry when He prophesied of the end times that "people will be terrified at what they see coming upon the earth, for the powers in the heavens will be shaken" (Luke 21:26). It is possible that such words could describe the force unleashed by one or more nuclear detonations.

Whether this is so, modern prophecy scholars often suggest the possibility of an eventual nuclear detonation on American soil.

This possibility exists because prophecy reveals that in the end times the balance of power will shift from the United States of America toward the United States *of Europe*—that is, toward a revived Roman Empire that will be headed up by the antichrist. This shift in the balance of power may indicate that the United States of America will somehow weaken in the end times.

Many possible scenarios could explain this weakening—two of the more likely are either a nuclear attack or an electromagnetic pulse (EMP) attack against the United States. Government advisors say that a nuclear attack on U.S. soil within the next ten years is more likely than not. Even if such an attack targeted just one major city, this would have a devastating and crippling effect on the already fragile U.S. economy for years to come.

Pondering the possibility of a nuclear attack against the United States is not the talk of mere sensationalists or alarmists. Some of the greatest thinkers in our land are sounding warning bells. National security experts say the risk of attack by weapons of mass destruction within the next decade may be as high as 70 percent. Some U.S. senators are saying that the United States faces an existential threat from terrorists who may get their hands on weapons of mass destruction. In the next decade, they say, we face the very real possibility of nuclear jihad.

One problem the United States faces is that it continues to have many easy entrances across its borders. It would not be difficult for a terrorist to smuggle a nuclear bomb into the country. A bomb could also be shipped into the United States. Some 50,000 cargo containers are shipped into the United States each day, and only about 5 percent of them get screened. That leaves 95 percent that remain unscreened. A bomb could easily make its way into the country in one of the unscreened containers.

It is also possible that some terrorist group could launch a nuclear weapon from a missile on a commercial ship off the coast of the United States. About 75 percent of the U.S. population is within 200 miles of the coast. With so many merchant ships sailing off U.S. coastal waters—over 130,000 from 195 countries—the nuclear danger is obvious.

The Nuclear Capabilities of North Korea

The United States also faces a threat from nuclear weapons delivered via intercontinental ballistic missiles (ICBMs). North Korea is rapidly becoming a major threat in this regard. Not long ago, North Korea released a four-minute video worldwide that threatens a nuclear attack against Washington, DC. It portrays an animated scene in which a North Korean submarine launches a missile that strikes near the Lincoln Memorial, triggering an explosion that annihilates the city. The video boasts: "If the American imperialists provoke us a bit, we will not hesitate to slap them with a preemptive nuclear strike."[1]

North Korea has released other videos that make similar threats. One portrays a nuclear attack on Manhattan. Another portrays our president and U.S. troops in flames. One of the videos proclaims: "The United States must choose! It's up to you whether the nation called the United States exists on this planet or not."[2]

The very day I am writing this chapter, a new report surfaced that North Korea has tested missiles that may become capable of reaching the United States. "North Korea has made no secret of its goal to produce an intercontinental ballistic missile capable of hitting the United States mainland, giving it the means to send a nuclear warhead to its archenemy." The expectation is that North Korea will have operational ICBMs within the next few years.[3]

Kim Jong-un, the "Supreme Leader" of North Korea, said: "Having witnessed with alarm what happened to Libya's Muammar

Kaddafi and Iraq's Saddam Hussein, North Korea is deadly serious in believing its nuclear weapons are the only guarantee that can ensure its survival against an invasion by the U.S."[4] Things are heating up.

The Nuclear Capabilities of Russia

Meanwhile, Russia is not only engaged in a major nuclear buildup but is also making significant preparations for surviving nuclear detonations on Russian soil. According to a recent article, there's a lot going on in Russia today: "Worrisome signs include increased talk about using nuclear weapons, more military maneuvers with nuclear arms, development of advanced nuclear munitions, and public discussion of a new war doctrine that accelerates the use of such weapons."[5]

Many see Russia's present activities as a direct challenge to the North Atlantic Treaty Organization (NATO), of which the United States is a member. Some speculate that Russia's rhetoric and surge in nuclear activity is intended to be a defiant warning to NATO to "restrain yourself from interfering with our business, or you might get hurt."[6]

Not backing down, the U.S. secretary of defense publicly stated (with Russia no doubt listening): "We're refreshing NATO's nuclear playbook to better integrate conventional and nuclear deterrence to ensure we plan and train like we'd fight, and to deter Russia from thinking it can benefit from nuclear use in a conflict with NATO."[7]

U.S. military experts note there are several ways nuclear weapons can be used, not the least of which is a massive and apocalyptic exchange. Another way such weapons could be used would be to "coerce a conventionally superior opponent to back off or abandon an ally during a crisis."[8] So, for example, if the Russians launched an attack against a small country that was a member of NATO, the

Russians might threaten nuclear consequences if a powerful member of NATO (such as the United States) sought to intervene.

Still another possible use of Russia's nuclear capabilities is to successfully attack U.S. stealth aircraft that are invisible to radar. U.S. intelligence has uncovered that Russia now has "nuclear-tipped supersonic anti-aircraft missiles that would create a large enough blast in the general vicinity to take out an entire formation of allied aircraft."[9] So, even if the Russians didn't land a direct hit against a formation of stealth aircraft, a nuclear weapon that detonated in the general vicinity of the aircraft would be sufficient to obliterate them all.

In like manner, Russia now has nuclear-tipped torpedoes and depth charges that could be used to destroy U.S. nuclear-armed submarines and aircraft carriers. In short, Russia is finding many different applications for nuclear weaponry. And there is little doubt that many of these applications are engineered to remove or at least weaken U.S. military capabilities.

It used to be that the doctrine of "mutually assured destruction" prevented both Russia and the United States from attacking each other. The idea was that if either attacked the other, a nuclear retaliation would occur and the populations of both nations would be destroyed. However, "Moscow is now taking steps to ensure that 100% of its population would be sheltered from such an attack."[10] They are accomplishing this by engaging in survival drills. A recent report informs us:

> Over 40 million Russians participated in the nuclear war drills, which lasted for four days. The drills include radiation resistance and forest survival activities. Participants also included students as young as fifth grade. The Russian government announced that the purpose of the drills was to provide security for their population.[11]

One wonders how all this relates to the nuclear-nonproliferation agreement the Russians and the United States signed a long time ago. It appears that current tensions may be rooted in the breakdown of U.S.–Russia talks on the fate of Syria. America's "unfriendly acts" toward the Russians have not been received well by Vladimir Putin and other Russian leaders.

Russia has now moved nuclear-capable missiles to its European enclave of Kaliningrad, and promises "'asymmetrical' and 'painful' actions against the U.S. should it decide to impose sanctions on Russia over Syria."[12] In view of the United States' "unfriendly acts," Russia's state-run media has been "ratcheting up anti-American rhetoric."[13] Even during the nuclear war drills, Russian media was denouncing the United States with headlines like, "Russia Is Tired of America's Arrogant Lies."

If you are in any way reluctant to accept all of this as a potential threat, consider a recent (2016) headline from *Newsweek* magazine: "War with Russia Looms, Says Former NATO General in New Book." In his novel, *2017 War with Russia,* General Sir Richard Shirreff argues that a belligerent Russia is the West's most pressing threat. Shirreff's book, while fictional, makes a nonfictional point: *Russia is a mega-threat to the United States.* "I'm worried, very worried, that we're sleepwalking into something absolutely catastrophic," Shirreff said.[14]

In keeping with this, James Stavridis, retired American admiral who served as the NATO Supreme Commander of Europe, and who wrote the foreword to Shirreff's book, said: "Of all the challenges America faces on the geopolitical scene in the second decade of the 21st century, the most dangerous is the resurgence of Russia under President Putin."[15] And yet, amazingly, most Americans are oblivious to this danger.

America's Defense Department is presently purchasing a "terminal high altitude area defense system"—a high-tech system designed to shoot down incoming missiles both inside and outside the atmosphere.[16] *National Defense* magazine also reports on the military's desire to use lasers to intercept missiles. However, "a viable system must be able to direct a laser beam at 'much longer ranges and much higher power' than any military laser capability that exists today... The missile defense chief hopes to have a laser demonstrator by 2021...The Pentagon is also pursuing rapid-fire, ground- and sea-based lasers."[17]

Bottom line: *Both the Russians and the United States are preparing for a nuclear exchange.*

Crippling America Through an EMP Attack?

Yet another potential danger to the United States is the incapacitation it would experience from an electromagnetic pulse (EMP) attack. This is a realistic possibility documented in a report issued in 2004 by a blue-ribbon commission created by Congress. In the report, titled "Commission to Assess the Threat to the United States from Electromagnetic Pulse Attack," some government officials lamented that the technology is now here to bring America's way of life to an end.

According to the report, a single nuclear weapon—delivered by a missile to an altitude of a few hundred miles over the United States—would yield catastrophic damage to the nation. Such a missile could easily be launched from a freighter off the coast of the United States. The commission explained that the higher the altitude of the weapon's detonation, the larger the affected geographic area would be. At a height of 300 miles, the entire continental United States would be exposed, along with parts of Canada and Mexico. A detonation about half that high would likely expose about half the United States or slightly more.

The electromagnetic pulse produced by such a weapon would likely severely damage or knock out electrical power systems, electronics, and information systems—all of which Americans depend on daily. At high risk would be the infrastructures for handling electric power, sensors and protective systems of all kinds, computers, cellphones, telecommunications, cars, boats, airplanes, trains, transportation, fuel and energy, banking and finance, emergency services, and even food and water. Anything electrical is at risk.

American society would be catastrophically affected since our infrastructure—both civilian and military—runs on electricity and electronic components. The commission estimated that it could take "months to years" to fully recover from such an attack.

It is entirely possible that starvation and disease could follow in some parts of the United States following a major EMP attack. Expert testimony presented before the U.S. Congress indicated that an EMP attack could reduce the United States to a pre-Industrial Age capacity in transportation and in the ability to provide food and water to the general population. Instead of cars, buses, and trains, people would be reduced to using bikes or perhaps horses and buggies.

What this means, practically speaking, is that food would no longer be transported to your local supermarket. Prescriptions would no longer be transported to your local pharmacies. Even if there was a way to transport food to a local supermarket, the lack of electricity would mean no operational refrigerators, so the food would spoil quickly. Because all communications would be cut off, there would be widespread confusion and panic. And since there's no way to contact your local police, it's pretty much up to each person to protect their rapidly diminishing stores of food.

In view of all this, allow me to revisit the threat from North Korea. North Korea recently detonated a low-yield H-bomb, which some media experts dismissed as being irrelevant. However, this is exactly the kind of bomb that can constitute a Super-EMP weapon that could knock out the United States' electrical grid and anything that runs on electricity. EMP expert Peter Vincent Pry has gone on record as saying that the low-yield detonation of the North Koreans is well within the requirements of a Super-EMP weapon.[18] In fact, four of North Korea's recent nuclear tests involved low-yield detonations that would be ideal for an EMP nightmare in the United States. Military experts have "long suggested that U.S. foes like Iran and North Korea have been eyeing an atmospheric nuclear explosion over the United States that could kill electricity to half the nation."[19]

In view of this danger, the House Homeland Security Committee in mid-2016 passed the "Critical Infrastructure Protection Act" that will soon explore ways to protect the electric grid.[20] This may be too little too late. As slow as things happen at the government level, one wonders if concrete action will be taken even in the next decade. Many continue to express concerns.[21]

The Continued Threat of Iran

Iran has long been on track to develop nuclear weapons, which creates two other threats to the vital interests of the United States. First, if Iran acquires nuclear weapons, it may proceed on the assumption that it is no longer vulnerable to American conventional military retaliation, and hence is free to pursue aggressive anti-American policies throughout the world.

Second, Iran's acquiring of nuclear weapons may serve as a spur for other nations to seek nuclear weaponry. There could end up being multiple nations in the Middle East with multiple nuclear warheads, thus increasing the threat and danger to multitudes of people worldwide.

There is also the possibility that Iran could become a supplier to third-party terrorists, thus greatly increasing the chances of the United States being attacked. Make no mistake about it: If terrorists got their hands on these weapons, there is virtually no doubt that they would use them.

In view of all this, the United States signed a nuclear deal with Iran in July 2015—the Joint Comprehensive Plan of Action. The agreement was engineered to prevent Iran from producing a bomb over the 15-year term of the agreement—and the agreement stipulated that Iran was to remain under international inspection beyond that.[22]

The problem is, the deal does not truly eliminate Iran's nuclear program. Specific details of the agreement surfaced about a year after it was signed. We now know that after the first ten years of the agreement's implementation, Iran will be permitted to begin replacing its mainstay centrifuges with more advanced equipment. Iran will end up with fewer centrifuges to enrich uranium with, but the new machines will be more efficient, capable of enriching uranium at more than twice the former rate.[23]

I believe the Iranians have every intention of developing nuclear weapons, and they are not being forthright with their true intentions. A senior Israeli security official was cited in the *Jerusalem Post* as saying, "History has shown that rogue nations tend to use diplomacy as a cover while they complete their work."[24] Jerome Corsi warns: "Iran will stay on track to develop nuclear weapons as fast as possible. Until then, sign any agreement, say anything, cheat—do whatever is necessary to throw the world off track."[25] He suggests that the mentality of the mullahs should be seen as cheating to buy time. "While buying time, the mullahs are willing to make whatever concessions they have to make, but they are resolved to never lose sight of their ultimate purposes—to get nuclear weapons, to defeat the United States and to wipe Israel from the face of the earth."[26]

Shortly after the signing of the deal, Iran's supreme leader, Ayatollah Khamenei, published a book titled *Palestine*. In the book, Khamenei argues that "Iran has a role to play in the destruction of Israel, and so must work to create and possess the strongest weapons possible."[27] Khamenei promised that Israel will not survive the next 25 years. In view of this, I feel justified in saying that any effects of the U.S. agreement with Iran will be short-term at best and not truly solve the problem.

One analysis I read suggested that we must continue to "be prepared to confront an Iranian regime just as hostile to the West as past ones…There are also real risks that a much bigger and broader war is brewing in the region."[28] I agree with this assessment. In fact, I believe that the bigger and broader war brewing in the region is none other than the prophesied Ezekiel invasion, which I will address later in this book. In that chapter, I will demonstrate that one day in the not-too-distant future, there will be a massive invasion into Israel involving not just Iran but also Turkey, Sudan, Libya, and other Muslim nations, in conjunction with Russia.

All eyes are on the Middle East.

POWDER KEG WITH A LIT FUSE: ISRAEL AND THE MIDDLE EAST CONFLICT

Israel and the Middle East have been like a powder keg, ready to blow up for decades. Wars in the region include the War of Independence (which brought Israel's statehood, 1947–1948), the Suez War/Sinai Campaign (1956), the Six-Day War (1967), the War of Attrition (1968–1970), the Yom Kippur/October War (1973), the Lebanese Civil War (1975–1976), the Iran-Iraq War (1980–1988), the Lebanon War (1982–1985), the Persian Gulf War (1991), the War on Terror (2001 to present), the War with Iraq (1991–2003), and the current war against the Islamic State of Iraq and Syria (ISIS). This represents 70 years of continual conflict.

It used to be that Americans didn't pay much attention to the Middle East. However, with 9/11 in our rearview mirror, four out of ten Americans now believe that conflicts in the Middle East are an indication that we are living in the last days. Moreover, over half of Americans (52 percent) agree that the rebirth of Israel in 1948 was a fulfillment of biblical prophecy. All of this—in conjunction with the escalating threat of terrorism from Middle East antagonists—has motivated Americans to pay more focused attention on events in the Middle East.

Much of the conflict centers on the city of Jerusalem. Indeed,

Jerusalem is the holiest of all cities for the Jews, and is the third holiest city for Muslims (behind Mecca and Medina). The conflict is hence as much a *religious* issue as it is a *political* issue for Jews and Muslims. After all, the Jews believe Jerusalem was promised to them by Yahweh, the God of the Bible. Muslims, by contrast, believe the city was promised to them by Allah, the God of the Quran. Because both sides are unbending in their religious devotion, conflict seems inevitable and unsolvable.

Muslim leaders—both old school and new school—have always held a hard line on Jerusalem. Anwar Sadat (1918–1981) in the 1970s proclaimed that "Jerusalem is the property of the Muslim nation... Nobody can ever decide the fate of Jerusalem. We shall retake it with the help of Allah."[1] Likewise, Yasser Arafat (1929–2004) in the 1990s promised that "whoever does not accept the fact that Jerusalem will be the capital of a Palestinian state, and only that state, can go drink from the Dead Sea." More recently, the Iranian head of the Strategic Research Center at the Expediency Council, Ali Akbar Velayati, stated in no uncertain terms that Iran will not recognize Israel because "it is a usurper entity." Indeed, "Iran believes Israel has stolen the Palestinians' land."[2] They want the land back. It belongs to them as a gift from Allah.

On the Jewish side, Israeli Prime Minister Benjamin Netanyahu—with equal vigor—has promised: "I will never allow Jerusalem to be divided again. *Never! Never!* We will keep Jerusalem united and...we will never surrender those ramparts." Netanyahu vowed in late 2016 "to keep Jerusalem united under Israeli control." Addressing the Knesset (Israel's parliament) to mark the 49th anniversary of the Israeli occupation of East Jerusalem, Netanyahu promised: "Our roots are deeper than any other nations, including to the Temple Mount. Jerusalem was ours and will remain ours."[3] Both Muslims and Jews remain unbending.

The Jewish Claim of Divine Right

From the very beginning, God provided very detailed land promises to the Jews. More specifically, God made a pivotal covenant with Abraham around 2100 BC. In this covenant, God promised Abraham a son and that his descendants would be as numerous as the stars in the sky (Genesis 12:1-3; 13:14-17). God also made specific land promises to Abraham: "I have given this land to your descendants, all the way from the border of Egypt to the great Euphrates River—the land now occupied by the Kenites, Kenizzites, Kadmonites, Hittites, Perizzites, Rephaites, Amorites, Canaanites, Girgashites, and Jebusites" (Genesis 15:18-21).

These land promises were confirmed with Abraham's son, Isaac. To Isaac, God promised: "I hereby confirm that I will give all these lands to you and your descendants, just as I solemnly promised Abraham, your father. I will cause your descendants to become as numerous as the stars of the sky, and I will give them all these lands" (Genesis 26:3-4).

The land promises were then confirmed with Isaac's son, Jacob. To Jacob, God promised: "The ground you are lying on belongs to you. I am giving it to you and your descendants. Your descendants will be as numerous as the dust of the earth! They will spread out in all directions—to the west and the east, to the north and the south" (Genesis 28:13-14). Much later, in Psalm 105:8-11, we are assured that

> God always stands by his covenant—
> > the commitment he made to a thousand generations.
> This is the covenant he made with Abraham
> > and the oath he swore to Isaac.
> He confirmed it to Jacob as a decree,
> > and to the people of Israel as a never-ending covenant:
> "I will give you the land of Canaan
> > as your special possession."

Clearly, the God of the Bible gave the Holy Land to the Jewish people as an eternal possession.

The Muslim Claim of Divine Right

Muslims claim that while the original Bible was the Word of God (the Word of Allah), and still retained its doctrinal purity by the time of Muhammad in the seventh century, it soon thereafter became corrupted by Jews and Christians. Since the time of Muhammad, the Bible has allegedly been mingled with many "untruths." Hence, the original and the fictitious, the divine and human are so intermingled that the grain cannot be separated from the chaff.

Muslims claim that the Jews inserted many things into the Old Testament that served to benefit them. More specifically, Muslims claim that while they are the true and rightful heirs of the promises made to Abraham through Ishmael (who, they claim, gave rise to the Arab nations), the Jews, for personal gain, concocted a story and inserted it into the manuscript copies of the Old Testament—to the effect that Isaac became Abraham's heir of the Palestinian land promises.

In this falsified Jewish version, Ishmael and his descendants became outcasts and thus have no right to the land. The original Old Testament, they say, did not have this concocted story. Muslims thus believe that the Holy Land truly belongs to them. They have vowed to keep fighting until they get the land back.

Of course, it is both inaccurate and unreasonable to claim that the Bible became corrupted soon after Muhammad's time. By the seventh century thousands upon thousands of manuscript copies of the Bible were dispersed over a large part of the world. To successfully corrupt the Bible, all these copies would have to be meticulously gathered, assuming people would be willing to surrender them (an impossible-to-believe scenario) and then the changes made.

Moreover, hundreds of years before Muhammad was even born, the Bible had already been translated into a number of languages. It is impossible to fathom that these various translations were identically altered all over the world so they would have a uniform corruption.

While Muslims may not like to admit it, God's land promises to Abraham, Isaac, Jacob, and the people of Israel have the support of thousands of reliable manuscript copies, some of which date to the second century AD, far before Muhammad was even born.

God's Promise of Jewish Restoration and Muslim Resentment

In the next chapter I will focus on the invasion of Muslim nations into Israel as foretold by the prophet Ezekiel. In that chapter, I'll also touch on Ezekiel's prophecies of Israel's rebirth and restoration to the land. Israel and its temple, of course, were destroyed by the Romans in AD 70. But God had promised the Jews: "I will gather you up from all the nations and bring you home again to your land" (Ezekiel 36:24; see also the vision of dry bones in Ezekiel 37). Herein lies the significance of 1948—the year Israel once again achieved statehood, after a long and worldwide dispersion.

Muslims view the entire existence of Israel as an aggression. The resettlement in the land was illegitimate to start with, they say, for the Jews had no right to return or come back to a land now under Islamic authority. Following Islamic logic, any territory that was at some time opened by a legitimate Islamic authority cannot revert to a non-Islamic authority. This means Israel cannot reemerge on Muslim land. It constitutes a grievous offense to Allah. The Muslims therefore want the land back.

Now, in the late nineteenth and early twentieth centuries, three significant ideologies emerged in the Middle East related to the current conflict over the land: Zionism, Arab Nationalism, and Islamic Fundamentalism. Let us take a brief look at these.

Zionism. Zionism gets its name from Mount Zion, the hill in ancient Jerusalem where King David's palace once stood. Zion became a symbol for Jerusalem during David's reign (2 Samuel 5:7). Zionism is another name for a type of Jewish nationalism that has the goal of reestablishing the Jewish ancestral homeland. It involves not just the idea that the Jews have returned to the land, but includes the return of Jewish sovereignty to the ancestral homeland. Zionism, then, is essentially a national liberation movement of the Jewish people. Christians who uphold the right of the Jewish people to return to the land and establish an independent state are often referred to as Christian Zionists.

Arab Nationalism. Arab Nationalism emerged in the late nineteenth and early twentieth centuries as a movement that seeks to unify Arabs as one people by appealing to their common history, culture, and language. This movement is secular, and seeks to gain and maintain Arab power in the Arab lands of the Middle East. In more recent decades, Arab nationalists have sought to end, or at least minimize, direct Western influence in the Arab world. As well, Israel is viewed as a cancerous tumor that must be removed.

Islamic Fundamentalism. Islamic fundamentalism is a religious philosophy that gained its strongest traction in the late twentieth century, and now seeks to establish Islamic dominance in the Middle East and eventually the rest of the world. Israel, a symbol of Jewish power, is viewed as a grievous insult to Allah and cannot be allowed to exist in the Islamic world. Israel must therefore be pushed into the sea.

The coexistence of Zionism, Arab Nationalism, and Islamic Fundamentalism is a powder keg with the fuse burning. It's a recipe for disaster. It's an explosion waiting to happen. And the explosive nature of this conflict shows no signs of decompressing.

Jewish Immigration and Repatriation/Palestinian Displacement

Jewish leadership in Israel presently seeks to grant Jewish immigration and repatriation rights to all Jews who wish to repatriate. This is based on an important piece of legislation adopted by the new state of Israel called the Law of Return—a law that provides all Jews the legal right to immigrate to Israel and immediately become citizens if they so choose. The Arabs, by contrast, say Jewish immigration to Palestine must stop.

As a result of the ongoing conflict between the Israelis and Arabs, many Palestinians have been displaced and have taken up residence in refugee camps in Jordan, the West Bank, and Gaza. Today there are millions of Palestinian refugees. While Jews from anywhere in the world are welcomed as Israeli citizens in Israel, Palestinian refugees are prevented from becoming citizens in neighboring Arab countries, except in Jordan.

The Israelis are willing to participate in a limited way in solving the refugee problem, but they do not want to allow millions of unhappy Palestinians into the Jewish state who could later become allies with Arab nations seeking to attack Israel. The most they have been willing to do is allow a limited number of Palestinians to live outside of Israel proper, segregate the Jews and Palestinians by a perimeter wall, and demilitarize the Palestinian area.

Palestinians have consistently sought permission to return to their former homes or be given compensation for choosing not to return. They claim Israel is not honoring the U.N. Security Council Resolutions 194 and 242, which grant repatriation and war reparations to the ousted Palestinians.

Neither side is budging. The conflict ever continues.

Current Arab and Muslim Groups in the Conflict

So many Arab and Muslim groups have emerged in the midst

of the Middle East conflict that it's hard to keep up with them all. Following is a brief primer on the most important of these groups, which will help us to see just how intensely Arabs and Muslims feel about Israel and about Israel's longtime ally—the United States.

The Palestine Liberation Organization. The Palestine Liberation Organization (PLO) was created by the Arab League in 1964. It was originally intended to be the primary Arabian vehicle for the annihilation of Israel. It utilized terrorist tactics in working toward its goal. The PLO undertook militant activities against both Israeli civilians and military targets. Hijackings, kidnappings, and assassinations were commonplace. All the while, the PLO was busy promoting a one-state doctrine: Arab Palestine. By the 1980s, the PLO shifted its strategy to gain more global political influence. The new goal was to (1) proclaim an independent Palestinian state, (2) renounce terrorism, and (3) recognize Israel's right to exist. This shift marked the beginning of a two-state doctrine: Palestine and Israel. Not unexpectedly, over the years that followed, talks broke down and the conflict continued.

Al Qaeda. Al Qaeda means "the base" (or military base) in Arabic. Al Qaeda has sought to diminish American influence in the Middle East, particularly in Israel and Iraq, and has sought to oust American troops from Saudi Arabian soil. The Al Qaeda network seeks to fund, recruit, train, and coordinate Islamic militants and extremist organizations across the globe. Many members of Al Qaeda envision the establishment of a caliphate—a single Islamic state ruled by a caliph, a successor of Muhammad—across all Muslim lands. While Al Qaeda has been on the run from the U.S. military, it is still alive and well.

As for the funding of Al Qaeda, the smoking gun points to the Saudis. Rachel Ehrenfeld, author of a groundbreaking book *Funding Evil: How Terrorism Is Financed—and How to Stop It*, says Al

Qaeda funding comes from the oil-rich Saudi royal family, Saudi charitable organizations, Saudi banks and financial networks, Saudi businesses (including real estate, publishing, software, and construction companies), and Saudi criminal activities (for example, credit card fraud, the pirating of compact discs, prostitution rings, and the sale of illegal drugs). Despite multiple sources of funding, the lion's share of the financing is rooted in Saudi oil money, clear and simple.[4]

Hezbollah. Hezbollah, literally, the "party of God," is a Lebanese umbrella organization of radical Islamic Shiites who hate Israel and oppose the West. Founded in 1982, they are deeply entrenched in terrorism. They believe Israel occupies land that belongs only to the Muslims, and they will resort to any level of violence and terror to rectify the situation. They advocate the establishment of Shiite Islamic rule in Lebanon and the liberation of all "occupied Arab lands," including Jerusalem. Hezbollah has thus continually vowed to destroy Israel and establish an Islamic state in Lebanon. They also seek to eliminate Jews worldwide.

Hezbollah's Secretary-General Hassan Nasrallah has openly acknowledged that it receives funds from oil-rich Tehran to support its terrorist activities against Israel. In earlier years, Iran provided some $60 to $100 million annually to Hezbollah, and then increased the amount in 2001 to $10 million per month. Iran provides this money specifically for terrorist activities against Israel. Iran also assists in providing weaponry, explosives, organizational aid, instructors, and political support.[5] Multiple news reports have indicated that Syria provides not only shelter and financing to Hezbollah, it also supplies the group with weaponry from its own stockpiles, as well as thousands of long-range rockets. Training facilities are also provided, along with logistical and technological support for attacks against Israel.

Hamas. Hamas is an Arabic term that means "Islamic resistance movement." The organization was founded by Sheikh Ahmed Yassin in 1987 in order to wage jihad to liberate Palestine and to establish an Islamic Palestinian state. Members of Hamas believe that negotiations with the Israelis are a waste of time because the Arabs and the Israelis cannot coexist. The military wing has committed countless terrorist attacks against Israel, including hundreds of suicide bombings. Yassin once called on Iraqis to "become human bombs, using belts and suitcases aimed at killing every enemy that walks on the earth and pollutes it."[6] Former President George W. Bush categorized Hamas as one of the deadliest terrorist organizations in the world. One often finds supporters carrying signs saying, "Death to USA." There is no question that Hamas has widespread funding, including from Iran, Saudi Arabia, the Gulf states, the United Arab Emirates, Syria, and Iraq, among other sources.

Palestinian Islamic Jihad. The Palestinian Islamic Jihad is a militant group based in Damascus, Syria. They are dedicated to the destruction of Israel and the establishment of an Islamic state in Palestine. It emerged in the 1970s, and has engaged in large-scale suicide bombing attacks against Israeli civilians as well as military targets. Not surprisingly, Iran's oil money helps to underwrite this organization. As well, Syria has provided safe haven, finances, arms, and training for the group. According to Palestinian intelligence documents discovered by the Israelis in 2002, money transferred from Iran and Syria to Palestinian terrorist groups is used for preparing terrorist attacks against Israel, supporting families of dead and detained terrorists, procuring arms, and purchasing physical equipment for terrorist attacks.[7]

ISIS. This is an acronym for the Islamic State in Iraq and Syria. It started as an Al Qaeda splinter group. ISIS aims to create an Islamic state called a caliphate across Iraq, Syria, and beyond. ISIS seeks to implement Sharia law, which is rooted in eighth-century Islam. The group has executed countless people—typically using cruel means—in enforcing its view of Sharia law. It is well known for using social media to promote its radical politics and religious fundamentalism. The group has also enslaved some of the peoples it has conquered, including women and girls who are sexually enslaved. As of late 2016, ISIS members have remained undeterred in killing the perceived enemies of their version of Islam. Their various attacks seem engineered to demonstrate that their reach is far and wide—including Belgium, Turkey, Bangladesh, Baghdad, and more.

The bottom line is that these various groups want to bring down the lesser Satan (Israel) and the greater Satan (the United States). All seek the dominance of Islam.

Failed Peace Efforts

Temporary peace has, on occasion, been achieved in the Middle East, such as that from the Oslo Accords in 1993. However, unresolved issues—invariably related to the city of Jerusalem—have always led to the reemergence of conflict.

A more substantial peace came with the Camp David Accords, signed in 1978, in which Jimmy Carter brought Anwar Sadat and Menachem Begin together at Camp David, Maryland. This meeting led to an Israeli agreement to withdraw from the Sinai in exchange for Egypt normalizing relations. The Camp David Accords changed the political landscape, but problems remained. While the Accords led to a peace treaty between Egypt and Israel, they did not result in peace between Israel and other Arab states. The two sides have been unable to make substantial progress on broader Arab-Israeli peace.

American presidents since then have consistently sought to initiate peace, but no lasting progress has resulted. To make matters worse, the vacuum created by the withdrawal of U.S. troops from the Middle East led to the emergence of ISIS, which has escalated the conflict to ever new heights.

The Present and the Near-Term Future

I believe the situation in the Middle East will continue to go from bad to worse. Prophetic Scripture tells us that Israel will increasingly be a sore spot in the world in the end times. In Zechariah 12:2 we read, "Behold, I am about to make Jerusalem a cup of staggering to all the surrounding peoples" (ESV). This can also be translated, "I am going to make Jerusalem a cup that sends all the surrounding peoples reeling" (NIV). The nations that surround Israel are Islamic. There's lots of staggering and reeling in the Middle East these days. And most of those who stagger are anti-Semitic.

As I write, the United States continues to call for immediate action to salvage a two-state solution to the Israeli-Palestinian conflict. U.S. representatives say that Israel's continued building of Jewish outposts on Palestinian land is corrosive to the cause of peace. Arab governments are obviously seeking to put a halt to Israeli settlements. Israel is meanwhile unbending in its possession and occupation of the land. No solution seems possible.

Meanwhile, Syria has become a massive thorn in the flesh in the Middle East. In the Syrian civil war, the Russians sided with Syrian leader Assad against Syrian rebels. Many are concerned that the Syrian civil war may lead to a wider regional war. Russia and the United States are presently at bitter odds with each other. Some are fearful that America and Russia will come to a point of war over the conflict. Tensions are at a fever pitch.

Turkey's relationship with NATO has chilled while it buddies up with Russia—a turn of events the U.S. government is not happy about. Russia is now friendly with Iran, Turkey, and Syria and wants to become the major influence in the region, a reality that bears directly on the eventual "Ezekiel invasion" into Israel (see next chapter).

And then there is ISIS. The problem Western leaders face with ISIS is that this group is like a recurring cancer. You can cut cancer out of a human body, but if you don't get 100 percent of it, it can regrow and become just as big as it was before (or bigger). Even though the U.S. and its regional allies have attacked and overcome a number of ISIS strongholds, the fear is that the group could regroup and regrow. Moreover, many wonder whether lone-ranger sympathizers not formally connected to ISIS will continue to engage in terrorist attacks around the world. Also of concern is whether ISIS members posing as immigrants will make their way into Europe and the United States and victimize innocent people.

One thing is certain: The multiple variables of the Middle East conflict seem to be cascading out of control. Taken in conjunction with the other signs of the times addressed in this book, can there be any doubt that we are living in the end times?

Many are crying out today for a leader who can take control of world crises and solve the Middle East problem. This yearning for a solution is setting the stage for what is to come, for Scripture prophesies that the antichrist—the leader of a revived Roman empire, a "United States of Europe"—will sign a covenant with Israel (Daniel 9:27). To the amazement of everyone, he will have solved the Middle East dilemma. The signing of this covenant will constitute the beginning of the tribulation period.

11

NORTHERN STORM RISING: THE COMING MUSLIM INVASION AGAINST ISRAEL

The Middle East is a powder keg waiting to explode. Multiple Muslim nations are presently aligned against Israel, and things are getting more heated with each passing year. *Israel exists in a constant state of threat.*

Bible prophecy has a great deal to say about all this. Ezekiel, in particular, prophesied that in the end times there would be an all-out invasion of Israel by a massive northern military assault force. The goal of the assault force will be to utterly obliterate the Jews. Ezekiel 38:1-6 even specifies the nations that will be involved in this invasion: Rosh,[1] Magog, Meshech and Tubal, Persia, Ethiopia, Put, Gomer, and Beth-togarmah.

Rosh likely refers to modern Russia. There is considerable historical evidence that a place known as Rosh—sometimes using alternate spellings such as Rus, Ros, and Rox—was very familiar in the ancient world, and was located in the territory now occupied by modern Russia. Rosh also appears as a place name in Egyptian inscriptions as Rash, dating as early as 2600 BC. One inscription that dates to 1500 BC refers to a land called Reshu that was located to the north of Egypt (as is the case with modern Russia). Rosh (or its equivalent) is found in a variety of other ancient documents as well. Placing Rosh in the area today known as Russia has long been a tradition in the Christian church, as early as AD 438. Finally, in Ezekiel 39:2 Rosh is said to be "from the distant north." The term *north* is to be understood in relation to Israel. If one draws a line from Israel and goes straight north, one ends up in Russia.

Magog refers to the geographical area in the southern portion of the former Soviet Union—probably including the former Soviet republics of Kazakhstan, Kyrgyzstan, Uzbekistan, Turkmenistan, Tajikistan, and possibly even northern parts of modern Afghanistan. Significantly, this entire area is Muslim-dominated, with more than enough religious motivation to move against Israel.

Meshech and *Tubal* refer to the geographical territory to the south of the Black and Caspian Seas of Ezekiel's day—what is today modern Turkey. Meshech and Tubal are apparently the same as the Mushki and Tabal of the Assyrians, and the Moschi and Tibareni of the Greeks, who inhabited the territory that constitutes modern Turkey. This is confirmed by the ancient historian Herodotus.

Persia is modern Iran. Persia became Iran in 1935 and the Islamic Republic of Iran in 1979. Note that the borders on the east and west sides of ancient Persia were wider than the modern borders of Iran. So *Persia* could refer to Iran plus territories to the west and the east, all of which are Islamic. Iran hates Israel and seeks to wipe Israel off the map.

Ethiopia refers to the geographical territory to the south of Egypt on the Nile River—what is today known as Sudan. Sudan is a hardline Islamic nation that is a kindred spirit with Iran in its venomous hatred of Israel. These nations are already such close allies that a mutual stand against Israel would not in the least be unexpected. This nation is infamous for its ties to terrorism and its harboring of Osama bin Laden from 1991 to 1996.

Put, a land to the west of Egypt, is modern-day Libya. However, ancient Put is larger than the Libya that exists today, and hence the boundaries of Put as referenced in Ezekiel 38–39 may extend beyond modern Libya, perhaps including portions of Algeria and Tunisia.

Gomer apparently refers to part of the geographical territory in modern Turkey. The ancient historian Josephus said Gomer founded those the Greeks called the Galatians. The Galatians of New Testament times lived in central Turkey. Hence, there is a direct connection of ancient Gomer to modern Turkey. Moreover, many claim Gomer may be a reference to the ancient Cimmerians or Kimmerioi. History reveals that from around 700 BC, the Cimmerians occupied the territory that is modern Turkey.

Beth-togarmah also apparently refers to modern-day Turkey. In Hebrew, *Beth* means "house." *Beth-togarmah* is a Hebrew term that literally means "the house of Togarmah." Ezekiel 38:6 refers to Beth-togarmah as being from the remote parts of the north. Hence, Beth-togarmah must be located to the north of Israel, as is present-day Turkey.

Now, here's something fascinating to think about. An alliance between many of the nations mentioned in Ezekiel 38–39 may not have made good sense back in Ezekiel's day. After all, these various nations are not even located near each other. However, such an alliance makes great sense today because the nations that make up the coalition are predominantly Muslim. Given Islamic hatred for Israel, that is more than enough reason for them to unify in attacking Israel. Of course, Islam did not exist in Ezekiel's day, so people back then would not have seen this connection. But today, the prophecy makes great sense.

When Does the Ezekiel Invasion into Israel Occur?

A few Bible expositors place the Ezekiel invasion in the past, in biblical history. In my thinking, such a view violates the specifics of the prophecy given to us by Ezekiel. Following are the reasons I believe the invasion is yet future:

First, there has never been an invasion into Israel on the scale of what is described in Ezekiel 38–39. Nor has there ever been an invasion into Israel involving the specific nations mentioned in the passage. Since it has not been fulfilled in the past, its fulfill-ment must yet be future. Even though the unique alignment of nations described in Ezekiel 38–39 has never occurred in the past, it is apparently occurring in modern days. (More on this shortly.)

Second, Ezekiel specifically stated that his prophecies would be fulfilled "in the latter years" (Ezekiel 38:8 ESV) and "in the latter days" (38:16 ESV) from the standpoint of his day. Such phrases point to the end times.

Third, Ezekiel stated that the invasion would occur *only* after Israel had been regathered from all around the earth—"gathered from many peoples" and "gathered from the nations" (Ezekiel 38:8,12 ESV)—to a land that had been a wasteland. Now, think through this with me. There were occasions in Israel's history where the Jews were regathered to the Holy Land from a nation where they had been held captive. The Jewish captivity in Babylon is a great example. When the Babylonian captivity was over, the Jews were gathered back to the Holy Land from a single nation (Babylon), not from many nations around the world. The only regathering of Jews from "many peoples" is that which is occurring in modern days—especially since 1948, when Israel achieved statehood. Ever since 1948, more and more Jewish people have been streaming back to the Holy Land from vir-tually every nation in the world. And Ezekiel says this must precede the Ezekiel invasion of Muslim nations into Israel.

Fourth, Since chapters 36–37 in Ezekiel are apparently being ful-filled literally (Israel became a nation again, and the Jews have been streaming back to Israel from every nation in the world), it is reasonable and consistent to assume that chapters 38–39, which speak of the invasion that follows Israel's rebirth, will likewise be literally fulfilled. This is in keeping with the well-established precedent of biblical prophecies throughout the Old Testament being literally fulfilled.

No One Will Come to Israel's Rescue

Ezekiel's prophecy reveals that Israel will stand alone when attacked by the massive northern military coalition. No nation will come to her rescue. It is true that some nations—apparently Saudi Arabia and perhaps some Western nations—will diplomatically inquire about the coalition's intentions (Ezekiel 38:13). But all they give is words with no action. Israel will stand utterly alone.

From a human perspective, then, it would appear that the odds of Israel's survival are nil. Israel will be vastly and overwhelmingly outnumbered. If this were a mere human battle, the outcome would be easy to predict. However, while Israel will appear weak and alone in the face of this Goliath invading force, God is strong! Ezekiel 38–39 reveals that the invading forces will be annihilated by God before any damage falls upon Israel. (More on this shortly.)

Russia and the Muslims Against Israel: The Precedent Has Already Been Set

We already know the Muslim nations are against Israel. But some might be surprised at the idea of the Russians partnering with the Muslims against Israel. However, the precedent for such a partnership has already been set. In 1973 Israel was attacked by Egypt, Syria, and some other Arab/Islamic countries. Russia provided the military muscle behind the attack, including weaponry, ammunition, intelligence, and military training to assist this Arabic coalition in their goal of destroying Israel. Of course, while Russia aided the Arabs, the United States helped Israel. Things began to heat up between Russia and the United States—more specifically, between Leonid Brezhnev and Richard Nixon. Long story short: Nixon told Brezhnev to back down or there would be "incalculable consequences." The Russians promptly backed down and Israel was able to fight off the invaders.

Even apart from working with the Muslims, we know that Russia has long had a goal of conquering Israel. During the 1967 Six-Day War, the Russians were poised to attack Israel and had been preparing to do so for a substantial time. Soviet warships, submarines, bombers, and fighter jets were mobilized and ready for action. However, President Johnson's ordering of the U.S. Sixth Fleet to steam toward Israel as a show of solidarity with Israel served to stare down the mighty Russian bear.

Later, in 1982, then-Israeli prime minister Menachem Begin revealed that a secret but massive cache of Russian weaponry had been discovered in deep underground cellars in Lebanon, apparently pre-positioned for a future invasion of Russia into Israel. Discovered were massive quantities of ammunition, armored vehicles, tanks, small arms, heavy weapons, communications devices, and other military paraphernalia. Much of what was discovered was highly sophisticated—equipment that crack military units would use. So much was found that it required virtually hundreds of trucks to remove it all. Israel's leaders admitted they had no idea that such extensive plans had been made for a future ground assault into Israel.

A Russia-Iran Partnership

Meanwhile, it is no secret that over the past decade, Russia and Iran have developed strong ties, largely military in nature. This is extremely relevant, for previously the relationship between Russia and Iran had been characterized by sheer hatred. But circumstances changed. Following the Iran-Iraq war (1980–1988), Iran needed to rebuild its military. Russia needed money from weapons sales. The rest is history.

These days Iran is streaming about half a billion dollars annually into Russia's wallet. Ilan Berman, in *Tehran Rising*, informs us: "In late 2000, buoyed by its expanding ties with the Kremlin, the Iranian government announced plans for a massive, twenty-five-year national military modernization program—one entailing upgrades to its air defense, naval warfare, land combat capabilities and built almost entirely around Russian technology and weaponry."[2] The modernization program includes the purchase of fighter aircraft, assistance in constructing military submarines, anti-aircraft missile systems, surface-to-air missile systems, radar stations, infantry fighting vehicles, naval landing craft, and patrol equipment.[3] Russia has also assisted Iran with its nuclear program.

A 2016 report affirms a new military agreement between Russia and Iran that allows Russian jets to use the Nojeh Airbase in western Iran for attacks against Syrian rebels. This is the first time that the Islamic regime in Iran has allowed a foreign power—in this case, Russia—to use Iranian territory as a base of operations for military offensives against another country in the region.[4]

It is also highly significant that Iran's anti-Semitism has today reached unprecedented levels. As of late 2016, Iranian leaders are declaring that Iran now possesses the capability to destroy Israel. The deputy commander of Iran's Revolutionary Guard Corps boasts that they have "more than 100,000 missiles" ready to strike at the heart of the Jewish nation.[5] Indeed, he says, "Today, the grounds for the annihilation and collapse of the Zionist regime are present more than ever."[6] A senior adviser to the Iranian Revolutionary Guards' elite unit Quds Force, Ahmad Karimpour, likewise affirmed that

"Iran could destroy Israel in eight minutes if the Supreme Leader, Ayatollah Ali Khamenei, gave the order."[7]

We are assured that "tens of thousands of other high-precision, long-range missiles, with the necessary destructive capabilities, have been placed in various places throughout the Islamic world. They are just waiting for the command, so that when the trigger is pulled, the accursed black dot will be wiped off the geopolitical map of the world, once and for all."[8]

Why do the Iranians so hate Israel? The Iranian head of the Strategic Research Center at the Expediency Council, Ali Akbar Velayati, says that Iran will not recognize Israel because "it is a usurper entity." Indeed, "Iran believes Israel has stolen the Palestinians' land."[9] They want the land back. It belongs to Allah.

New Friends: Russia and Turkey

Russia has been busy forging ties with other Muslim nations aside from Iran. Interestingly, Russia and Turkey have been cozying up in recent days—something unexpected given Turkey's commitment to NATO. Here's how things developed:

- An attempted coup in Turkey sent shockwaves not only throughout Turkey but throughout the Middle East.

- Vladimir Putin, the Russian president, gave Turkey's president Recep Tayyip Erdogan a heads-up about an hour before the attempted coup, giving Erdogan time to escape immediate danger.

- Meanwhile, Erdogan felt let down by his NATO allies (including the United States) for not showing sufficient support following the attempted coup. Then-U.S. secretary of state John Kerry warned the Turkish government that it would be unwise to stand against Turkey's

military personnel, for "the actions could have consequences for the NATO alliance."[10]

- It is now apparent that the attempted coup was directed
by former Turkish imam Fethullah Gülen, the founder
of the Gülen movement, and who is now residing in
self-imposed exile in Saylorsburg, Pennsylvania. Following the coup, Erdogan wanted him extradited to Turkey,
but U.S. officials said it must go through the U.S. legal
process. This further displeased Erdogan.

- Erdogan called Vladimir Putin "my dear friend" during
a subsequent news conference and pledged close relations for the future, including a military alliance.

- Not unexpectedly, this set off alarm bells in Washington.

One Middle East analyst suggests that "Erdogan's recent cozying
up to Putin sends the message to the United States and its allies that
Turkey can make new friends in the region. It certainly appears that
the Russian leader took advantage of cracks in the NATO alliance."[11]
Another Middle East expert warns:

> It is a very dynamic situation. I think Turkish President
> Erdogan basically has given up on NATO and even
> on the EU [European Union]—he is pivoting more
> towards the East at this point. For Turkey and Russia
> now to begin to talk as they are—particularly in terms
> of military alliances—this offers a whole new opportu-
> nity for not only bilateral cooperation [between the two],
> but also regional cooperation in a very intriguing sense.[12]

Yet another analyst put it this way:

> Turkey and Iran are simultaneously moving toward
> Russia, while Russia is expanding its global military and

strategic reach, all to the detriment of the United States and our allies. This will have a major impact across the region, potentially leaving U.S. ally Israel isolated to face a massive hostile alliance armed with nuclear weapons... Believers in Bible prophecy see this new alignment as a step closer to the alliance mentioned in Ezekiel 37–38.[13]

God Will Be Israel's Defender

It now seems that the stage is being set for the Ezekiel invasion. In the not-too-distant future, a massive northern military coalition will launch an unprecedented invasion into Israel. It will seem like an unstoppable force.

Of course, Scripture reveals that God is always watchful over Israel—"Indeed, he who watches over Israel never slumbers or sleeps" (Psalm 121:4)—and He will be Israel's defender against the invasion. The invaders may think their success is all but guaranteed, but God sees all, and Israel's attackers ultimately stand no chance of success.

Recall that God had earlier promised His people that "no weapon turned against you will succeed" (Isaiah 54:17). In fulfilling this promise, we often witness God in the Old Testament playing the definitive role in battling Israel's enemies (see, for example, Exodus 15:1-3 and Psalm 24:7-10). God is even sometimes described in military terms—"the LORD of Heaven's Armies" (2 Samuel 6:2,18).

Ezekiel 38:17-19 reveals that God's attitude toward the northern military invaders will involve "fury" and "blazing anger." Such words express the sheer and seemingly unrestrained intensity of God's vengeance against those who attack His people.

God's multifaceted defeat of the northern military coalition is described for us in Ezekiel 38:17–39:8. God's judgment is fourfold:

First, a catastrophic earthquake will cause many troops to die. Transportation will be disrupted, and the armies of the multinational forces will be thrown into utter chaos (Ezekiel 38:19-20).

Second, God will cause an outbreak of friendly fire among the invading troops (Ezekiel 38:21). This may be partially due to the confusion and chaos following the massive earthquake. Adding to the confusion is the fact that the armies of the various nations speak different languages, including Russian, Farsi, Arabic, and Turkic, and communication will be difficult at best. It may also be that the Russians and Muslim nations turn on each other. Perhaps amid the chaos, they suspect that the other is double-crossing them, and they respond by opening fire on each other. In any event, there will be countless casualties.

Third, there will be a sudden and massive outbreak of disease (Ezekiel 38:22a). Following the earthquake and friendly fire, countless dead bodies will be lying around everywhere. Transportation will be disrupted so it will be difficult if not impossible to transfer the wounded or bring in food and medicine. Meanwhile, myriad birds and other predatory animals will feast on this unburied flesh. All this is a recipe for the outbreak of pandemic disease, which according to Ezekiel will take many more lives.

Fourth, God will rain down hailstones, fire, and burning sulfur upon the invading troops (Ezekiel 38:22b). The powerful earthquake may set off volcanic deposits in the region, thrusting into the atmosphere a hail of molten rock and burning sulfur (volcanic ash) that then falls upon the enemy troops, thereby utterly destroying them.

God will also "rain down fire" on the southern part of the former Soviet Union, as well as "your allies who live safely on the coasts" (Ezekiel 39:6). These sobering words have led prophecy expert Joel Rosenberg to comment:

> This suggests that targets throughout Russia and the former Soviet Union, as well as Russia's allies, will be supernaturally struck on this day of judgment and partially or

completely consumed. These could be limited to nuclear missile silos, military bases, radar installations, defense ministries, intelligence headquarters, and other government buildings of various kinds. But such targets could very well also include religious centers, such as mosques, madrassas, Islamic schools and universities, and other facilities that preach hatred against Jews and Christians and call for the destruction of Israel. Either way, we will have to expect extensive collateral damage, and many civilians will be at severe risk.[14]

This judgment will serve to nullify any possible reprisal or future attempts at invasion. No further attack against Israel by these evil forces will be possible!

A Resulting Shift in the Balance of Power

God will utterly destroy this massive northern military coalition—Russia, Iran, Turkey, Sudan, Libya, and the other participating Muslim nations. When He does this, there will be a shift in the balance of power in the world both politically and religiously. This shift will ultimately make things much easier for the antichrist.

For one thing, the destruction of the northern invaders will make it much easier for the antichrist to assume global power. With Russia and a number of oil-wealthy Muslim nations now out of the way, there will be far fewer nations with political clout to challenge his authority when he comes into power early in the tribulation period. As prophecy scholar Arnold Fruchtenbaum puts it, "the eastern balance of power will collapse with the fall of Russian forces and her Muslim allies in Israel and the destruction of Russia itself. With the eastern power destroyed, this will open the way for a one world government."[15]

The antichrist's peace pact with Israel also becomes much easier to enforce following the destruction of Muslim invaders (Daniel 9:27). Muslim forces will no longer be a threat to Israel. As well, this likely explains why Israel is able to build its temple on the temple mount. After all, if the Muslims were still in power, it would be very difficult for Israel to build its temple on the temple mount in Jerusalem. But if the Muslim armies are largely destroyed by God, then this major obstacle to Israel's rebuilding of the temple is removed.

Looking to the Future

Today, the stage is being set for virtually all of this. The prophecies are casting their shadows before them:

- Multiple Islamic nations are positioned to attack Israel.

- Their motive is sheer hatred of the Jews. They want the Holy Land back—land they believe was promised to them by Allah.

- Russian alliances with these Muslim nations continue to grow and solidify.

- The precedent has been set for the Russians partnering with Muslim nations against Israel.

- Meanwhile, plans are already being made to rebuild the Jewish temple. (More on this in the next chapter.)

Israel presently remains on high alert.

READY TO REBUILD
THE JEWISH TEMPLE

At the heart of Jewish worship is the Jewish temple. In Old Testament times, David sought to build the first temple for God, though it was not to happen. David was a warrior, and this served to disqualify him. It was through his son Solomon that this temple was eventually built (1 Kings 6–7; 2 Chronicles 3–4).

Solomon's temple had a layout based on instructions that came directly from God. It had both a Holy Place and a Holy of Holies or Most Holy Place. In the Holy Place (the main outer room), we find the golden incense altar, the table of showbread, five pairs of lampstands, as well as various utensils used for sacrifice. Double doors led into the Most Holy Place, in which was found the Ark of the Covenant. The Ark was placed between two wooden cherubim overlaid with gold, each standing ten feet tall. God manifested Himself in the Most Holy Place in a cloud of glory (1 Kings 8:10-11). Tragically for the Jewish people, Solomon's temple was eventually destroyed by King Nebuchadnezzar and his Babylonian empire in 587 BC. Nebuchadnezzar's men looted all the valuable utensils found within the temple.

Following the Babylonian exile, which lasted 70 years, King Cyrus of Persia allowed the Jews to return to Jerusalem and construct a smaller and leaner version of Solomon's temple. The Jews were permitted to take with them the various temple utensils Nebuchadnezzar's men had looted.

The returned exiles started out well but soon ran out of steam. They got discouraged, and the prophets Haggai and Zechariah had to work hard to encourage them. This temple was finally completed in 515 BC. However, it was not nearly as magnificent as Solomon's original temple. Scripture tells us, "Many of the older priests, Levites, and other leaders who had seen the first Temple wept aloud when they saw the new Temple's foundation" (Ezra 3:12). It had little of its former glory and was a dim reflection of the original. This temple was also without the Ark of the Covenant, which had never been recovered. It also had only one seven-branched lampstand (Solomon's ten lampstands were never recovered). This lesser temple lasted about 500 years.

Israel's next temple in Jerusalem was built by King Herod the Great. Herod believed this ambitious building program, initiated in 19 BC, would be a great way to earn favor with his Jewish subjects as well as impress the Roman authorities. Completed in AD 64, it was much larger and more resplendent (with more gold) than even Solomon's temple. It was an enormous, cream-colored temple that shone exceedingly bright during the day. It measured 490 yards (north to south) by 325 yards (east to west).

This magnificent temple was destroyed in AD 70 along with the rest of Jerusalem by Titus and his Roman warriors, a mere six years after the project was completed. How ironic that those Herod sought to impress in Rome were the instigators of the temple's destruction.

The Tribulation Temple

Prophetic Scripture reveals that another Jewish temple will exist during the future seven-year tribulation. It's important to note that *there can be no rebuilt Jewish temple unless there is first a Jewish land (a reborn Israel) in which to rebuild the temple.* Israel, of course, was reborn as a nation in 1948, and Jews have been streaming back to the Holy Land from all over the world ever since (see Ezekiel 36–37). Now that the Jews are back in their own land, it makes sense that they would eventually want another temple.

How do we know that another Jewish temple will be built? There are several scriptural indicators. First, Jesus in the Olivet Discourse warned of a catastrophic event that would take place during the future tribulation period that assumes the existence of another temple: "The day is coming when you will see what Daniel the prophet spoke about—the sacrilegious object that causes desecration standing in the Holy Place…Then those in Judea must flee to the hills" (Matthew 24:15-16). This "sacrilegious object that causes desecration" refers to the desecration of the Jewish temple by the antichrist, who not only will personally sit within the temple, but will also set up an image of himself within the temple at the midpoint of the tribulation (Revelation 13:14-15; 14:9-11; 15:2; 16:2; 19:20; 20:4). Those who witness this act will experience outrage or horror at this barbaric idolatry within God's holy temple. It will utterly profane and desecrate the temple. The Hebrew word used to describe this horrendous act literally means "to make foul" or "to stink." It refers to something that makes one feel nauseated, and by implication, something morally abhorrent and detestable.

An abomination on a much lesser scale took place in 168 BC. At that time, Antiochus Epiphanies, who ruled the Seleucid Empire from 175 BC until his death in 164 BC—and who was a cruel persecutor of the Jews—erected an altar to Zeus in the temple at Jerusalem and sacrificed a pig, an unclean animal, on it. Antiochus may be considered a prototype of the future antichrist.

It is fascinating to ponder the scriptural affirmation that the false prophet will "give life" to the image of the beast (or antichrist) so that "it could speak" (Revelation 13:15). Some believe the beast's image will merely give the impression of breathing and speaking by mechanical means, like computerized talking robots today. Others suggest that perhaps a holographic deception may be employed. Still others see the supernatural involved. Do not forget that Satan has great intelligence, and also has the limited ability to manipulate the forces of nature, as happened when he afflicted Job (see Job 1–2). So, perhaps with his scientific knowledge and his ability to manipulate the forces of nature, he is able to give the appearance of the image being alive in some deceptive way. Whatever the explanation, many people on earth will be deceived by what they perceive to be supernatural.

The apparent animation that the false prophet gives the image of the beast sets it apart from typical idols in Old Testament times. As we read in Psalm 135:15-17,

> The idols of the nations are merely things of silver and gold,
>   shaped by human hands.
> They have mouths but cannot speak,
>   and eyes but cannot see.
> They have ears but cannot hear,
>   and mouths but cannot breathe.

Likewise, Habakkuk 2:19 says,

> "What sorrow awaits you who say to wooden idols,
>   'Wake up and save us!'
> To speechless stone images you say,
>   'Rise up and teach us!'
>   Can an idol tell you what to do?
> They may be overlaid with gold and silver,
>   but they are lifeless inside."

Contrary to such dead idols, this idolatrous image of the antichrist will seem to be very much alive, even god-like.

The goal of placing this supernatural image of the antichrist within the Jewish temple will be to induce people around the world to worship the antichrist. Keep in mind that since the antichrist puts himself in the place of Christ, he seeks the same kind of worship Jesus Himself received many times during His three-year ministry on earth.

Recall also the scriptural command: "You must worship no other gods, for the LORD, whose very name is Jealous, is a God who is jealous about his relationship with you" (Exodus 34:14). Because the antichrist demands worship, he is placing himself in the position of deity. The image in the temple is a symbol of his alleged deity. It is this that will utterly defile and desecrate the temple, as prophesied by Jesus (Matthew 24:15).

I find it significant that Jesus speaks of the desecration of the temple in Matthew 24:15, because in verses 1 and 2, He affirmed that the *present* temple—the great temple built by Herod, which was the temple of Jesus' day—would soon be utterly destroyed: "Do you see all these buildings? I tell you the truth, they will be completely demolished. Not one stone will be left on top of another!" (Matthew 24:2). This prophecy was literally fulfilled in AD 70 when Titus and his Roman warriors overran Jerusalem and the Jewish temple. The only conclusion that can be reached is that even though the temple of Jesus' day would be destroyed, the abomination of desolation would occur in a yet-future tribulation temple.

We also know there will be a tribulation Jewish temple in view of the prophecy about the antichrist in Daniel 9:27:

> "The ruler [the antichrist] will make a treaty with the
> people for a period of one set of seven, but after half

this time, *he will put an end to the sacrifices and offerings.* And as a climax to all his terrible deeds, he will set up a sacrilegious object that causes desecration, until the fate decreed for this defiler is finally poured out on him" (insert for clarification and emphasis added).

The very fact that at the midpoint of the tribulation period the antichrist will "put an end to the sacrifices and offerings" means that sacrifices and offerings were permitted during the first part of the tribulation, and they can be permitted *only within the Jewish temple.*

Why will the antichrist cut off all offerings and sacrifices at the midpoint of the tribulation period? The answer is simple. At this juncture the antichrist will set himself up as God, and *he alone* will now be the permitted object of worship for all who live on earth. Second Thessalonians 2:4 speaks of the antichrist as the one who "will exalt himself and defy everything that people call god and every object of worship. He will even sit in the temple of God, claiming that he himself is God." The antichrist—the world dictator—will demand that the world worship and pay idolatrous homage to him. Any who refuse will be persecuted and even martyred. The false prophet, who is the antichrist's first lieutenant, will see to this.

The fact that the antichrist claims to be god is in keeping with the reality that he is energized by Satan (2 Thessalonians 2:9), who himself had earlier sought godhood (Isaiah 14:13-14). The antichrist takes on the character of the one who energizes him.

There is something else to notice here. Recall that during His three-year ministry, Jesus *cleansed* the temple (Mark 11:15-19). By contrast, the antichrist will *defile* the temple when he takes his seat "in the temple of God, claiming that he himself is God" (2 Thessalonians 2:4). Truly the antichrist is the antithesis of Christ. And when he claims to be god, things will turn south rapidly for the Jews in Jerusalem.

Jesus Himself, in the Olivet Discourse, points to how bad things will be, and how Jews living in Jerusalem will need to flee for their lives (Matthew 24:15-21):

> "The day is coming when you will see what Daniel the prophet spoke about—the sacrilegious object that causes desecration standing in the Holy Place." (Reader, pay attention!) "Then those in Judea must flee to the hills. A person out on the deck of a roof must not go down into the house to pack. A person out in the field must not return even to get a coat. How terrible it will be for pregnant women and for nursing mothers in those days. And pray that your flight will not be in winter or on the Sabbath. For there will be greater anguish than at any time since the world began. And it will never be so great again."

When these horrific circumstances quickly unfold in Jerusalem, Jesus urges that the Jews living there should have no concern for personal belongings. Rather, they should make haste to get out of town. Time spent gathering personal belongings might mean the difference between life and death. Jesus indicates that the distress for Jewish people is about to escalate dramatically and rapidly (Jeremiah 30:7).

Preparations in the Present Day

Even today various Jewish individuals and groups have been working behind the scenes to prepare materials for the future temple: the menorah of pure gold, the pure gold crown worn by the high priest, fire pans and shovels, the vessel used to transport the blood of sacrificial offerings, the copper laver, linen garments of the priests, stone vessels to store the ashes of the red heifer, and the like. These items are being prefabricated by the Temple Institute in Jerusalem so that when the temple is finally rebuilt, everything will be ready for it.

The Temple Institute recently released a video proposing the rebuilding of the third Temple. The video tells us: "The Temple Institute is dedicated to doing everything possible to build the third Jewish Temple on the Temple Mount…It is incumbent on every one of us, at all times, to prepare for the rebuilding of the Holy Temple. With the work of the Temple Institute over the last three decades, preparation for the Temple is no longer a dream, it's a reality, in which everyone can play a part."[1]

Rabbi Ben-Dahan added that the rebuilding of Jerusalem would not be complete until the Temple too is rebuilt and the Temple Mount redeemed: "We are all here to declare that we have returned to Jerusalem, and God-willing we will prepare the hearts [of the people] to return to the Temple Mount as well and to rebuild the Temple. We aren't embarrassed to say it: We want to rebuild the Temple on the Temple Mount."[2]

A key indicator that the rebuilding of the temple is imminent is the reestablishment of the Sanhedrin after 1600 years of absence. In Bible times, the Sanhedrin was the supreme court and legislative body of the Jews that was made up of 71 rabbis. Prophecy expert Thomas Ice says, "The reinstitution of the Sanhedrin is seen as a harbinger for the rebuilding of the Temple and the coming of Messiah. Orthodox Jews believe that a body like the Sanhedrin is needed today to oversee the rebuilding of the Temple and to identify Messiah should he appear on the scene."[3] The new Sanhedrin met in October 2004, and the council now meets monthly in Jerusalem. Presumably, the council will seek to become the supreme governing body for modern Israel.

It seems that the stage is being set for the soon rebuilding of the Jewish temple. As prophecy scholar Arnold Fruchtenbaum puts it, "The Temple Institute in Jerusalem has reconstructed the instruments for Jewish Temple worship; Jewish men determined to be descendants of Aaron, known as the Kohanim, are being trained in ritual practices to serve as Temple priests; and now we have the establishment of an authoritative body to speak to the nation of Israel on matters of Jewish religion."[4] It's all coming together in our day.

Significantly, the new Sanhedrin has issued a call for architectural plans to rebuild the temple.[5] To accomplish this, "the group will establish a forum of architects and engineers to begin plans for rebuilding the Temple—a move fraught with religious and political volatility."[6] Meanwhile, they are "calling on the Jewish people to contribute toward the acquisition of materials for the purpose of rebuilding the Temple—including the gathering and preparation of prefabricated, disassembled portions to be stored and ready for rapid assembly, 'in the manner of King David.'"[7]

Of course, there is a problem that must be dealt with. Prophecy scholar Mark Hitchcock is correct in his assessment that "the main impediment to the rebuilding of a temple in Jerusalem is the presence of the Muslim Dome of the Rock—the mosque of Omar—on the place where the temple must be rebuilt. Also on the Temple Mount is the Al-Aqsa Mosque, which was built in AD 715 and is regarded as the third holiest place in Islam (after Mecca and Medina). Muslims consider the Dome of the Rock to be the crown of the Temple Mount."[8] Somehow, the Dome of the Rock must be removed so the Jewish temple can be rebuilt.

I believe this will be made possible as a result of the Ezekiel invasion, discussed previously in this book. If the Muslims were still in power in the early part of the tribulation period, it would be very difficult for Israel to build its temple on the Temple Mount. But if all the Muslim armies are destroyed by God prior to the beginning of the tribulation period (or *right at* the beginning of the tribulation period), then this major obstacle to Israel's rebuilding of the temple is removed. There would be little to no Muslim resistance.[9]

A feasible scenario is that the antichrist himself—following God's destruction of the Muslim invaders—will grant permission to the Jews to rebuild their temple on the Temple Mount as a part of the "strong covenant" he will make with the Jews (Daniel 9:27 ESV). As Thomas Ice notes, "This would mean that the Jews would be free to remove the [Muslim] Dome of the Rock and construct their Third Temple on that site. I would estimate, depending on how long it would take to properly remove the Dome of the Rock, that Israel could construct their Temple by the end of the first year, after the start of the seven-year period." It may be that the rebuilding of the temple will be supervised supernaturally by the two prophetic witnesses of Revelation 11 during the first half of the tribulation. Since, from a scriptural perspective, the temple does not need to be rebuilt until the middle of the tribulation period (Daniel 9:27), this scenario fits the biblical chronology quite well.[10]

Randall Price, who has written a definitive book on the rebuilding of the temple titled *The Coming Last Days Temple*, closes his book with these inspiring words:

> What does this say to you and me? It says that not only have the Jews already begun the ascent to their goal, but they are only one step away from accomplishing it!… The current conflict over the Temple Mount and the resolve of the Jewish activists to prepare for the conclusion of this conflict have provided the momentum for the short distance that remains of "the climb." We live in a day that is on the brink of the rebuilding effort, and with it the beginning of the fulfillment of the prophecies that will move the world rapidly to see as a reality the coming Last Days Temple.[11]

Thomas Ice speaks fondly of his tour of the Temple Institute in West Jerusalem. As noted previously, the orthodox Jews affiliated with this institute are now busy prefabricating implements for the tribulation temple. When the tour guide was asked how the temple would be built upon the currently occupied Temple Mount, she said "she had no idea but knew that the Lord would bring it to pass in order for the end of days to unfold."[12]

Indeed, the Lord will bring it to pass!

13

THE COMING CASHLESS WORLD

In our day, we are witnessing major steps toward globalism. We are witnessing the merging of banks as well as the centralization of financial regulations. Even in the United States, we have witnessed steps away from national sovereignty and toward solutions to problems that are more globalist in orientation (more on this in chapter 15). One begins to wonder if the antichrist is now waiting in the wings, ready to fill his role as the ultimate CEO of the end times, controlling the world and its economy.

When the antichrist emerges on the scene in the tribulation period, the world will embrace him with open arms. He will appear to have solutions to all the problems that afflict humankind. He will promise stability and order, and it will appear that he has the power and wisdom to accomplish it. But later, his iron hand will fall upon humanity, and during the last half of the tribulation, a policy will be enforced in which no one will be able to buy or sell without taking his mark (Revelation 13:16-18).

A modern development that will help facilitate all this is that we are rapidly moving toward being a cashless world. The technologies now in place will no doubt be utilized in the future by the forces of the antichrist in bringing about this cashless reality. To be sure,

Scripture does not come right out and say that the world in the end times will be "cashless," but it is a clear and unmistakable inference.

The book of Revelation portrays two beasts—the antichrist and the false prophet (Revelation 13). This diabolical duo will subjugate the entire world so that no one can buy or sell who does not receive the mark of the beast. We read that the false prophet "required everyone—small and great, rich and poor, free and slave—to be given a mark on the right hand or on the forehead. And no one could buy or sell anything without that mark, which was either the name of the beast or the number representing his name" (verses 16-17).

The false prophet will seek to force human beings to worship the antichrist, elsewhere identified as the "man of lawlessness" (2 Thessalonians 2:3). His squeeze play will force them to make the following choice: Either receive the mark of the beast and worship the antichrist—or starve, with no ability to buy or sell.

Later, in Revelation 14:1, we read: "Then I saw the Lamb [the Lord Jesus] standing on Mount Zion, and with him were 144,000 who had his name and his Father's name written on their foreheads." It would seem that the antichrist's mark is a parody of God's sealing of the 144,000 witnesses of Revelation 7 and 14. Prophecy experts Thomas Ice and Timothy Demy suggest that "God's seal of His witnesses most likely is invisible and for the purpose of protection from the antichrist. On the other hand, antichrist offers protection from the wrath of God—a promise he cannot deliver—and his mark is visible and external." They note, "For the only time in history, an outward indication will identify those who reject Christ and His gospel of forgiveness of sins."[1]

Receiving the mark reveals an implicit approval of the antichrist as a leader and an implicit agreement with his purpose. No one will take this mark by accident. One must choose to do so, with all the facts on the table. It will be a deliberate choice with eternal consequences. Those who choose to receive the mark will do so with the full knowledge of what they have done.

This will cause a radical polarization among human beings during the tribulation period. There is no possible middle ground. One chooses either *for* or *against* the antichrist. One chooses either *for* or *against* God. While people in our day think they can avoid God and His demands upon their lives by feigning neutrality, no such neutrality will be possible during the tribulation, for one's very survival will be determined by a decision for or against God. One must choose to either receive the mark and live (being able to buy and sell and eat), or reject the mark and face suffering and possible death by starvation.

Woe to any who receive the mark of the beast. We read an angel's pronouncement in Revelation 14:9-10: "Anyone who worships the beast and his statue or who accepts his mark on the forehead or on the hand must drink the wine of God's anger. It has been poured full strength into God's cup of wrath. And they will be tormented with fire and burning sulfur in the presence of the holy angels and the Lamb." We are likewise told in Revelation 16:2: "The first angel left the Temple and poured out his bowl on the earth, and horrible, malignant sores broke out on everyone who had the mark of the beast and who worshiped his statue."

There is no escaping the fact that *any* who express loyalty to the antichrist and his cause will suffer the wrath of our holy and just God. How awful it will be for these people to experience the full force of God's divine anger and unmitigated vengeance (Psalm 75:8; Isaiah 51:17; Jeremiah 25:15-16).

Believers in the Lord Jesus Christ will refuse to receive the mark of the beast, and they will be saved forever. Revelation 20:4 tells us: "I saw the souls of those who had been beheaded for their testimony about Jesus and for proclaiming the word of God. They had not worshiped the beast or his statue, nor accepted his mark on their foreheads or their hands. They all came to life again, and they reigned with Christ for a thousand years."

The Mark of the Beast: A Commerce Passport

What is the mark that will be placed on human beings? Apparently, people in that day will somehow be branded, just as animals today are branded—and as slaves, soldiers, and religious devotees were once branded back in Bible times. Bible scholar Robert Thomas explains it this way:

> The mark must be some sort of branding similar to that given soldiers, slaves, and temple devotees in John's day. In Asia Minor, devotees of pagan religions delighted in the display of such a tattoo as an emblem of ownership by a certain god. In Egypt, Ptolemy Philopator I branded Jews, who submitted to registration, with an ivy leaf in recognition of their Dionysian worship (cf. 3 Mace. 2:29). This meaning resembles the long-time practice of carrying signs to advertise religious loyalties (cf. Isa. 44:5) and follows the habit of branding slaves with the name or special mark of their owners (cf. Gal. 6:17). *Charagma* ("mark") was a [Greek] term for the images or names of emperors on Roman coins, so it fittingly could apply to the beast's emblem put on people.[2]

This branding—the mark of the beast—will be a commerce passport during the future tribulation period. Prophecy scholar Arnold Fruchtenbaum suggests that the mark of the beast "will be given to all who submit themselves to the authority of the Antichrist and accept him as god. The mark will serve as a passport for business (v. 17a). They will be able to neither buy nor sell anything unless they have the mark."[3]

The Mark Itself Is Not High Technology

A number of prophecy enthusiasts in the past have claimed that the mark will be a high-tech chip (or something similar) inserted under the skin. While I believe that modern technology will make it possible for the antichrist and false prophet to *enforce* the mark of the beast (with no buying or selling without the mark), we should differentiate between this technology and the mark of the beast, for the technology itself is not the mark.

The mark, which Scripture says is "on" the right hand or forehead, not "in" or "under" the skin (Revelation 13:16), will identify allegiance to the antichrist. But that is separate and distinct from the technology that enables him to enforce his economic system. My former prophecy mentor John F. Walvoord, now with the Lord in heaven, commented on how technology will make it possible for such economical control, based on whether people have received the mark: "There is no doubt that with today's technology, a world ruler, who is in total control, would have the ability to keep a continually updated census of all living persons and know day-by-day precisely which people had pledged their allegiance to him and received the mark and which had not."[4] It is highly likely that "chip implants, scan technology, and biometrics will be used as tools to enforce his policy that one cannot buy or sell without the mark."[5]

Goodbye Greenbacks

Certain aspects of our society have already gone cashless. For example, if you take a flight on American Airlines, as I do dozens of times each year, the flight attendant will tell you they've got sandwiches for sale, but you cannot use cash. "American Airlines has gone cashless," travelers are informed. Other airlines have likewise gone cashless, including Southwest, Alaska, JetBlue, AirTran, Virgin America, and Midwest.

Meanwhile, as one cruises down toll roads, smart technologies automatically charge one's credit card or bank account so that one does not have to slow down and manually give cash at a tollbooth. It all happens behind the scenes, and people are not even aware of the instant and seamless financial transaction that takes place as they traverse those toll roads.

Cash has met the beginning of its demise. Economists tell us that the amount of real cash in circulation today is rapidly waning. In fact, the amount of cash being used today is less than half that used in the 1970s. Why so? Because more and more people are using cashless options, such as credit cards, debit cards, Apple Pay, and Android Pay. Radio Frequency Identification (RFID) chips, which can be implanted underneath the skin and can store financial data, are another possible means of making cashless payments. All of this is the wave of the future. Even the few who choose to use checks today typically have their checks read by a scanner that instantly transfers money from their bank account to the vendor to whom they wrote the check.

Presently, over 70 percent of all consumer payments are electronic in nature. More than two billion credit cards are in use in the United States alone. In view of this, an economist observes: "The long-predicted 'cashless society' has quietly arrived, or nearly so. Electronic money is cheaper than cash or checks…[and] it is more convenient…We have crossed a cultural as well as an economic threshold when plastic and money are synonymous."[6]

Some economists suggest that cash could soon become obsolete. Dollar bills and coins will be relegated to the history books. It is entirely possible, as one financial leader recently noted, that retail establishments will soon assess surcharges every time you use cash in their stores.

Providential Developments and the
Fulfillment of Biblical Prophecy

In studying Bible prophecy, keep in mind that while the prophecies are quite specific, people living during the time of the prophets often had no awareness of the providential circumstances that would one day emerge to bring about the fulfillment of that prophecy. For example, Micah 5:2 prophesied that the Messiah would be born in Bethlehem. But Joseph and Mary lived in Nazareth. So how would Joseph and Mary end up in Bethlehem so that the prophecy could be fulfilled?

Luke 2:1 gives us the answer: "At that time the Roman emperor, Augustus, decreed that a census should be taken throughout the Roman Empire." Luke 2:3 then tells us that people had to register for this census in their original hometown. Bethlehem was Joseph's hometown. While they were in Bethlehem at government request, Mary gave birth to Jesus.

Back in Micah's day, though, people had no idea that this government census would facilitate the prophecy being fulfilled. Only God Himself knew that detail.

We might say the same thing about Zechariah 12:10, which speaks of the Messiah as Him "whom they have pierced." But how would the Messiah be pierced? This prophecy was written hundreds of years before crucifixion was Rome's chosen method of execution. So people in Zechariah's day were unaware of the providential circumstances that would one day emerge to bring about the fulfillment of that prophecy (execution by piercing or crucifixion).

Likewise, when the Bible prophesies about the one-world economy and the antichrist's control of the economy in the tribulation period, no mention is made of computers or cyberspace or the Internet or a cashless society. But very clearly these new technologies, for the first time in human history, make it possible for these prophecies to be fulfilled. Now all becomes clear.

I don't think there is any doubt that a cashless system will be the means by which the antichrist controls who can buy or sell during the tribulation period. After all, if the world economy were still cash-based, then people who possessed cash could still buy and sell. It would be impossible for the antichrist to enforce who can buy or sell in such a cash-based society. Only in a cashless world—with a centralized electronic transaction system, where all is controlled electronically—would such control be possible. "It is obvious that any leader wanting to control the world's economy would avail themselves of the power that an electronic cashless system holds as a tool for implementing total control."[7]

I've noted a number of times in this book that prophecies often cast their shadows before them. Hence, as Bible expositor David Jeremiah has put it, "We are on the cutting edge of having all the technology that the antichrist and false prophet would need to wire this world together for their evil purposes. Right now it is well within the range of possibility for a centralized power to gain worldwide control of all banking and purchasing." Jeremiah further exhorts, "As we see things that are prophesied for the tribulation period beginning to take shape right now, we are made aware of the fact that surely the Lord's return is not far off."[8]

Super Computers and a Cashless World

It is downright amusing to watch science fiction shows created in the 1970s. I say this because my MacBook Pro is immensely faster than the computer system on the *Starship Enterprise*, where green words appear on a dark computer screen about as fast as an old teletype machine.

What makes the *Enterprise* computer even more comical (by

comparison) are the super-fast computers that exist today. They are *so* fast that it is hard to adequately describe them. IBM has developed a supercomputer—the Sequoia—that is so fast that it can easily do 20,000 trillion calculations per second. How fast is that? Well, if you had billions of people on earth all using an electronic calculator to work together on one massive calculation—and they were all working 24/7, 365 days a year—it would take them over 300 years to do what Sequoia can do in a single hour.[9]

There is plenty of computer power available today to monitor and even control a global, one-world economy. We do not need to invent anything new to make it all possible. The technology that exists *today* is more than sufficient for the antichrist's future control of the world.

The Lure of a Cashless Society

The strong movement toward a cashless society exists because, in the perception of many, a cashless society has numerous benefits. Technology makes things easier. Using telephones to communicate is easier than yelling down the street. Driving cars to the store is easier than walking. Flushing a toilet is easier than using an outhouse. Air conditioners offer more comfort and convenience than handheld fans. Likewise, going cashless is easier and more convenient than carrying around paper bills and coinage.

There are very few places where one cannot use a credit card or debit card. The great majority of grocery store purchases in our day are put on cards. Internet purchases are put on cards. Many bills are paid via online banking. Cashless options are already widely available because they are so convenient, and that will only increase in the future.

As well, federal authorities tell us that over $100 million of counterfeit money is removed from circulation each year. Over a ten-year period, that amounts to a billion dollars in counterfeit money. In a cashless society, counterfeit money will become a thing of the past.

In addition, a cashless world would make it impossible for would-be thieves to rob a store's cash register. There cannot be cash robberies in a cashless world.

Various forms of crime would also go down. In a recent op-ed in the *Wall Street Journal*, Harvard economics professor Kenneth Rogoff lists various crimes that are presently facilitated by paper money: "Racketeering, extortion, money laundering, drug and human trafficking, corruption of public officials, and terrorism."[10] All of these and more become far less likely in a cashless world.

Moreover, in a cashless society, no one will become infected with germs that are passed back and forth on dollar bills and coins. *Scientific American* ran a recent article providing scientific proof that dollar bills can be veritable reservoirs for flu viruses—and such viruses can survive on the dollar bill for as long as 17 days.[11] So going cashless might help keep you healthier.

Still further, in a cashless society, losing your wallet or purse is less painful because you don't lose any cash. Besides, cashless options are plain old convenient. *Fast and easy.*

There's one more thing. Many workers today are involved in service businesses that take cash payments—and lots of those cash payments don't end up being reported on tax returns. This kind of tax fraud would become a thing of the past in a cashless society. That alone is especially appealing to the government.

Simply because a cashless world will make it possible during the tribulation period for the antichrist to gain economic control over the world does not mean these technologies are evil in themselves. Technology can be used for good or for evil, and is hence morally neutral. So it is fine and good for all of us to use smartphones and credit cards and online banking and the like. My only point to you is that *the stage is being set in our day for what the ancient prophets predicted would take place in the future tribulation period.* These are unquestionably days for discernment.

The Present and the Future

The trend is clear. We are headed toward becoming a cashless planet. A recent article titled "Cash Not Welcome Here" tells us: "To get a glimpse of the future of commerce in America, look no further than Sweden…The Scandinavian country is largely a cashless society, with consumers relying on mobile phone payments or plastic. While the U.S. is still far from achieving the same level of cash-free existence, increasing numbers of restaurants and retailers are now snubbing the lowly dollar bill."[12] One reason the United States government may be in favor of going cashless is that our country spends $200 billion each year to keep cash in circulation. Going cashless would save us a whole lot of time and money.

It might seem odd that some retail establishments are snubbing the dollar bill. But it's really happening out there. One economist muses: "If you wanted to buy a scarf, maybe one that's on sale for about $50, don't bother paying with cash. The store won't take your Benjamins—or Hamiltons, Jacksons, or Grants…The oddity of a no-cash policy does make you think. How much closer, really, are we to a cashless society?" Indeed, we are "on the edge of seeing more and more businesses that don't take cash."[13]

In a 2016 Gallup poll, "62 percent of Americans said they believe the country would be a cashless society in their lifetimes. The belief is fueled by the expanded use of credit cards, debit cards, and other electronic payments options. In short, the survey found that more people are becoming comfortable without cash in their pockets." The Gallup poll concluded that "cash is becoming less a part of American's purchasing behavior."[14]

A number of countries have recently been exploring the possibility of developing a digital currency. "The central banks of China, the UK, and Canada, to name just a few, have been investigating the possibility of creating digital currencies." What is the appeal? "Issuing digital currency would be far cheaper than printing and distributing notes and coins...It would also enable nations to more accurately track developments in the economy—including inflation."[15]

One *Forbes* magazine staff writer described her view with a spin on the popular John Lennon song "Imagine": "Imagine there's no loose change (it's easy, if you try). No paper money; to ATM fees, say goodbye. Imagine all the people, living life cash free (aah-ah). You may say I'm a dreamer, but I'm not the only one."[16]

My friends, the prophetic stage is now being set for events that will transpire during the future tribulation period. We're going cashless!

BIOMETRICS AND THE LOSS OF PERSONAL PRIVACY

The term *biometrics* derives from two Greek words: *bios* (meaning "life") and *metrikos* (meaning "measure"). Biometrics is a technology that enables the identification of people by measuring and analyzing biological data and behavioral traits. More specifically, it identifies people by measuring and analyzing one of their bodily characteristics, such as their fingerprints, facial patterns, or iris pattern. (I'll discuss these and others in detail in a moment.) Behavioral traits used for identifying people include typing rhythms, gait, and use of voice. Granted, one would naturally think that a person's voice is more of a physiological trait than a behavioral trait, but this aspect of the science studies the behavioral way a person speaks. Some have coined the term behaviometrics to refer to the behavior-trait aspect of biometrics. Experts note that a biometric system based on a physiological characteristic is typically more reliable than one based on a behavioral characteristic.

Biometrics technology goes hand in hand with our emerging cashless world. After all, this technology serves to guarantee that *I am who I claim to be*, and therefore instant monetary transfers from my bank account to any vendor is secure and trustworthy. I believe this will be one of the technologies used in the end times as the antichrist seeks to control who can buy and sell during the tribulation period.

Biometrics Today

For years now, biometric technology has been used in a variety of contexts. Some laptops, personal computers, and smartphones have a fingerprint scanner, which guarantees that the only person who can sign on to that computer or smartphone is the owner.[1] The technology is also used to control access to private corporate networks where there is confidential data. As well, it is used to seek out and identify individuals in groups that are under surveillance.

In the United Kingdom, students pay for meals by giving a thumbprint scan. They simply put their thumb on the scanner and funds are withdrawn from an account already set up by the students' parents. The automated thumbprint system also sends nutrition reports regarding the food purchased to a student's parents. Also in the UK, over 60 hospitals use fingerprint biometrics to access patient files.

Meanwhile, Australians use biometrics with visas and passports. Canadians use it for border security and immigration purposes. Israelis use it with a new high-tech ID card. The Dutch use it with both passports and ID cards.

Finger imaging is used in different parts of the world to verify identity at ATM machines and to prevent check-cashing fraud. Hand-scanning biometrics is used in various parts of the world to verify credit card purchases, to prevent welfare fraud, and in immigration procedures at the airport.

The United States and the European Union are both considering new biometric methods for border-crossing procedures. Moreover, biometrics may play an increasing role in travel for many countries around the world.

Biometric passenger identification will soon find its way into U.S. airports. The Department of Homeland Security (DHS) is seeking contractors for a $7.2 billion biometric system "that will track travelers' arrivals and departures by scanning their unique biometric features."[2] We are assured this will be a great benefit to airport security.

It appears that the science of biometrics is here to stay.

What Makes Biometrics Convenient and Reliable

Certain things must be true about a personal characteristic for it to work in a biometric context. For example:

- *Universality*—the characteristic must be common to all people. Almost everyone has a thumb, so a thumbprint works well in biometric contexts. The same is true of an iris.

- *Collectability*—it must be easy to acquire the needed measurement. Today there are convenient, easy-to-use thumb scanners. There are also easy to use iris scanners.

- *Uniqueness*—a person's measurement must be different from that of other people. My thumbprint is unlike that of any other person. It uniquely belongs to me alone. The same is true of my iris.

- *Permanence*—people must retain the characteristic as time passes. Again, a thumbprint and iris scan are ideal because these do not change over time.

- *Performance*—the technology must be fast and accurate. Such technology already exists today.

- *Acceptability*—the technology must be widely accepted as reliable. There has been some initial resistance to biometric technology, but overall, people are more open to it with each passing year, especially since traditional usernames and passwords have proven unreliable. Over half of all people surveyed prefer biometrics to traditional usernames and passwords.[3]

A recent study reveals that among "600 security professionals surveyed across 15 industries in the U.S., the vast majority (69%) believe usernames and passwords are insecure...In fact, nearly three-quarters believe that by 2025, passwords will have been phased out."[4]

One of the big problems today is that many people use highly predictable passwords. For example, a substantial percentage of people use their mother's maiden name as a password.[5] Studies reveal that over 750,000 computer users have the password "123456." Also often used are personal names and birth dates. Only 25 percent of computer users use complex and secure passwords.[6]

Furthermore, a substantial number of computer users use the *same* password for different accounts. Security software company Kaspersky Lab found that "nearly a quarter of the consumers it surveyed used just five passwords for almost 20 accounts. For hackers, this is the gift that keeps on giving, since the weak and recycled passwords they steal will unlock even more websites they can loot."[7] Hence the appeal of biometrics.

Because of the increasing acceptance of biometrics, the fingerprint, voice, and facial recognition industries are predicted to be worth $12 billion, $11 billion, and $1 billion, respectively.[8] It's now big business.

The Two Primary Applications of Biometrics

Security experts tell us that there are two primary applications of biometrics—identification and verification. *Identification* involves a "one to many" comparison—that is, the measured characteristic (such as a thumbprint or an iris scan) is compared to a massive database of other fingerprinted or iris-scanned individuals. In a company context, for example, every employee would have a fingerprint profile or an iris-scan profile. As an employee, every time you enter the building, the scanners distinguish you as "you" as opposed to someone else. That's because every person has a distinct fingerprint or iris-scan profile.

Verification, by contrast, is a "one to one" comparison—that is, the measured characteristic (a thumbprint or iris-scan) is compared to the person's previously recorded and stored fingerprint profile or iris-scan profile in order to verify that the person is who he or she claims to be. Obviously, verification is a faster biometric process than identification because it does not require a massive database search.

What makes biometric identification and verification useful is that unique body characteristics cannot be borrowed, stolen, or forgotten—and hence one's biometric identity cannot be forged. It is for this reason that many believe biometrics is preferable to usernames and passwords.

The Initial Scan

When a person first utilizes a biometric device, biometric information about that person, such as from a thumbprint, iris scan, or hand scan, is recorded. Based on this data, a biometric profile—sometimes called a "template"—is formulated for that person and is electronically stored. From thence forward, biometric scans are compared against this initial data. So subsequent iris scans are compared to the stored iris scan in the computer database to identify a person or to verify his or her identity.

A Wide Range of Biometric Technologies

Today there is a wide range of biometric technologies, some in widespread use, others in an experimental phase. Here is a sampling:

Thumbprint or fingerprint. Digital images of fingerprints are easy to facilitate, and because fingerprints are unique, they constitute a reliable biometric scan. Since fingerprint biometric devices cost less than 20 dollars today, this is a popular biometric device and is often used for computer security.

Retina. Retina recognition—which requires a retina scan—is based on the reality that each person has a unique vascular configuration in the retina. This is a very secure biometric since it is not possible to change one's vascular configuration.

Iris. Each person's iris has a complex and unique pattern with many distinctive features. Iris scans are easier than retina scans because a retina scan requires looking into a lens, whereas an iris scan can be facilitated from several yards away. Increased verification is possible by measuring the iris in light conditions (irises change in light). This is a very reliable biometric.

Palm print. Palm prints are unique to each person, and because they are larger than fingers, they can be even more reliable than fingerprints—measuring ridge and valley features, principal lines, and wrinkles in the palm.

Hand geometry. This technology measures the dimensions of fingers in conjunction with finger joints and the overall shape and size of the hand. This biometric measure has been used for close to five decades now. Because hand geometry is not highly distinctive, it is best used for verification of identities as opposed to identifying a person from a large population.

Vein print. This technology, also called "finger-vein ID," scans the unique vein pattern of users' fingers as a means of identification.

Face. This is a nonintrusive biometric method that is suitable for both covert and noncovert identity purposes. A popular facial recognition approach measures the location and shape of such facial features as the eyes, eyebrows, nose, lips, and chin, and their overall relationship to each other. The combined effect of these features makes for a unique biometric. Some experts question whether a person's face alone is sufficient to identify with a high level of confidence one person from a large population of faces. One problem is that a person's face can change due to weight gain or loss, and people can put a variety of expressions on their faces, thereby possibly invalidating the biometric process.

Facial-recognition technology is being used on some of today's mobile phones. The software is fast and accurate, and replaces passwords and PINs.[9] In 2016 "MasterCard announced a new mobile app that lets customers identify themselves with selfies anytime they buy something online. And e-commerce giant Amazon.com filed for a patent for a biometric technology that would let customers authorize purchases with a photo of themselves."[10]

Voice. People have unique voices, and voice recognition distinguishes a person by measuring his or her voice against a voice profile or template stored in a database. The first time the system is used, the individual must go through a training period (sometimes more than one) until the voice template is complete. The template is a digital model of a person's voice—essentially a voice print.

Ear. Our ears are distinctive:

> Just like finger printing, passport photos, and eye recognition, our ears too can be scanned at airports to prove our identity…Researchers have discovered that every person has uniquely-shaped ears and have formulated a way to scan them to compare them with images already compiled in a database…There are a whole load of structures in the ear that you can use to get a set of measurements that are unique to an individual…The ear scan system is said to be 99.6 percent accurate. It maps the curves and wrinkles of the skin, cartilage, and lobes.[11]

Gait. Technology exists that measures the peculiar way each person walks. While gait is not as distinctive as a fingerprint or an iris scan, it is considered sufficient in low-security applications. One drawback of this technology is that as a person grows older, he or she might walk a bit differently. This is considered a behavioral biometric. Some have suggested that this technology might be useful for catching terrorists.

Infrared thermogram. This technology can be used to capture the pattern of heat radiated from some part of the human body, such as the face, hand, or a hand vein. The radiated pattern of each person is unique. This technology can even be used for covert recognition—that is, without the person realizing he or she is being scanned.

DNA. DNA contains the genetic blueprints of life, and because DNA is unique to each person, it is a reliable biometric. In fact, it is probably the most reliable biometric. There are a few problems to note, however. First, one could feasibly steal DNA from another person. Second, it is not practical, since it requires complex chemical procedures performed by experts, and thus takes longer than other biometric technologies. At present, then, this biometric technology has limited applications.

Signature. The way a person signs his or her name is generally unique. Signatures are thus a behavioral biometric. The problem is that peoples' signatures can change over time, and people who know they're being watched can purposefully write differently. Hence this is not a premium biometric.

Keystroke. This technology measures the way a person types on a keyboard. Because every person types in a characteristic way, this mode of identification is sufficient in lower security applications. This, too, is considered a behavioral biometric.

As you can see, there are multiple biometric technologies available that can accurately identify you. In some contexts, such technology can be useful, but there is also potential for great abuse. It's possible you could be biometrically watched and identified without you even knowing you are being watched.

A Benefit to Law Enforcement

Many today believe that facial recognition technology might benefit law enforcement efforts. Such technology allows a large crowd of people to be scanned, after which facial images could be measured against a master database, providing a quick read-out of names and addresses of people in the crowd and flagging potential bad guys. The obvious downside is the invasion of privacy of innocent people. How would you like it if you were in a crowd, and you knew your face was being scanned and measured against a master database of bad guys. No thank you.

Nevertheless, in a world riddled with the threat of terrorism, such technology might make things safer for all of us. Biometrics could ultimately save lives. Facial recognition technology could make our airports safer.[12] Advocates in favor of this technology for law enforcement reasons point out that it has already been used to keep German Olympians safe. If the technology works in this context, it can work in any context. So, some say, get over your privacy paranoia and get with the program!

Benefits to the Military

Our military is already using biometric technologies successfully. Here's a typical scenario: "Within minutes of knocking down the door of a suspected bomb maker in Iraq, U.S. troops can fingerprint everyone they find inside, send the scans across a satellite link, and find out if the subjects are suspected terrorists."[13]

The U.S. military, with the assistance of biometric technologies, has been able to put a damper on terrorists who are building explosive devices. "Biometric tools, when used on raids of suspected bomb makers' safe houses, have helped to kill or capture individuals who are involved in the construction of improvised explosive devices at the average rate of two per day for the last two years."[14]

Here's how it works: "Collector ID kits" are used to gather fingerprints and mugshots, after which those records are sent via a small satellite dish to three databases—the Defense Department's Biometrics Fusion Center, the Army's National Ground Intelligence Center, and the FBI's automated fingerprint identification system. At present the Defense Department has about 2.2 million files, and the FBI has 58 million. Once data is sent off by satellite, the goal is to have a response back in no later than 15 minutes (the average is under 5 minutes). This makes operations fast and smooth. Using this technique, the military has thwarted lots of bad guys.

Present and Future Dangers

More than a few people are concerned that biometric technology could be used for purposes other than identification and verification. Such technology could be used to infringe upon a person's privacy.

Though the 2002 movie *Minority Report* was a fictional story, it illustrated what *could* happen as a result of biometric technology. In the movie, iris scanners were scattered throughout the city, keeping track of people no matter where they went. That data, tied into a master database containing lots of information about each person (including their personal tastes and buying patterns), would cause customized advertisements to pop up in the person's vicinity, typically at the point of sale. The main character eventually changes his biometric identity by having an eye-transplant procedure. In the movie, it was difficult to go anywhere without "big brother" watching and knowing exactly where one was.

Granted, this was fiction. However, if facial recognition

technology improves to the degree that surveillance cameras can easily and routinely recognize people, then privacy becomes a thing of the past. Even in our day, it bothers many people who work in major U.S. cities that they are being recorded daily by a variety of surveillance cameras scattered about the city.

In my research, I came across one article titled "Biometric ID that 'Gives Big Brother a Passport to Your Privacy.'" The article warns: "Perhaps your firm already has your fingerprints on file so you can get into the office without any hassle. But although you may think nothing of it, giving over this type of information could be leaving you open to Big Brother-type surveillance." Indeed, "volunteering fingerprint and DNA information, and even eye scans, could lead to racial or social profiling and invasion of privacy." We are warned that "biometrics are put forward as a way of enhancing personal security, but the use of biometrics requires people to give up pieces of their body, effectively. The ubiquity of biometrics begs the question whether any of us can lead truly private lives anymore."[15]

In London, cameras are routinely used to scan the faces of people who enter parks to check them against a crime database. Understandably, this has not gone over well with many people. After all, those who live in the UK are already the most watched people on planet Earth—with a typical person in downtown London being caught on camera some 3000 times each week (there are surveillance cameras just about everywhere).

Some people express concern that innocent folks could conceivably be convicted of a crime. As one person put it, "If you are an innocent person who happens to look a bit like a criminal, I would be worried about what the response would be. What would happen if you were wrongly added to this database?...It's overthrowing the presumption of innocence from the start."[16]

Another danger that might emerge due to biometric systems involves the possibility of attack or mutilation. For example, in an effort to break into a corporation, an executive might be kidnapped and forced to yield to a fingerprint scan so the bad guys can get in. One case already on file involves the bad guys cutting off the finger of a good guy executive so the bad guys could get into the corporation's offices.

Still another real danger is that technology designed to make things more convenient for people could end up being used to control people. The book of Revelation indicates that the antichrist will one day wield absolute control over the world during the tribulation period. People will ask, "Who is as great as the beast?" and "Who is able to fight against him?" (Revelation 13:4). "He was given authority to rule over every tribe and people and language and nation" (13:7). The false prophet will require "everyone—small and great, rich and poor, free and slave—to be given a mark on the right hand or on the forehead. And no one could buy or sell anything without that mark" (13:16-17).

The technologies we are talking about in this chapter—along with the reality of a cashless world—will make it easy for the antichrist to wield absolute control.

15

GLOBALISM ON THE HORIZON

The antichrist will one day attain global dominion, but he will do so through the springboard of first ruling over a revived Roman Empire. The two questions that therefore face us in this chapter are: (1) Do we see the stage being set for a revived Roman Empire or a new United States of Europe? (2) Do we witness the stage being set for the eventual emergence of globalism on planet Earth?

A Revived Roman Empire—Phase 1 of World Dominion

The book of Daniel provides substantial information about the future revived Roman Empire over which the antichrist will one day rule. In Daniel's vision, he witnessed four beasts—representing four kingdoms—that play an important role in biblical prophecy (Daniel 7:1-8). We read in verse 3: "Four huge beasts came up out of the water, each different from the others." These four beasts reveal much about prophetic chronology.

The first beast, Daniel indicated, was "like a lion with eagles' wings," but "its wings were pulled off" (Daniel 7:4). This imagery apparently represents Babylon, its lion-like quality indicating power and strength. It is interesting to observe that winged lions guarded the gates of Babylon's royal palaces. It is also interesting that some biblical passages represent Nebuchadnezzar as a lion (Jeremiah 4:7;

50:17). The wings on the lion indicate rapid mobility, while the wings being pulled off indicates a removal of mobility—perhaps a reference to Nebuchadnezzar's insanity or to Babylon's deterioration following his death.

Daniel said the second beast "looked like a bear. It was rearing up on one side, and it had three ribs in its mouth between its teeth" (Daniel 7:5). This kingdom is Medo-Persia. The fact that the bear was "rearing up on one side" indicates that the Persians maintained the higher status in the Medo-Persian alliance. The three ribs in its mouth are vanquished nations—apparently Babylon (conquered 539 BC), Lydia (conquered 546 BC), and Egypt (conquered 525 BC). Medo-Persia was well-known for its strength and fierceness in battle (see Isaiah 13:17-18).

Daniel said the third beast "looked like a leopard. It had four bird's wings on its back, and it had four heads. Great authority was given to this beast" (Daniel 7:6). The leopard was known for its swiftness, cunning, and agility. This imagery represents Greece under Alexander the Great (born in 356 BC). The "four heads" are the four generals who divided the kingdom following Alexander's death, ruling Macedonia, Asia Minor, Syria, and Egypt.

Daniel then refers to the fourth beast that was a mongrel beast composed of parts of a lion, bear, and leopard and was more terrifying and powerful than the three preceding beasts. This beast was "terrifying, dreadful, and very strong" (Daniel 7:7). Daniel describes the beast this way:

> It devoured and crushed its victims with huge iron teeth and trampled their remains beneath its feet. It was different from any of the other beasts, and it had ten horns.
>
> As I was looking at the horns, suddenly another small horn appeared among them. Three of the first horns were torn out by the roots to make room for it. This little

horn had eyes like human eyes and a mouth that was boasting arrogantly (Daniel 7:7-8).

This wild imagery refers to the Roman Empire. Regarding the imagery of a "horn," a horn on an animal is used by that animal as a weapon (see Genesis 22:13; Psalm 69:31). For this reason, the horn eventually became a symbol of power and might. As an extension of this symbol, horns in biblical times were sometimes used as emblems of dominion, representing kingdoms and kings, as is the case in the books of Daniel and Revelation (see Daniel 7:7-8; Revelation 12:3; 13:1,11; 17:3-16).

Rome already existed in ancient days, but it fell apart in the fifth century AD. It will be revived, however, in the end times, apparently comprised of ten nations ruled by ten kings (ten horns). It is noteworthy that Rome has never consisted of a ten-nation confederacy with ten co-rulers. If it has not happened in the past, this means the prophecy must deal with the future. The final form of the Roman Empire will be prominent during the future tribulation period.

In Daniel 7, an eleventh horn—a small horn (the antichrist)— starts out apparently in an insignificant way, but grows powerful enough to uproot three of the existing horns (kings). He eventually comes into absolute power and dominance over this revived Roman Empire.

In the book of Daniel, King Nebuchadnezzar also had a vision from God about this revived Roman Empire. In his vision, the end-times Roman Empire was pictured as a mixture of iron and clay (Daniel 2:41-43). Daniel, the great dream-interpreter, saw this as meaning that just as iron is strong, so this latter-day Roman Empire would be strong. But just as iron and clay do not mix with each other, so this latter-day Roman Empire would have some weaknesses. The union would not be completely integrated.

Today's European Union

Many modern biblical interpreters—myself included—see today's European Union as a primary prospect for the fulfillment of this prophecy. Prophecy scholar Thomas Ice notes that "the goal of the European Union is to unite all of Europe into one union that will also promote peace, harmony, and prosperity and prevent future world conflicts. This 'European Dream,' as it is often labeled, proposes a single government that will eliminate national rivalries and conflicts within Europe."[1] Some have suggested that the ultimate goal of today's European Union has never been to merely unify Europe, but rather to use this union as a steppingstone for eventual global governance by the Europeans.[2] This may indeed be the case.

In Daniel 2, it may be that the clay mixed with iron points to the diversity (race, religion, and politics) of the peoples in the ten nations that make up the empire. The clay and iron indicate weakness and strength at the same time, something that is true of the European Union even today. The European Union possesses great economic and political strength, but the nations that comprise this union are diverse in culture, language, and politics, and hence are not perfectly united. At present, the European Union has its own parliament, a rotating presidency, a supreme court, a common currency used in many member nations, allows for unrestricted travel of citizens among member nations, and is working toward a unified military.

Perhaps the stage is being set for the ultimate fulfillment of Daniel 2 and 7. As prophecy expert Mark Hitchcock puts it, "The basic governmental and economic components are in place for one man to come on the scene in the EU and ascend to tremendous power. The events we see in Europe today seem to be the prelude to the reunited Roman Empire prophesied by Daniel over 2,500 years ago."[3] This is so, despite the fact that the United Kingdom is leaving the European Union. I believe that what is transpiring in Europe today is setting the stage for an eventual ten-nation confederacy—a United States of Europe.

An Eventual Globalized Government and Globalized Economy

Prophetic Scripture reveals that the antichrist will eventually come into global dominion. He will rule the entire world, not just the revived Roman Empire. Globalism is clearly indicated in Revelation 13. We are told that "the whole world...gave allegiance to the beast" (verse 3). The antichrist "was given authority to rule over every tribe and people and language and nation. And all the people who belong to this world worshiped the beast" (verses 7-8). We are also told that the false prophet "required all the earth and its people to worship the first beast" (verse 12). This is where the infamous "mark of the beast" comes into play. Revelation 13:16-17 tells us that the false prophet "required everyone—small and great, rich and poor, free and slave—to be given a mark on the right hand or on the forehead. And no one could buy or sell anything without that mark, which was either the name of the beast or the number representing his name." Again, then, there will be a globalized political union, religious union, and economic union.

Current Movements Toward Globalism

Even in our day, we are witnessing major steps toward globalism. We see globalist policies emerging in economics, banking, commerce and trade, business, management, manufacturing, environmentalism, population control, education, religion, agriculture, information technologies, the entertainment industry, the publishing industry, science and medicine, and even government. The book of Revelation tells us that the antichrist will ultimately lead a global union—an anti-god union (see Revelation 13:3-18).

Multiple Cascading Problems

When one considers the multiple problems now facing humanity—including the Middle East conflict, terrorism, overpopulation, starvation, pollution, famine, national and international crime, cyberwarfare, and economic instability—it is entirely feasible that increasing numbers of people will come to believe that such problems can be solved only on a global level. They may think that the only hope for human survival is a strong and effective world government.

As the danger mounts, people worldwide are yearning for a leader who can take control and fix everything. The global economy is reeling, people are suffering, and there is a sense of urgency for a powerful leader who can chart a clear global course toward stability. Such a leader is coming, and he may already be alive in the world. Scripture identifies him as the antichrist.

Of great significance is the fact that the technology that makes possible a world government—including instant global media via television and radio, cyberspace, and super-computers—is now in place. In other words, technology has greased the skids for the emergence of globalism in our day.

The Central Role of Economics

Economics is an especially important factor in regard to the globalism predicted in biblical prophecy. Even as I write, the world is moving more and more toward a globalized economy. A number of financial advisors to the U.S. president have gone on record as affirming that a global economy is inescapable. There is every possibility, they say, that the world's consistent financial problems may lead to a financial new world order.

Many today believe that a global solution is needed because we have a global crisis. Some financial leaders are even speaking about the possibility of a global economic "policeman" (or a police-like financial regulatory commission) to watch over the globe's financial affairs and to ensure that we never again get engulfed by a financial tsunami. The nation-state system—with separate economies—is not working, many believe. People are ready for a new system, a global system.

In the new age of cyberspace, the respective economies of different nations are more deeply interconnected and intertwined than ever before. Each of our economies is built on global trade, global capital markets, and global communication. Our respective economies rise or fall together. What is good for one is good for all. What is bad for one is bad for all.

Today if there is an economic crisis in one country, the economy of the entire world is affected. From an economic perspective, nations do not rise or fall alone. Because of our current interconnected technologies, economic woes in one country are felt almost instantly in other countries. "An economic eruption or disturbance in New York sends financial shockwaves throughout the globe. The economic scene is highly complex, technologically integrated, and extremely unstable."[4]

In keeping with all this, people from a variety of countries—including Germany, Russia, China, and Brazil—are calling for a new way of doing things. Voices from around the world are saying the same thing: We need some kind of global financial regulation. Some countries, such as Russia and China, are open to the creation of a globalized currency to replace America's ailing dollar. Many claim the days of nation-states protecting their own economic interests in an isolationist fashion are over; everything must be done now with a view to what is good for the global economy. That is the mindset of many today.

Many also insist that we need tougher global laws and regulations on big banks and financial institutions—laws and regulations that ensure global economic stability and growth instead of protecting the interests of nation-state economies. Meanwhile, various nations are forming alliances with a view to collectively staying afloat in these uncertain times. Globalism is taking shape before our very eyes.

The Contribution of Modern Academia

Modern academia has made a notable impact on today's openness to globalism. Consider the following analysis:

> Academia in the United States is dominated by those who reject the Bible as God's revelation to mankind. Therefore, they are left with only humanistic assumptions and theories about people and society like evolution…Social theorists reject the Genesis account of creation and therefore think that society has evolved from the individual to a family; from the family to tribes; from tribes to larger communities, from communities to cities; from cities to states; and finally from nationalism to globalism. They argue that nationalism produced a time of the greatest wars in the history of mankind (the twentieth century). This occurred because nations could not settle their disputes among them without wars. Thus, nationalism only produces wars that bring great destruction and famine on mankind. This is why we need to take the next step and move on to globalism so that we will be able to eliminate the basis for division among ourselves (i.e., nationalism).[5]

Those who oppose the view of the academics are portrayed as unenlightened morons. It appears that modern academia is helping to prepare the stage for what will unfold during the tribulation period.

The Role of the Rapture

Consider how the rapture of the church may affect all this. After millions of Christians vanish off the planet, the entire globe will be negatively impacted economically. Mortgages, loans, and college tuitions will go unpaid worldwide. Millions of people will not show up for work. In their panic, the people who are left behind will stop buying. The world economy will likely collapse. Politically and economically, an eventual globalized system will seem to be the only solution. And the antichrist will be the one who assumes control. Things seem to be taking shape just as the ancient prophets predicted.

Globalism and the United States

The United States will likely be subsumed in the globalism that will emerge and prevail during the tribulation period. In his book *The Late Great United States*, Mark Hitchcock says that "the United States is slowly, subtly, yet relentlessly being drawn away from national sovereignty into a globalist order. NATO, the UN, GATT, NAFTA, the WTO, and many other acronyms signal the startling trend away from U.S. sovereignty and toward our submission to multinational treaties, organizations, and courts of law."[6] It appears that the United States has embraced the role of being "a citizen of the world."

The Enforcement of Globalism

Today's high-tech weaponry—including laser-guided missiles, nuclear submarines, fighter jets with cyber technologies built in, smart bombs, GPS technology applications on the battlefield, and cyberattacks—may well play a key role in the antichrist's enforcement of obedience to his world government. Much like shoot-'em-up video games, many attacks against opponents can be launched conveniently from a computer console. The antichrist will do whatever it takes to protect his turf—*the entire globe*. Just the threat of possible attack will be enough to keep most nations in check regarding the antichrist's globalist agenda.

The Role of Satan

Regardless of the various human leaders seeking to bring about a globalized government in the end times, behind it all is Satan— "[the man of lawlessness] will come to do the work of Satan with counterfeit power and signs and miracles. He will use every kind of evil deception to fool those on their way to destruction" (2 Thessalonians 2:9-10). My late mentor, John F. Walvoord, explained it this way:

> In the revelation concerning Satan's fall from his original holiness in eternity past as discussed in Isaiah 14:13-16, we find that his ambition was to be exalted like God. It is Satan's purpose not only to take the place of God in worship and obedience but also to establish a worldwide kingdom in competition to the prophetic program of the millennial kingdom in which Christ will reign supreme. Accordingly, in the end time prior to the second coming of Christ, Satan will achieve his purpose of having a world government that will be empowered by him and will produce almost universal worship of himself. As such, the final world government preceding the Second Coming will be Satan's final "attempt to supplant Christ and replace him with the worship and service of Satan himself."[7]

I think Walvoord is correct. Recall Satan's five "I wills" found in Isaiah 14:13-14 (NIV):

"I will ascend to the heavens." Apparently Satan wanted to abide in heaven and desired equal recognition alongside God Himself.

"I will raise my throne above the stars of God." The "stars" likely refer to the angels of God. Satan apparently desired to rule over the angelic realm with the same authority as God.

"I will sit enthroned on the mount of assembly." Scripture elsewhere indicates that the "mount of assembly" is a reference to the center of God's kingdom rule (Isaiah 2:2; Psalm 48:2). The phrase is sometimes associated with the Messiah's future earthly rule in Jerusalem during the millennial kingdom. Hence, it may be that Satan desired to rule over humans in place of the Messiah.

"I will ascend above the tops of the clouds." In the Bible, clouds often metaphorically represent the glory of God (Exodus 13:21; 40:34-38; Matthew 26:64; Revelation 14:14-16). Apparently Satan sought a glory equal to that of God Himself.

"I will make myself like the Most High." Scripture describes God as the creator and possessor of heaven and earth (Genesis 14:18-19). Apparently Satan sought the supreme position of the universe for Himself. Satan wanted to be as powerful as God. He wanted to exercise the authority and control in this world that rightfully belongs only to God. His sin was a direct challenge to the power and authority of God.

While it is the antichrist who emerges into power during the tribulation period, *Satan is the one who will energize him.* Second Thessalonians 2:9 tells us that the antichrist "will come to do the work of Satan." The NIV translates the verse, "The coming of the lawless one will be in accordance with how Satan works." The ESV translates it, "The coming of the lawless one is by the activity of Satan." The NET Bible translates it, "The arrival of the lawless one will be by Satan's working." The Amplified Bible puts it, "The coming of the [Antichrist, the lawless] one is through the activity of Satan."

This means that just as Satan sought global dominion, so now the antichrist—*as energized by Satan*—will seek global dominion.

Ultimately, the antichrist will be a puppet leader. This is why Revelation 13:2 tells us that "the dragon gave the beast his own power and throne and great authority." The dragon is Satan, while the beast is the antichrist. We might paraphrase the verse: "Satan gave the antichrist his own power and throne and great authority."

Conclusion

Two key prophecies are of interest in this chapter: (1) Prophetic Scripture predicts a revived Roman Empire, which may now exist in embryonic form in the European Union. (2) Prophetic Scripture predicts an eventual globalized government. Even today, the stage is being set for this globalized government. The end-time prophecies are casting their shadows before them.

HOW THEN SHALL WE LIVE?

Our journey is ended. We've taken a fascinating look at end-times super trends and have considered the relevance of specific end-times prophecies for our own day.

In the introduction of this book, I noted that if these are truly the last days, then we would expect to see certain developments in the world that relate specifically to the end times as prophesied in Scripture. These developments include a falling away from the truth, the widespread embracing of doctrinal error, a significant moral decline, a growing tolerance for all things evil, a widespread outbreak of a variety of sexual sins and perversions, the steady diminishing of religious freedom, the global persecution of God's people, Israel being a sore spot in the world, ever-escalating conflict in the Middle East, efforts being made to rebuild the Jewish temple, the stage being set for a massive invasion of Muslim nations into Israel, the steady rise of globalism, political and economic steps toward the establishment of a revived Roman Empire (a United States of Europe), the emergence of a cashless world in preparation for the antichrist's control of the world economy during the tribulation, and much more. It is sobering—even a bit frightening—to recognize that *all of these are trending in our day*.

I like to tell people that we are witnessing the "convergence factor." What I mean by this is that many ancient prophecies of the end times seem to be converging either today or at a point in the not-too-distant future. The end times are upon us. The day of our redemption is drawing very near.

Having said all this: *How, then, shall we live?* More specifically, in view of what we have learned...

- Should we be discouraged about world events?
- Should we be worried about the future?
- Should we change the way we live?
- What should be our attitude as we live in the end times?

The Bible provides great insights on these issues.

Avoid Unhealthy Thinking

It is sad to recognize that some people have taken unhealthy paths as a result of their understanding of Bible prophecy. I know of one person who, because he believed the Lord was coming shortly, put off going to college. I know of another person who stopped saving money for the future because he believed the Lord was coming soon. I read about another person who chose not to go to the doctor to address some serious symptoms because he believed the rapture would occur soon. To avoid such unhealthy decisions, I always advise people to follow a simple principle: *Live your life as though the rapture could happen today, but plan your life as if you will be here for your entire life expectancy. That way you are prepared for both time and eternity.*

Pray Always, Love Always

We find much wisdom in 1 Peter 4:7-10 regarding how we ought to live in view of biblical prophecy. Consider these words:

The end of the world is coming soon. Therefore, be earnest and disciplined in your prayers. Most important of all, continue to show deep love for each other, for love covers a multitude of sins. Cheerfully share your home with those who need a meal or a place to stay.

God has given each of you a gift from his great variety of spiritual gifts. Use them well to serve one another.

It is unfortunate that many people become sensationalistic and alarmist about end-time prophecies. They get so focused on the finer points of prophecy that they forget to pray and love other people. Don't let that happen. *Pray always. Love always.*

Don't Be Troubled

Jesus speaks words of great comfort to His disciples in John 14:1-3:

> "Don't let your hearts be troubled. Trust in God, and trust also in me. There is more than enough room in my Father's home. If this were not so, would I have told you that I am going to prepare a place for you? When everything is ready, I will come and get you, so that you will always be with me where I am."

John F. Walvoord has a great insight on this passage:

> These verses are the Bible's first revelation of the rapture, in which Christ will come back to take His own to heaven. He exhorted the disciples not to be troubled. Since they trusted the Father, they also should trust Christ, whose power was demonstrated in His many miracles…They need not be anxious about His leaving because later He would return for them.[1]

No matter what happens in this world, we need not be troubled. We need not fear. Jesus is now preparing our eternal homes, and He's coming for us soon. That future reality is enough to strengthen us through any present difficulties.

Live Righteously

When God reveals the future to us, He does not do so to show off. God does not give us prophecy to teach us mere intellectual facts about eschatology. It is highly revealing that many verses in the Bible that deal with prophecy follow with an exhortation to personal purity. As we study Bible prophecy, it ought to change the way we live. It ought to have an effect on our behavior. Consider the apostle Paul's exhortation in Romans 13:11-14, which is in a context of biblical prophecy:

> This is all the more urgent, for you know how late it is; time is running out. Wake up, for our salvation is nearer now than when we first believed. The night is almost gone; the day of salvation will soon be here. So remove your dark deeds like dirty clothes, and put on the shining armor of right living. Because we belong to the day, we must live decent lives for all to see. Don't participate in the darkness of wild parties and drunkenness, or in sexual promiscuity and immoral living, or in quarreling and jealousy. Instead, clothe yourself with the presence of the Lord Jesus Christ. And don't let yourself think about ways to indulge your evil desires.

We also see the connection between biblical prophecy and purity in 2 Peter 3:10-14:

> The day of the Lord will come as unexpectedly as a thief. Then the heavens will pass away with a terrible noise, and

the very elements themselves will disappear in fire, and the earth and everything on it will be found to deserve judgment.

Since everything around us is going to be destroyed like this, what holy and godly lives you should live, looking forward to the day of God and hurrying it along. On that day, he will set the heavens on fire, and the elements will melt away in the flames. But we are looking forward to the new heavens and new earth he has promised, a world filled with God's righteousness.

And so, dear friends, while you are waiting for these things to happen, make every effort to be found living peaceful lives that are pure and blameless in his sight.

First John 3:2-3 likewise instructs:

Dear friends, we are already God's children, but he has not yet shown us what we will be like when Christ appears. But we do know that we will be like him, for we will see him as he really is. And all who have this eager expectation will keep themselves pure, just as he is pure.

John is here referring to the rapture. What a glorious day that will be. Walvoord put it this way: "The hope of the rapture, when we will meet the Savior, should be a sanctifying force in our lives. We will be made completely like Him then; so we should endeavor with His help to serve Him faithfully now and to lead lives of purity."[2]

We find an analogy in ancient Jewish marriage customs. In biblical times, following the marriage betrothal, the groom would go to his father's house to prepare a place for the new couple to stay. Meanwhile, the betrothed woman would eagerly await the coming of her groom to take her away to his father's house in marriage celebration. During this time of anticipation, the bride's loyalty to her groom was tested. Likewise, as the Bride of Christ (the church) awaits the coming of the messianic Groom (Jesus), the church is motivated to live in purity and godliness until He arrives at the rapture. Let us daily choose purity.

Meanwhile—Never Set Dates

God Himself controls the timing of end-time events, and He has not provided us the specific details. In Acts 1:7 we read Jesus' words to the disciples before He ascended into heaven: "The Father alone has the authority to set those dates and times, and they are not for you to know." This means that we can be accurate observers of the times, as Jesus instructed (Matthew 24:32-33; Luke 21:25-28), but we do not have precise details on the timing. We must simply resolve to trust God with those details.

Let us not forget that Christians who get caught up in date-setting can do damage to the cause of Christ. Humanists enjoy scorning Christians who have put stock in end-time predictions—especially when specific dates have been attached to specific events. Why give ammo to the enemies of Christianity? We can be excited about events that appear to be setting the stage for the eventual fulfillment of prophecy without engaging in such sensationalism (Mark 13:32-37).

Bible Prophecy Points to the Awesome Greatness of God

I never tire of reminding Bible students that biblical prophecy constantly and relentlessly points to the awesome greatness of God. For example, in Isaiah 44:6-8 we read:

> This is what the LORD says—Israel's King and Redeemer,
> the LORD of Heaven's Armies:
> "I am the First and the Last;
>   there is no other God.

Who is like me?
>   Let him step forward and prove to you his power.
> Let him do as I have done since ancient times
>   when I established a people and explained its future.
> Do not tremble; do not be afraid.
>   Did I not proclaim my purposes for you long ago?
> You are my witnesses—is there any other God?
>   No! There is no other Rock—not one!"

In the book of Daniel, we read:

> "Praise the name of God forever and ever,
>   for he has all wisdom and power.
> He controls the course of world events;
>   he removes kings and sets up other kings.
> He gives wisdom to the wise
>   and knowledge to the scholars.
> He reveals deep and mysterious things
>   and knows what lies hidden in darkness,
>   though he is surrounded by light."
>   (Daniel 2:20-22)

Can there be any doubt that our God is an awesome God? The Bible reveals some phenomenal facts about this awesome God. Let us meditate on these truths as they relate to the unfolding of God's prophetic plan on earth.

God Is Eternal

One theologian describes God as "the eternal without beginning, He who is above the whole course of time, He who in harmony beyond explanation possesses unity and life, the Father, the Son, and the Holy Spirit, the basis of eternity, the Living One, the only God."[3] God transcends time altogether. He is above the space-time universe.

As an eternal being, He has always existed. He is the eternal King (1 Timothy 1:17) who alone is immortal (6:16). He is "the Alpha and the Omega" (Revelation 1:8) and "the First and the Last" (Isaiah 44:6; 48:12). He exists "from beginning to end" (Psalm 90:2). He lives forever from eternal ages past (Psalm 41:13; 102:12,27; Isaiah 57:15). So, while events transpire daily here on planet Earth, and while prophecies are fulfilled temporally, God Himself is beyond time altogether.

One comfort related to God's eternal nature is the absolute confidence that God will never cease to exist. He will always be there for us. His continued providential control of our lives is thereby assured. Human leaders come and go. Countries come and go. But God is eternal and is always there! The prophetic future is in His eternal hands.

God Is Everywhere-Present

The reality that God is everywhere-present does not mean that He is diffused throughout space, as if part of Him is here and part of Him is there. Rather God in His whole being is in every place. There is nowhere one can go where God is not present (Psalm 139:7-8; Jeremiah 23:23-24; Acts 17:27-28). Hence, whether one is in the United States or Iran or Russia or anywhere in the entire universe, *God is there.*

While the world in these last days often seems to be spinning out of control, how comforting to know that no matter where we go, we will never escape the presence of our beloved God. Because He is everywhere-present, we can be confident of His real presence at all times. We will always know the blessing of walking with Him in every trial and circumstance of life.

God Is All-Knowing

Because God transcends time—because He is above time—He

can see the past, present, and future as a single act. God's knowledge of all things is from the vantage point of eternity, so that the past (Isaiah 41:22), present (Hebrews 4:13), and future (Isaiah 46:10) are all encompassed in one ever-present "now" to Him. God knows all things, both actual and possible (Matthew 11:20-24). Because He knows all things, there can be no increase or decrease in His knowledge. Psalm 147:5 affirms that "His understanding is beyond comprehension" (see also Psalm 33:13-15; 139:11-12; Proverbs 15:3; Isaiah 40:14; Acts 15:18; Hebrews 4:13; 1 John 3:20). This is why we can trust God when He communicates prophecies about the future to us. God knows all!

God Is All-Powerful

Scripture portrays God as being all-powerful (Jeremiah 32:17). He has the power to do all that He desires and wills. Scripture declares some 56 times that God is almighty (for example, Revelation 19:6). God is abundant in strength (Psalm 147:5) and has incomparably great power (2 Chronicles 20:6; Ephesians 1:19-21). No one can hold back His hand (Daniel 4:35). No one can reverse Him (Isaiah 43:13) and no one can thwart Him (Isaiah 14:27). Nothing is impossible with Him (Matthew 19:26; Luke 1:37) and nothing is too difficult for Him (Genesis 18:13-14; Jeremiah 32:17,27). The Almighty reigns (Revelation 19:6). None of the nations of the world are beyond God's control. No matter what threat one nation might make against another—such as Iran threatening Israel—we must remember that our God, who is all-powerful, is in control. No one can thwart His plans. His prophetic plan will unfold just as He decreed.

God Is Sovereign

Scripture portrays God as being absolutely sovereign. He rules the universe, controls all things, and is Lord over all (Ephesians 1). There is nothing that can happen in this universe that is beyond the reach of His control. All forms of existence are within the scope of His absolute dominion. Psalm 66:7 affirms that "by his great power he rules forever." We are assured in Psalm 93:1 that "the LORD is king!" God asserts, "Everything I plan will come to pass, for I do whatever I wish" (Isaiah 46:10). God assures us, "It will all happen as I have planned. It will be as I have decided" (Isaiah 14:24). Proverbs 16:9 tells us, "We can make our plans, but the LORD determines our steps." Proverbs 19:21 says, "You can make many plans, but the LORD's purpose will prevail."

Supreme peace in the heart is the natural result of trusting that God sovereignly oversees all that comes into our lives. No matter what we may encounter—no matter how much we may fail to understand why certain things happen and no matter how horrible the newspaper headlines may often seem to be—the knowledge that our sovereign God is in control is like a firm anchor in the midst of life's storms. We can be at peace no matter what the future may hold.

God Is Holy

God's holiness means not just that He is entirely separate from all evil but also that He is absolutely righteous (Leviticus 19:2). He is pure in every way.

The Scriptures lay great stress upon this attribute of God:

- "Who is like you…glorious in holiness?" (Exodus 15:11).
- "No one is holy like the LORD!" (1 Samuel 2:2).
- "The LORD our God is holy!" (Psalm 99:9).
- "What a holy, awe-inspiring name he has!" (Psalm 111:9).
- "Holy, holy, holy is the LORD of Heaven's Armies!" (Isaiah 6:3).
- "You alone are holy" (Revelation 15:4).

One important ramification of God's holiness is that He will not allow persons or nations to get away with sinful actions. So, for example, when the northern military coalition launches a massive invasion into Israel, as prophesied in Ezekiel 38–39, God responds to this defiant sinful act by utterly destroying them.

God Is Just

God carries out His righteous standards justly and with equity. There is never any partiality or unfairness in God's dealings with people (Genesis 18:25; Psalm 11:7; Zephaniah 3:5; John 17:25; Romans 3:26; Hebrews 6:10). The fact that God is just is both a comfort and a warning. It is a comfort for those who have been wronged in life. They can rest assured that God will right all wrongs in the end. It is a warning for those who think they have been getting away with evil. Justice will prevail in the end. God's end-time judgments will see to that!

Maintain an Eternal Perspective

Does it not create excitement in each of our hearts that we, as Christians, will live for all eternity in heaven with our wondrous God? No matter what takes place on this earth, we each have a splendorous destiny ahead. I never tire of saying that a daily pondering of the incredible glory of the afterlife is one of the surest ways to stay motivated to live faithfully during our relatively short time on earth. We are but pilgrims on our way to another land—to the final frontier of heaven where God Himself dwells (Hebrews 11:16).

J.I. Packer, whose writings have greatly impacted my life, says that the "lack of long, strong thinking about our promised hope of glory is a major cause of our plodding, lackluster lifestyle." He points to the Puritans as a much-needed example for us, for they believed that "it is the heavenly Christian that is the lively Christian."

The Puritans understood that we "run so slowly, and strive so lazily, because we so little mind the prize…So let Christians animate themselves daily to run the race set before them by practicing heavenly meditation."[4]

Puritan Richard Baxter's daily habit was to "dwell on the glory of the heavenly life to which one was going." Baxter daily practiced "holding heaven at the forefront of his thoughts and desires." The hope of heaven brought him joy, and joy brought him strength. Baxter once said, "A heavenly mind is a joyful mind; this is the nearest and truest way to live a life of comfort…A heart in heaven will be a most excellent preservative against temptations, a powerful means to kill thy corruptions."[5]

Such comments reflect the exhortation of the apostle Paul in Colossians 3:1-2: "Since you have been raised to new life with Christ, set your sights on the realities of heaven, where Christ sits in the place of honor at God's right hand. Think about the things of heaven, not the things of earth." The original Greek of this verse is intense, communicating the idea, "diligently, actively, single-mindedly think on the things of heaven." Moreover, the present tense in the original Greek communicates the idea, "perpetually *keep on* thinking on the things of heaven…Make it an ongoing process." This ought to be our attitude every single day.

It is also wise to keep in mind the temporal nature of this life. We ought to pray with the psalmist: "Teach us to realize the brevity of life, so that we may grow in wisdom" (Psalm 90:12). And: "LORD, remind me how brief my time on earth will be. Remind me that my days are numbered—how fleeting my life is" (Psalm 39:4). Those Christians who wisely ponder their mortality are most often the ones who maintain the eternal perspective described above.

Come soon, Lord!

APPENDIX

IF YOU ARE NOT A CHRISTIAN

A personal relationship with Jesus is the most important decision you could ever make. It is unlike any other relationship.
If you go into eternity without this relationship, you will spend eternity apart from Him.

If you will allow me, I would like to tell you how you can come
into a personal relationship with Jesus.

First you need to recognize that...

God Desires a Personal Relationship with You

God created you (Genesis 1:27). And He did not create you just
to exist all alone and apart from Him. He created you with a view
to coming into a personal relationship with Him.

God has fellowshipped with His people throughout Bible times
(for example, Genesis 3:8-19). Just as God fellowshipped with them,
so He desires to fellowship with you (1 John 1:5-7). God loves you
(John 3:16). Never forget that fact.

The problem is...

Humanity Has a Sin Problem that Blocks
a Relationship with God

When Adam and Eve chose to sin against God in the Garden of

Eden, they catapulted the entire human race—to which they gave birth—into sin. Since that time, every human being has been born into the world with a propensity to sin.

The apostle Paul affirmed that "when Adam sinned, sin entered the world. Adam's sin brought death, so death spread to everyone" (Romans 5:12). We are told that "because one person disobeyed God, many became sinners" (Romans 5:19). Ultimately this means that "death came into the world through a man" (Adam), and "everyone dies because we all belong to Adam" (1 Corinthians 15:21-22).

Jesus often spoke of sin in metaphors that illustrate the havoc sin can wreak in one's life. He described sin as blindness (Matthew 23:16-26), sickness (Matthew 9:12), being enslaved in bondage (John 8:34), and living in darkness (John 8:12; 12:35-46). Moreover, Jesus taught that this is a universal condition and that all people are guilty before God (Luke 7:36-50).

Jesus also taught that both inner thoughts and external acts render a person guilty (Matthew 5:27-28). He taught that from within the human heart come evil thoughts, sexual immorality, theft, murder, adultery, greed, malice, deceit, envy, slander, arrogance, and folly (Mark 7:20-23). Moreover, He affirmed that God is fully aware of every person's sins, both external acts and inner thoughts; nothing escapes His notice (Matthew 22:18; Luke 6:8; John 4:15-19).

Of course, some people are more morally upright than others. However, we all fall short of God's infinite standards (Romans 3:23). In a contest to see who can throw a rock to the moon, I am sure a muscular athlete would be able to throw it much farther than I could. But all human beings fall short of the task. Similarly, all of us fall short of measuring up to God's perfect holy standards.

Though the sin problem is a serious one, God has graciously provided a solution.

Jesus Died for Our Sins and Made Salvation Possible

God's absolute holiness demands that sin be punished. The good news of the gospel, however, is that Jesus has taken this punishment on Himself. God loves us so much that He sent Jesus to bear the penalty for our sins!

Jesus affirmed that it was for the very purpose of dying that He came into the world (John 12:27). Moreover, He perceived His death as being a sacrificial offering for the sins of humanity (Matthew 26:26-28). Jesus took His sacrificial mission with utmost seriousness for He knew that without Him, humanity would certainly perish (Matthew 16:25; John 3:16) and spend eternity apart from God in a place of great suffering (Matthew 10:28; 11:23-24; 23:33; 25:41; Luke 16:19-31).

Jesus therefore described His mission this way: "The Son of Man came not to be served but to serve others and to give his life as a ransom for many" (Matthew 20:28). "The Son of Man came to seek and save those who are lost" (Luke 19:10). "God sent his Son into the world not to judge the world, but to save the world through him" (John 3:17).

Please beware that the benefits of Christ's death on the cross are not automatically applied to your life. *To receive the gift of salvation, you must...*

Believe in Jesus Christ the Savior

By His sacrificial death on the cross, Jesus took the sins of the entire world on Himself and made salvation available for everyone (1 John 2:2). But this salvation is not automatic. Only those who choose to believe in Christ are saved. This is the consistent testimony of the biblical Jesus. Listen to His words:

- "For this is how God loved the world: He gave his one and only Son, so that everyone who believes in him will not perish but have eternal life" (John 3:16).

- "For it is my Father's will that all who see his Son and believe in him should have eternal life. I will raise them up at the last day" (John 6:40).

- "I am the resurrection and the life. Anyone who believes in me will live, even after dying" (John 11:25).

Choosing *not* to believe in Jesus, by contrast, leads to eternal condemnation: "There is no judgment against anyone who believes in him. But anyone who does not believe in him has already been judged for not believing in God's one and only Son" (John 3:18).

Free at Last: Forgiven of All Sins

When you believe in Christ the Savior, a wonderful thing happens. God forgives you of all your sins. All of them! He puts them completely out of His sight. Ponder for a few minutes the following verses, which speak of the forgiveness of those who have believed in Christ:

> He is so rich in kindness and grace that he purchased
> our freedom with the blood of his Son and forgave our
> sins.
> > (Ephesians 1:7)

> Then [the Holy Spirit] says,
> > "I will never again remember
> > their sins and lawless deeds."
> > (Hebrews 10:17)

> Oh, what joy for those
> > whose disobedience is forgiven,
> > whose sin is put out of sight!
> Yes, what joy for those
> > whose record the Lord has cleared of guilt,
> > whose lives are lived in complete honesty!
> > (Psalm 32:1-2)

For his unfailing love toward those who fear him
   is as great as the height of the heavens above
   the earth.
He has removed our sins as far from us
   as the east is from the west.
       (Psalm 103:11-12)

Such forgiveness is wonderful indeed, for none of us can possibly work our way into heaven or be good enough to warrant God's good favor. Because of what Jesus has done for us, we can freely receive the gift of salvation. It is a gift provided solely through the grace of God (Ephesians 2:8-9). It becomes ours by placing our faith in Jesus.

Don't Put It Off

It is a dangerous thing to put off turning to Christ for salvation, for you do not know the day of your death. What if it happens this evening? "Everyone dies—so the living should take this to heart" (Ecclesiastes 7:2).

If God is speaking to your heart now, then now is your door of opportunity to believe. "Seek the Lord while you can find him. Call on him now while he is near" (Isaiah 55:6).

Follow Me in Prayer

Would you like to place your faith in Jesus for the forgiveness of sins, thereby guaranteeing your eternal place in heaven along His side? If so, pray the following prayer with me. Keep in mind that it is not the prayer itself that saves you. It is the faith in your heart that saves you. So let the following prayer be a simple expression of the faith that is in your heart:

Dear Jesus:
I want to have a relationship with You.

I know I cannot save myself, because I know I am a sinner.
Thank You for dying on the cross on my behalf.
I believe You died for me, and I accept Your free gift of salvation.

Thank You, Jesus.
Amen.

Welcome to God's Forever Family

On the authority of the Word of God, I can now assure you that you are a part of God's forever family. If you prayed the above prayer with a heart of faith, you will spend all eternity by the side of Jesus in heaven. Welcome to God's family! I will one day see you in heaven.

What to Do Next

1. Purchase a Bible and read from it daily. Read at least one chapter a day, followed by a time of prayer. If you've not read the Bible before, I recommend that you obtain an easy-to-read translation, such as the New Living Translation (NLT). I also recommend starting with the Gospel of Luke.

2. Join a Bible-believing church. Get involved in it. Join a Bible study group at the church so you will have regular fellowship with other Christians.

3. Send me an email at ronrhodes@earthlink.net. I would love to hear from you if you have made a decision for Christ.

BIBLIOGRAPHY

Allen, John. *The Global War on Christians: Dispatches from the Front Lines of Anti-Christian Persecution*. New York: Image, 2016.

Ankerberg, John, and Dillon Burroughs. *Middle East Meltdown*. Eugene, OR: Harvest House, 2007.

Barna, George. *America at the Crossroads: Explosive Trends Shaping America's Future and What You Can Do About It*. Grand Rapids, MI: Baker, 2016.

Barnhouse, Donald Grey. *Revelation: An Expository Commentary*. Grand Rapids, MI: Zondervan, 1971.

The Bible in America: The Changing Landscape of Bible Perceptions and Engagement, ed. Barna Group. Ventura, CA: Barna Group, 2016.

Block, Daniel. *The Book of Ezekiel: Chapters 25-48*. Grand Rapids, MI: Wm. B. Eerdmans, 1998.

Briggs, Kenneth. *The Invisible Bestseller: Searching for the Bible in America*. Grand Rapids, MI: Wm. B. Eerdmans, 2016.

Dyer, Charles. *The Rise of Babylon: Sign of the End Times*. Chicago: Moody, 2003.

Feinberg, Charles. *The Prophecy of Ezekiel*. Eugene, OR: Wipf and Stock, 2003.

Fruchtenbaum, Arnold. *The Footsteps of the Messiah*. San Antonio, TX: Ariel, 2004.

Geisler, Norman. *Systematic Theology: Church/Last Things*, vol. 4. Minneapolis, MN: Bethany House, 2005.

Hays, J. Daniel, J. Scott Duvall, and C. Marvin Pate. *Dictionary of Biblical Prophecy and End Times*. Grand Rapids, MI: Zondervan, 2007.

Hindson, Ed. *Revelation: Unlocking the Future*. Chattanooga, TN: AMG, 2002.

Hitchcock, Mark. *Bible Prophecy*. Wheaton, IL: Tyndale House, 1999.

———. *The Coming Islamic Invasion of Israel*. Sisters, OR: Multnomah, 2002.

———. *Iran: The Coming Crisis*. Sisters, OR: Multnomah, 2006.

———. *Is America in Bible Prophecy?* Sisters, OR: Multnomah, 2002.

———. *The Late Great United States*. Colorado Springs, CO: Multnomah, 2009.

———. *The Second Coming of Babylon*. Sisters, OR: Multnomah, 2003.

Hoyt, Herman. *The End Times*. Chicago: Moody, 1969.

Ibrahim, Raymond. *Crucified Again: Exposing Islam's New War on Christians*. Washington: Regnery, 2013.

Ice, Thomas, and Randall Price. *Ready to Rebuild: The Imminent Plan to Rebuild the Last Days Temple*. Eugene, OR: Harvest House, 1992.

Ice, Thomas, and Timothy Demy. *Prophecy Watch*. Eugene, OR: Harvest House, 1998.

———. *What the Bible Says About Heaven and Eternity*. Grand Rapids, MI: Kregel, 2000.

———. *When the Trumpet Sounds*. Eugene, OR: Harvest House, 1995.

Jeremiah, David. *Escape the Coming Night: An Electrifying Tour of the World as It Races Toward Its Final Days*. Dallas: Word, 1990.

Kinnaman, David, and Gabe Lyons. *Good Faith: Being a Christian When Society Thinks You're Irrelevant and Extreme*. Grand Rapids, MI: Baker, 2016.

LaHaye, Tim. *The Beginning of the End*. Wheaton, IL: Tyndale House, 1991.

———. *The Coming Peace in the Middle East*. Grand Rapids, MI: Zondervan, 1984.

LaHaye, Tim, and Jerry Jenkins. *Are We Living in the End Times?* Wheaton, IL: Tyndale House, 1999.

LaHaye, Tim, and Thomas Ice. *Charting the End Times*. Eugene, OR: Harvest House, 2001.

The MacArthur Study Bible, ed. John MacArthur. Nashville, TN: Thomas Nelson, 2003.

Newell, William. *Revelation Chapter-by-Chapter*. Grand Rapids, MI: Kregel, 1994.

Pache, Rene. *The Future Life*. Chicago: Moody, 1980.

Pentecost, J. Dwight. *Prophecy for Today*. Grand Rapids, MI: Discovery House, 1989.

———. *Things to Come*. Grand Rapids, MI: Zondervan, 1964.

———. *The Words and Works of Jesus Christ*. Grand Rapids, MI: Zondervan, 1978.

Pink, Arthur W. *The Antichrist: A Study of Satan's Christ*. Blacksburg, VA: Wilder, 2008.

The Popular Bible Prophecy Commentary, eds. Tim LaHaye and Ed Hindson. Eugene, OR: Harvest House, 2006.

The Popular Encyclopedia of Bible Prophecy, eds. Tim LaHaye and Ed Hindson. Eugene, OR: Harvest House, 2004.

Price, Randall. *Fast Facts on the Middle East Conflict*. Eugene, OR: Harvest House, 2003.

———. *Jerusalem in Prophecy*. Eugene, OR: Harvest House, 1998.

———. *Unholy War*. Eugene, OR: Harvest House, 2001.

Price, Walter K. *The Coming Antichrist*. Neptune, NJ: Loizeaux Brothers, 1985.

Prophecy Study Bible, ed. Tim LaHaye. Chattanooga, TN: AMG, 2001.

Rhodes, Ron. *40 Days Through Daniel: Revealing God's Plan for the Future*. Eugene, OR: Harvest House, 2013.

———. *40 Days Through Revelation: Uncovering the Mystery of the End Times*. Eugene, OR: Harvest House, 2013.

———. *The Coming Oil Storm*. Eugene, OR: Harvest House, 2010.

———. *Five Views on the Rapture: What You Need to Know*. Eugene, OR: Harvest House, 2011.

———. *Is America in Bible Prophecy? What You Need to Know*. Eugene, OR: Harvest House, 2011.

———. *The Middle East Conflict: What You Need to Know*. Eugene, OR: Harvest House, 2009.

———. *Northern Storm Rising: Russia, Iran, and the Emerging End-Times Military Coalition Against Israel*. Eugene, OR: Harvest House, 2008.

———. *The Popular Dictionary of Bible Prophecy*. Eugene, OR: Harvest House, 2010.

———. *The Topical Guide of Bible Prophecy*. Eugene, OR: Harvest House, 2010.

Richardson, Joel. *The Islamic Antichrist*. Los Angeles: WND Books, 2009.

Robison, James. *The Stream: Refreshing Hearts and Minds, Renewing Freedom's Blessings*. Franklin, TN: Worthy, 2016.

Rosenberg, Joel. *Epicenter: Why Current Rumblings in the Middle East Will Change Your Future*. Carol Stream, IL: Tyndale House, 2006.

Ruthven, Jon Mark. *The Prophecy That Is Shaping History: New Research on Ezekiel's Vision of the End*. Fairfax, VA: Xulon, 2003.

Ryrie, Charles. *Basic Theology*. Wheaton, IL: Victor, 1986.

———. *Dispensationalism Today*. Chicago: Moody, 1965.

The Ryrie Study Bible, ed. Charles Ryrie. Chicago: Moody, 2011.

Sanders, J. Oswald. *Heaven: Better by Far*. Grand Rapids, MI: Discovery House, 1993.

Showers, Renald. *Maranatha: Our Lord Come!* Bellmawr, NJ: Friends of Israel Gospel Ministry, 1995.

Toussaint, Stanley. *Behold the King: A Study of Matthew*. Grand Rapids, MI: Kregel, 2005.

Unger, Merrill F. *Beyond the Crystal Ball*. Chicago: Moody, 1978.

Walvoord, John F. *End Times*. Nashville, TN: Word, 1998.

———. *The Millennial Kingdom*. Grand Rapids, MI: Zondervan, 1975.

———. *The Prophecy Knowledge Handbook*. Wheaton, IL: Victor, 1990.

———. *The Return of the Lord*. Grand Rapids, MI: Zondervan, 1979.

Walvoord, John F., and John E. Walvoord. *Armageddon, Oil, and the Middle East Crisis*. Grand Rapids, MI: Zondervan, 1975.

Walvoord, John F., and Mark Hitchcock. *Armageddon, Oil, and Terror*. Carol Stream, IL: Tyndale House, 2007.

Wood, Leon J. *The Bible and Future Events: An Introductory Summary of Last-Day Events*. Grand Rapids, MI: Zondervan, 1973.

Woodward, Kenneth. *Getting Religion: Faith, Culture, and Politics from the Age of Eisenhower to the Era of Obama*. New York: Convergent, 2016.

Yamauchi, Edwin. *Foes from the Northern Frontier: Invading Hordes from the Russian Steppes*. Eugene, OR: Wipf and Stock, 1982.

NOTES

Introduction—End-Times Super Trends

1. George Barna, *America at the Crossroads* (Grand Rapids, MI: Baker Books, 2016), 9.

2. Ibid., 9-10.

3. Randall Price, "The Divine Preservation of the Jewish People," *World of the Bible Ministry Update*, October 1, 2009.

4. Randall Price, *Jerusalem in Prophecy: God's Final Stage for the Final Drama* (Eugene, OR: Harvest House, 1998), 220.

5. Robert P. Lightner, *Evangelical Theology* (Grand Rapids, MI: Baker Books, 1986), 57.

Chapter 1—A Departure from the Faith: End-Times Apostasy

1. The Barna Group, *The Bible in America: The Changing Landscape of Bible Perceptions and Engagement* (Ventura, CA: Barna Group, 2016), 19.

2. George Barna, *America at the Crossroads* (Grand Rapids, MI: Baker Books, 2016), 41.

3. Ibid., 39-40.

4. David Kinnaman and Gabe Lyons, Good *Faith: Being a Christian When Society Thinks You're Irrelevant and Extreme* (Grand Rapids, MI: Baker Books, 2016), 12-13.

5. Barna, *America at the Crossroads*, 29,38-39.

6. David Voas, "Are Americans Becoming as Godless as Europeans?," *Newsweek*, September 17, 2016, online edition.

7. The Barna Group, *The Bible in America*, 8,56. See also The Barna Group, "Bible Engagement in a New World," May 18, 2016, online report, www.barna.com.

8. The Barna Group, "The Bible in America: 6-Year Trends," June 15, 2016, online report, www .barna.com.

9. The Barna Group, *The Bible in America*, 57,58.

10. Barna, *America at the Crossroads*, 51.

11. Kenneth Briggs, *The Invisible Bestseller: Searching for the Bible in America* (Grand Rapids, MI: Eerdmans, 2016), 1.

12. Ibid., 5.

13. See Barna, *America at the Crossroads*, 33,67.

14. www.recoveringfromreligion.org/.

15. Alan Freeman, "Can an Atheist Lead a Protestant Church? A Battle Over Religion in Canada," *Washington Post*, September 29, 2016, online edition.

16. Shelby Webb, "Religious 'Free-Thinkers' as Old as the Country, But Becoming the New Norm," *Houston Chronicle*, October 26, 2016, online edition.

17. For a refutation of this claim, see my book *Reasoning from the Scriptures with Muslims*, published by Harvest House.

18. For more information on her and others like her, see my book *The Truth Behind Ghosts, Mediums, and Psychic Phenomena*, published by Harvest House.

19. Brian D. McLaren, *A Generous Orthodoxy* (Grand Rapids, MI: Zondervan, 2006), 19-20.

20. Brian D. McLaren, *The Last Word and the Word After That* (San Francisco: Jossey-Bass, 2008), 35.

21. Alan Jones, *Reimagining Christianity* (Hoboken, NJ: John Wiley and Sons, 2004), 132.

Chapter 2—Alternative Religions in the End Times

1. See, for example, *The Challenge of the Cults and New Religions, Find It Quick Handbook on Cults and New Religions, Correcting the Cults, Reasoning from the Scriptures with Jehovah's Witnesses, Reasoning from the Scriptures with Mormons, Reasoning from the Scriptures with Masons, Reasoning from the Scriptures with Muslims, The 10 Most Important Things You Can Say to a Jehovah's Witness, The 10 Most Important Things You Can Say to a Mormon, The 10 Things You Need to Know About Islam, Conversations with Jehovah's Witnesses*, and others.

2. Pauline Chiou, "Listening to the Voices of Ghosts," *CBS News*, February 3, 2006.

3. Marcia Montenegro, "I See Dead People," *Christian Research Journal*, vol. 25, no. 1, 2003.

4. Brooks Alexander, cited in John Ankerberg and John Weldon, *Cult Watch* (Eugene, OR: Harvest House Publishers, 1991), 249.

5. The Barna Group, "New Research Explores Teenage Views and Behavior Regarding the Supernatural," *Barna.com*, January 23, 2006.

Chapter 3—Anything Goes: End-Times Moral Decline

1. Elliot Miller, "Breaking Through the 'Relativity Barrier,'" *Christian Research Journal*, Winter/Spring 1988, 7.

2. David Kinnaman and Gabe Lyons, *Good Faith: Being a Christian When Society Thinks You're Irrelevant and Extreme* (Grand Rapids, MI: Baker, 2016), 114.

3. Carl F.H. Henry, cited in Russell Chandler, *Understanding the New Age* (Dallas: Word Publishing, 1991), 252.

4. Chandler, *Understanding the New Age*, 258.

5. Ibid., 263.

6. The Barna Group, *The Bible in America: The Changing Landscape of Bible Perceptions and Engagement* (Ventura, CA: Barna Group, 2016), 9.

7. Michael Foust, "One-Third of Practicing Christians Say Morality Is Relative, Shocking Poll Shows," *Christian Examiner*, May 31, 2016, online edition.

8. Kinnaman and Lyons, *Good Faith*, 57,59.

9. These statistics are based on George Barna, *America at the Crossroads* (Grand Rapids, MI: Baker Books, 2016), 126.

10. "Euthanasia Acceptable to Solid Majority of Americans: Poll," *New China*, June 26, 2016, online edition.

11. Kim Kuo, "Assisted Suicide and Real Death with Dignity," *Christianity Today*, September 15, 2015, online edition.

12. Steve Weatherbe, "Porn Still 'Morally Unacceptable' to Most Americans: Gallup," *LifeSiteNews.com*, June 23, 2016.

13. Colleen Dulle, "Organizations Combat Trend Toward Moral Acceptance of Pornography," *Catholic News Service*, July 13, 2016, online edition.

14. Yasmin Alibhai-Brown, "Revenge Porn Is Just One Part of Our Loss of Privacy," *iNews*, September 7, 2016, online edition.

15. Barna, *America at the Crossroads*, 127.

16. Jennifer Harper, "73 Percent of Americans Say the Nation's Moral Values Have Declined: Gallup Poll," *Washington Times*, May 26, 2016, online edition.

17. See Kinnaman and Lyons, *Good Faith*, 60.

18. The Barna Group, "The End of Absolutes: America's New Moral Code," *Barna.com*, May 25, 2016.

19. Stephen Leeb, *The Coming Economic Collapse* (New York: Warner, 2006), 30.

Chapter 4—Tolerance for All: The New Golden Rule

1. David Kinnaman and Gabe Lyons, *Good Faith: Being a Christian When Society Thinks You're Irrelevant and Extreme* (Grand Rapids, MI: Baker Books, 2016), 11.

2. Ibid., 14.

3. William D. Watkins, "Is Tolerance a Virtue?," *Christian Research Journal*, Summer 1995, online edition.

4. D.A. Carson, cited in Mollie Ziegler Hemingway, "Tolerance—Or Else: Coercive Attempts to Impose Secular Beliefs," *Christianity Today*, April 16, 2012, online edition.

5. See Francis J. Beckwith, "Deconstructing Liberal Tolerance," *Christian Research Journal*, vol. 22, no. 3, 2000, online edition.

6. Daniel Taylor, "Are You Tolerant? (Should You Be?)," *Christianity Today*, January 11, 1999, online edition.

7. Bob Unrah, "Armageddon for Christian Colleges," *WorldNetDaily*, May 29, 2016, online edition.

8. Beckwith, "Deconstructing Liberal Tolerance."

9. Cited in Watkins, "Is Tolerance a Virtue?"

10. See Hank Hanegraaff, "Should Christians Be Tolerant?," *Christian Research Journal*, vol. 30, no. 6, 2007, online edition.

11. Taylor, "Are You Tolerant? (Should You Be?)."

12. Elliot Miller, "The 1993 Parliament of the World's Religions: The Fundamentalism of Tolerance," *Christian Research Journal*, Winter 1994, online edition.

13. Beckwith, "Deconstructing Liberal Tolerance."

Chapter 5—The Steady Deterioration of Religious Freedom

1. Sydney E. Ahlstrom, *A Religious History of the American People* (New York: Image Books, 1975), 30.

2. J.E. Wood, "Separation of Church and State," in *Dictionary of Christianity in America*, ed. Daniel G. Reid (Downers Grove, IL: InterVarsity Press, 1990), 268.

3. James Madison, cited by Wood, 267.

4. The Barna Group, *The Bible in America: The Changing Landscape of Bible Perceptions and Engagement* (Ventura, CA: Barna Group, 2016), 11.

5. Veronica Neffinger, "Supreme Court Justice Warns Religious Freedom Is in Danger," *Crosswalk .com*, June 29, 2016, www.crosswalk.com/blogs/christian-trends/supreme-court-justice-warns-religious-freedom-is-in-danger.html/.

6. Frank Camp, "Religious Freedom Group Demands Air Force Major Be 'Visibly and Aggressively Punished' for Bible," *Independent Journal Review*, August 21, 2016, online edition.

7. Anugrah Kumar, "Ex-Atlanta Fire Chief Removed for Faith: Gov't the Biggest Threat to Religious Freedom," *Christian Post*, July 18, 2016, online edition.

8. David Kinnaman and Gabe Lyons, *Good Faith: Being a Christian When Society Thinks You're Irrelevant and Extreme* (Grand Rapids, MI: Baker Books, 2016), 51.

9. Humanist Manifesto II, https://americanhumanist.org/what-is-humanism/manifesto2/.

10. James Hitchcock, *What Is Secular Humanism?* (Ann Arbor, MI: Servant Books, 1982), Introduction.

11. Isaac Asimov, *Free Inquiry*, Spring 1982; cited at https://en.wikiquote.org/wiki/Isaac_Asimov.

12. Carl Sagan, *Cosmos* (New York: Ballantine Books, 1985), 1.

13. Isaac Asimov, *Isaac Asimov's Book of Science and Nature Quotations* (New York: Weidenfeld and Nicolson, 1988), xvi.

14. Frederick Edwords, "The Humanist Philosophy in Perspective," *The Humanist*, January/February 1984 (n.p.).

15. Paul Kurtz, *Forbidden Fruit: The Ethics of Humanism* (Buffalo, NY: Prometheus Books, 1988), 243.

16. Humanist Manifesto II.

17. Brandon Showalter, "74 Percent of World's Population Live in Religious Freedom Violating Country, New Report Finds," *CP Politics*, August 13, 2016, online edition.

18. Ibid.

19. Angelina E. Theodorou, "Religious Restrictions Among the World's Most Populous Countries," Pew Research Center, June 28, 2016, online edition.

20. Ibid.

21. Ibid.

22. Sutirtho Patranobis, "China Removes Bible Extract from Textbooks," *Hindustan Times*, June 3, 2016, online edition.

23. Heather Tomlinson, "Prayer and Religion Banned in Chinese Hospitals," *Christianity Today*, August 21, 2016, online edition.

24. Ibid.

25. Ibid.

26. Stoyan Zaimov, "Seminary Students in China Forced to Deny God, 'Obey Communist Party,'" *Christian Post*, July 26, 2016, online edition.

27. Ibid.

28. Sarah Eekhoff Zylstra, "Russia's Ban on Evangelism Is Now in Effect," *Christianity Today*, July 21, 2016, online edition.

29. Ibid.

30. Ibid.

31. Ibid.

32. Theodorou, "Religious Restrictions Among the World's Most Populous Countries."

33. Ed Stetzer, "Islam a Threat to Religious Freedom? New Data from Lifeway Research," *Christianity Today*, June 30, 2015, online edition.

34. Raymond Ibrahim, *Crucified Again: Exposing Islam's New War on Christians* (Washington, DC: Regnery Publishing, 2013).

Chapter 6—The Rising Persecution and Martyrdom of Christians

1. Robert J. Morgan, "The World's War on Christianity," *The Huffington Post,* March 16, 2014, online edition.

2. Ruth Gledhill, "Report on Freedom of Religion Shows Horrific Persecution of Christians Worldwide," *Christianity Today,* July 1, 2016, online edition.

3. Section 295-C of the Pakistan penal code, cited in Aakar Patel, "Pakistan's Blasphemy Law," *The Express Tribune,* August 26, 2012, online edition.

4. Fred Barbash, "'She Wouldn't Listen': A Wrenching Story of an 'Honor Killing' in Pakistan," *Washington Post,* October 5, 2016, online edition.

5. Norman Byrd, "Christian Man's Arms Chopped Off for Not Embracing Islam," *Inquisitr,* July 17, 2016, online edition.

6. Raymond Ibrahim, *Crucified Again: Exposing Islam's New War on Christians* (Washington, DC: Regnery Publishing, 2013), 195.

7. "Pakistan's Persecution of Christians Escalates," *Peter Tatchell Foundation,* July 6, 2016, online edition.

8. Hazel Torres, "Pakistan Textbooks Teach Children to Hate Christians, Describing Them as 'Outsiders, Unpatriotic, and Inferior,'" *Christianity Today,* August 8, 2016, online edition.

9. "Pakistan's Persecution of Christians Escalates," *Peter Tatchell Foundation.*

10. Carey Lodge, "Beaten and Abused for their Faith in Jesus: Christian Persecution in India," *Christianity Today,* July 5, 2016, online edition.

11. Ruth Gledhill, "Massive Increase in Persecution Against Christians in India," *Christianity Today,* July 25, 2016, online edition.

12. Heather Tomlinson, "5 Countries Where You Might Not Know that Christians Face Persecution," *Christianity Today,* August 12, 2016, online edition.

13. Ibrahim, *Crucified Again,* 7-8.

14. Ibid., 22.

15. Andre Mitchell, "Humanitarian Warns of the 'Elimination' of Christianity in the Middle East," *Christianity Today,* July 12, 2016, online edition.

16. Maria Abi-Habib, "For Many Christians in Middle East, Intimidation or Worse," *Wall Street Journal,* July 26, 2016, online edition.

17. Julie Bourdon, "Coptic Christians Face Rising Persecution," *Mission Network News,* August 12, 2016, online edition.

18. Cited in Andre Mitchell, "Christians in Egypt Reaching 'Breaking Point' after Experiencing So Much Persecution," *Christianity Today,* September 7, 2016, online edition.

19. Harry Farley, "Christian Persecution Intensifies in DRC as 36 Tied Up and Hacked to Death," *Christianity Today,* August 16, 2016, online edition.

20. Samuel Smith, "Christian Mother of 7 Hacked to Death in Nigeria While Preaching," *Christian Post,* July 12, 2016, online edition.

21. Ibrahim, *Crucified Again,* 98-99.

22. "Jihad Comes to Church," *Christian Concern,* July 29, 2016, online edition.

23. Oliver Lane, "The Islamic State's Dehumanization of Christians Is Nothing New," *Breitbart,* August 10, 2016, online edition.

24. See Steve Byas, "Mary Eberstadt's Book 'It's Dangerous to Believe': The Growing Persecution of U.S. Christians," *New American,* August 10, 2016, online edition.

25. Joseph Hayes, "Christians Should Stand Up, Not Shy Away from Persecution," *Times Herald*, May 27, 2016, online edition.

26. Lea Singh, "How Bad Will It Get? Bracing for Religious Persecution in the West," *LifeSite News*, July 13, 2016, online edition.

27. Cited in Singh, "How Bad Will It Get?"

Chapter 7—Marriage and the Family Unit in a Sexually Dysfunctional Society

1. Archith Seshadri, "The Changing Face of Family," *CNN*, February 7, 2016, online edition.

2. Ibid.

3. Alanna Vagianos, "Redefining the 'Traditional' American Family in 7 Stunning Images," *Huffington Post*, February 2, 2016, online edition.

4. "Same-Sex Marriages in U.S. Up, Domestic Partnerships Down: Gallup," *Reuters*, June 22, 2016, online edition.

5. Joe Dallas, "Now What? Same-Sex Marriage and Today's Church," *Christian Research Journal*, vol. 37, no. 1 (2014), online edition.

6. Ibid.

7. Kate Shellnutt, "ChristianMingle Lawsuit Forces Site to Add Options for Gay Daters," *Christianity Today*, July 6, 2016, online edition.

8. Samuel Smith, "Pastor Saying Premarital Sex Is OK Pushes People Away from God, Greg Laurie Warns," *Christian Post*, August 29, 2016, online edition.

9. These reviews and endorsements are posted at Amazon.com.

10. Farley Goodman, "Millennials More Accepting of Premarital Sex, Have Fewer Partners," *BlogHer*, June 5, 2016, online edition.

11. The Barna Group, "What Americans Believe About Sex," January 14, 2016, online edition.

12. The Barna Group, "No Thanks, Maybe Later," July 9, 2016, www.barna.com, online report.

13. Leonardo Blair, "America's Fall Away from God Is More About Sex than Unbelief, Christian Author Frank Turek Says," *Christian Post*, October 14, 2016, online edition.

14. Aldous Huxley, cited in Blair, "America's Fall Away from God Is More About Sex than Unbelief."

15. Lee Strobel, cited in Norman Geisler and Frank Turek, *I Don't Have Enough Faith to Be an Atheist* (Wheaton, IL: Crossway Books, 2004), 163.

16. Lee Strobel, *The Case for Faith* (Grand Rapids, MI: Zondervan, 2000), 226.

17. J. Budziszewski, "Why I Am Not an Atheist," in *Why I Am a Christian*, ed. Norman L. Geisler and Paul K. Hoffman (Grand Rapids, MI: Baker Books, 2006), 57.

18. Rodney Pelletier, "2015 Porn Stats Show Alarming Trends," *ChurchMilitant.com*, January 17, 2016, online edition.

19. David Kinnaman and Gabe Lyons, *Good Faith: Being a Christian When Society Thinks You're Irrelevant and Extreme* (Grand Rapids, MI: Baker Books, 2016), 122.

20. Reported by Morgan Lee, "Here's How 770 Pastors Describe Their Struggle with Porn," *Christianity Today*, January 26, 2016, online edition.

21. Ibid.

22. Maria Cowell, "Porn: Women Use It Too," *Christianity Today*, October 19, 2016, online edition.

23. Ibid.

24. Ibid.

25. Kinnaman and Lyons, *Good Faith*, 123.

26. Cowell, "Porn: Women Use It Too."

27. Kyle Roberts, "6 Reason Why Kids Sext," *Educate Empower Kids*, October 9, 2016, online edition.

28. Ibid.

29. Michael Allen, "Poll: Nearly Half OK with Transgender, Christians Upset," Michael Allen Blog, July 28, 2016, online edition.

30. Ibid.

31. Ibid.

32. Stoyan Zaimov, "Obama Uses Bible, Christian Faith to Defend Transgender Bathroom Directive to Schools," *Christian Post*, June 3, 2016, online edition.

33. Czarina Ong, "Macy's Fires Christian Store Detective for Questioning Transgender Bathroom Policy," *Christianity Today*, July 28, 2016, online edition.

34. J.I. Packer, *Knowing Christianity* (Wheaton, IL: Harold Shaw, 1995), 138.

35. Matthew Barrett, "Martin Luther on Marriage as a School of Character," *Gospel Coalition*, August 3, 2011, www.thegospelcoalition.org/article/martin-luther-on-marriage-as-a-school-of-character.

36. Walter Martin, *The New Cults* (Ventura, CA: Regal Books, 1980), 28.

37. Dallas, "Now What? Same-Sex Marriage and Today's Church."

Chapter 8—E-Madness: The Escalation of Cyberattacks and Cyberwarfare

1. "One in Three Americans Hacked in the Past Year," *Business Wire*, September 13, 2016, online edition.

2. "A No-Rules Cyberwar Is Well Underway," *San Francisco Chronicle*, August 7, 2016, online edition.

3. Brian Becker, "Cyber Warfare: Hackers Steal NSA Weapons, Offer Them to the Highest Bidder," *Loud & Clear*, August 19, 2016, online edition.

4. Leo Sun, "10 Stats About Cybersecurity That Will Alarm You," *The Motley Fool*, June 25, 2016, online edition.

5. Tim Johnson, "When Does a Cyber Attack Become an Act of War?" *McClatchy DC*, July 15, 2016, online edition.

6. *Cyberpower and National Security*, ed. Franklin Kramer, Stuart Starr, and Larry Wentz (Washington: Potomac Books, 2009), xvi; see also p. 4.

7. Richard Clarke, *Cyber War: The Next Threat to National Security and What to Do About It* (New York: HarperCollins, 2010), 66-68.

8. Jim Setde, cited in Thomas Ice and Timothy Demy, *The Coming Cashless Society* (Eugene, OR: Harvest House, 1996), 146.

9. *Cyberpower and National Security*, 438.

10. See Gerald Posner, "China's Secret Cyberterrorism," *Combined Arms Center Blog*, January 13, 2010.

11. Diana Manos, "Cyber Jihadists Are Gaining Momentum, Report Says," *CIO Briefing Room*, June 29, 2016, online edition.

12. Ibid.

13. Bradley A. Blakeman, "Cyber Warfare More Dire and Likely Than Nuclear," *The Hill*, May 27, 2016, online edition.

14. Jeffrey Carr, *Inside Cyber Warfare* (Sebastopol, CA: O'Reilly Media, 2009), 22.

15. Mary Alice Davidson, "The Many Faces of Malware," *Security Management*, vol. 51, no. 8, September 2007, 120-23, Questia.

16. See John Viega, *The Myths of Security: What the Computer Security Industry Doesn't Want You to Know* (Sebastopol, CA: O'Reilly Media, 2009), 9-10.

17. Anne Layne-Farrar, "The Law and Economics of Software Security," *Harvard Journal of Law and Public Policy*, vol. 30, no. 1 (2006): 283-87, Questia.

18. See Clarke, *Cyber War,* 91-92.

19. See *Cyberpower and National Security*, 25.

20. See, for example, Paul D. Berg, "Dominant Air, Space and Cyberspace Operations," *Air & Space Power Journal*, vol. 21, no. 1 (2007), Questia.

21. Johnson, "When Does a Cyber Attack Become an Act of War?"

22. Carr, *Inside Cyber Warfare*, 1-2.

23. Ibid.; see also Arnaud de Borchgrave, "Silent Cyberwar," *Washington Times*, February 19, 2009, online edition.

24. Clarke, *Cyber War,* 70-71; see also Huba Wass de Czege, "Warfare by Internet: The Logic of Strategic Deterrence, Defense, and Attack," *Military Review*, vol. 90, no. 4 (2010): 85-87, online edition, Questia.

25. "The Cyber-Security Menace Grows," *Compliance Week*, July 1, 2010, HighBeam Research.

26. Dan Tynan, "Cyberwar Is Not Coming to the U.S.—It's Already Here," *The Guardian*, August 4, 2016, online edition.

Chapter 9—The Growing Nuclear and Electromagnetic Pulse Threat

1. Curt Mills, "North Korea Threatens Nuke Strike on Washington," *Examiner*, March 26, 2016, online edition.

2. Ibid.

3. Anna Fifield, "Did North Korea Just Test Missiles Capable of Hitting the U.S.? Maybe," *Washington Post*, October 26, 2016 online edition.

4. "N. Korea's Nuclear Threat Growing after Latest Test," *Manila Bulletin*, September 21, 2016, online edition.

5. Oren Dorell, "U.S. Allies Worry: Russia's Missile Exercise May Be Tip of Nuclear Iceberg," *USA Today*, October 21, 2016, online edition.

6. Ibid.

7. Ibid.

8. Ibid.

9. Ibid.

10. Alex Lockie, "Russia Is Preparing for Nuclear War," *Business Insider*, October 25, 2016, online edition.

11. Rubelle Carmeli Tan, "Russia vs. USA War: Russia Ready for Nuclear Attacks," *Morning Ledger*, October 26, 2016, online edition.

12. Lockie, "Russia Is Preparing for Nuclear War."

13. Ibid.

14. Alexander Nazaryan, "War with Russia Looms, Says Former NATO General in New Book," *Newsweek*, August 1, 2016, online edition.

15. Ibid.

16. Jon Harper, "North Korea, Iran's Advances Fuel Demand for Regional Missile Defense," *National Defense*, April 1, 2016, online edition.

17. Ibid.

18. Paul Bedard, "Expert: North Korea's H-Bomb Is 'Super-EMP' Weapon," *Washington Examiner*, January 6, 2016, online edition.

19. Paul Bedard, "Feds: EMP Hit on Electric Grid Threatens National Security," *Washington Examiner*, May 19, 2016, online edition.

20. Bedard, "Expert: North Korea's H-Bomb Is 'Super-EMP' Weapon."

21. See Bedard, "Feds: EMP Hit on Electric Grid Threatens National Security."

22. Elaine Sciolino, "A Journalist's Dark Perspective on the Nuclear Deal with Iran," *Washington Post*, October 21, 2016, online edition.

23. Frances Martel, "Fact-Check: Iran Deal Does Not 'Eliminate' Nuclear Program," *Breitbart Live*, October 4, 2016, online edition.

24. Ali Ansari, *Confronting Iran* (New York: Basic Books, 2006), 2.

25. Jerome Corsi, *Atomic Iran* (Nashville, TN: WND Books, 2005), 180.

26. Ibid.

27. Martel, "Fact-Check: Iran Deal Does Not 'Eliminate' Nuclear Program."

28. Sciolino, "A Journalist's Dark Perspective on the Nuclear Deal with Iran."

Chapter 10—Powder Keg with a Lit Fuse: Israel and the Middle East Conflict

1. Some of the quotations in this and the next paragraph are from Randall Price, *Unholy War: The Truth Behind the Headlines* (Eugene, OR: Harvest House, 2001), 344.

2. "Iranian Official: We Will Not Recognize Israel," *Middle East Monitor*, June 30, 2016, online edition.

3. "Netanyahu: 'Jerusalem Was Ours and Will Remain Ours,'" *Middle East Monitor*, June 2, 2016, online edition.

4. Rachel Ehrenfeld, *Funding Evil: How Terrorism Is Financed—and How to Stop It* (Chicago: Bonus Books, 2005), 35.

5. Ibid., 125-26.

6. Ophir Falk and Henry Morgenstern, *Suicide Terror: Understanding and Confronting the Threat* (New York: John Wiley and Sons, 2009), 53.

7. Ehrenfeld, *Funding Evil*, 133.

Chapter 11—Northern Storm Rising: The Coming Muslim Invasion Against Israel

1. Some may wonder why the term "Rosh" does not appear in the ESV, NIV, NET, HCSB, and NLT translations except as a marginal reading. The Hebrew word in this verse can be taken as either a proper noun (a geographical place called Rosh) or as an adjective (meaning "chief"). If

it's an adjective, it qualifies the meaning of the word prince, so that it is translated "*chief* prince." Hebrew scholars debate the correct translation. I believe Hebrew scholars C.F. Keil and Wilhelm Gesenius are correct in saying Rosh refers to a geographical place. The evidence suggests that the errant translation of Rosh as an adjective ("*chief* prince") can be traced originally to an early Jewish translator, and later popularized in the Latin Vulgate, translated by Jerome—who himself admitted that he did not base his translation on grammatical considerations. Jerome resisted translating *Rosh* as a proper noun primarily because he could not find it mentioned as a geographical place anywhere else in Scripture. Hebrew Scholar Clyde Billington observes: "Jerome's incorrect translation of Rosh as an adjective has been followed by many of today's popular translations of the Bible. It is clear that this translation originated with the Jewish translator Aquila [and] was adopted by Jerome in the Vulgate." (See "Clyde Billington, "The Rosh People in History and Prophecy," part 1, *Michigan Theological Journal*, 3:1, Spring 1992, 65.) Taking Rosh as a geographical place is the most natural rendering of the original Hebrew (as reflected in the ASV and NASB translations). I see no legitimate linguistic reason for taking it as an adjective.

2. Ilan Berman, *Tehran Rising* (New York: Rowman and Littlefield, 2005), 57-58.

3. Ibid.

4. Kenneth R. Timmerman, "The Turkey-Russia-Iran Axis," *Front Page*, August 22, 2016, online edition.

5. Hazel Torres, "Iran Ready for 'Annihilation' of Israel: More than 100,000 Missiles Ready to Strike at the Heart of Jewish Nation," *Christianity Today*, July 7, 2016, online edition.

6. Ibid. See also Majid Rafizadeh, "Iran: 'More than 100,000 Missiles Are Ready to Strike Israel,'" *Front Page*, July 12, 2016, online edition.

7. Rafizadeh, "Iran: 'More than 100,000 Missiles are Ready to Strike Israel.'"

8. Elad Benari, "Iranian Commander: Ground Is Ready to Destroy 'Zionist Regime,'" *Arutz Sheva*, July 7, 2016, online edition.

9. "Iranian Official: We Will Not Recognize Israel," *Middle East Monitor*, June 30, 2016, online edition."

10. "As Russia and Turkey Cozy Up, U.S. Influence at Stake in Middle East," *Kansas City Star*, August 18, 2016, online edition.

11. Ibid.

12. Sergei Karpukhin, "US Apoplectic as Turkey Pivots Eastward," *RT Op-Edge*, August 19, 2016, online edition.

13. Timmerman, "The Turkey-Russia-Iran Axis."

14. Joel Rosenberg, *Epicenter* (Carol Stream, IL: Tyndale House, 2006), 63.

15. Arnold G. Fruchtenbaum, *The Footsteps of the Messiah* (San Antonio, TX: Ariel Ministries, 2004), Logos Bible Software edition.

Chapter 12—Ready to Rebuild the Jewish Temple

1. Arutz Sheva Staff, "Preparation for Temple No Longer a Dream," *Temple Mount*, August 8, 2016, online edition.

2. Eliran Aharon, "We're Not Embarrassed to Say It: We Want to Rebuild the Temple," *Temple Mount*, August 15, 2016, online edition.

3. Thomas Ice, "Is It Time for the Temple?," article posted at Pre-Trib Research Center, www.pre-trib.org/.

4. Arnold Fruchtenbaum, *Ariel Ministries Newsletter* (Fall 2004/Winter 2005), 4.

5. "New 'Sanhedrin' Plans Rebuilding of Temple: Israeli Rabbinical Body Calls for Architectural Blueprint," *WorldNetDaily.com,* June 8, 2005.

6. Ibid.

7. Ibid.

8. Mark Hitchcock, *101 Answers to the Most Asked Questions about the End Times* (Colorado Springs, CO: Multnomah Books, 2001), iBooks.

9. It is entirely possible that the Ezekiel invasion takes place years prior to the beginning of the tribulation period. I thoroughly document this possibility in my book *Northern Storm Rising* (Eugene, OR: Harvest House, 2008).

10. Thomas Ice, "The Tribulation Temple," article posted at Pre-Trib Research Center, www.pre-trib.org/.

11. Randall Price, *The Coming Last Days Temple* (Eugene, OR: Harvest House, 1999), 592.

12. Ice, "Is It Time for the Temple?"

Chapter 13—The Coming Cashless World

1. Thomas Ice and Timothy Demy, *The Coming Cashless Society* (Eugene, OR: Harvest House, 1996), 125-26 and 80.

2. Robert Thomas, cited in Thomas Ice and Timothy Demy, *Fast Facts on Bible Prophecy from A to Z* (Eugene, OR: Harvest House, 2004), 129.

3. Arnold Fruchtenbaum, *Footsteps of the Messiah* (San Antonio, TX: Ariel Ministries, 2003), 250-51.

4. John F. Walvoord, *Prophecy: 14 Essential Keys to Understanding the Final Drama* (Nashville, TN: Thomas Nelson, 1993), 125.

5. Ice and Demy, *The Coming Cashless Society*, 132.

6. Robert Samuelson, cited in David Jeremiah, *The Coming Economic Armageddon: What Bible Prophecy Warns About the New Global Economy* (New York: Faith Words, 2010), 162-64.

7. Ice and Demy, *The Coming Cashless Society*, 85-86.

8. Jeremiah, *The Coming Economic Armageddon,* 162-64.

9. Mark Hitchcock, *Cashless: Bible Prophecy, Economic Chaos, and the Future Financial Order* (Eugene, OR: Harvest House, 2010), 75-76.

10. As cited in "Will the U.S. Become a Cashless Society?" *Chicago Tribune*, September 9, 2016, online edition.

11. Cited in Jeremiah, *The Coming Economic Armageddon,* 162-64.

12. Aimee Picchi, "Cash Not Welcome Here," *Moneywatch*, August 12, 2016, online edition.

13. Susan Tompor, "A Cashless Society? Some Retailers Turn Noses Up at Currency," *Detroit Free Press*, September 5, 2016, online edition.

14. "Cash Is Losing Its Luster Among Consumers," *BJBiz*, July 18, 2016, online edition.

15. Fernando Florez, "Cashless Society: The Shape of Things to Come," *Accounting and Business*, July/August 2016, online edition.

16. Maggie McGrath, "Death to Greenbacks? Majority of Americans Say U.S. Will Go Cashless in Their Lifetimes," *Forbes*, July 15, 2016, online edition.

Chapter 14—Biometrics and the Loss of Personal Privacy

1. Michael Morisy, "Password Deathwatch? Banks Increasingly Adopt Biometrics to Keep Customers (More) Secure," *Windows IT Pro*, June 26, 2016, online edition.

2. "Biometrics Coming to US Airports," *i-HLS*, June 29, 2016, online edition.

3. "Survey Says 52 Percent of Consumers Prefer Biometrics Over Passwords When Logging into Online Accounts," *Business Wire*, June 28, 2016, online edition.

4. Helen Leggatt, "Age of the Password Almost Over, Security Pro's Favor Behavioral Biometrics," *BizReport*, July 5, 2016, online edition.

5. Praseeda Nair, "Can You Trust Biometrics?" *Growth Business*, August 11, 2016, online edition.

6. See Jason Rose, "Consumer Brands Must Ditch Passwords; Find Future in Biometrics," *MarTech Advisor*, June 24, 2016, online edition.

7. Laura Hautala, "Use Your Eyes, Voice—and Thoughts—to Replace Passwords," *CNET*, July 4, 2016, online edition.

8. "Survey Says 52 Percent of Consumers Prefer Biometrics Over Passwords When Logging into Online Accounts," *Business Wire*.

9. "New Software Brings Facial-Recognition Technology to Mobile Phones," *NewsRx Health and Science*, November 12, 2010, Questia.

10. Hautala, "Use Your Eyes, Voice—and Thoughts—to Replace Passwords."

11. "Now, Ears Too Can be Used for Airport Security ID Checks," *Asian News International*, October 11, 2010, Questia.

12. See Mark Hitchcock, *Cashless: Bible Prophecy, Economic Chaos, & the Future Financial Order* (Eugene, OR: Harvest House, 2010), 74.

13. Stew Magnuson, "Defense Department Under Pressure to Share Biometric Data," *National Defense Magazine*, January 2009, online edition.

14. Ibid.

15. Ian Carey, "Biometric ID that 'Gives Big Brother a Passport to Your Privacy,'" *Daily Mail*, November 5, 2009, Questia.

16. Jaya Narain, "Big Brother Cameras Scan Faces at Car Park," *Daily Mail*, August 7, 2010, Questia.

Chapter 15—Globalism on the Horizon

1. Thomas Ice, "The Emerging Global Community," article posted at the Pre-Trib Research Center, www.pre-trib.org.

2. Ibid.

3. Mark Hitchcock, *Seven Signs of the End Times* (Colorado Springs, CO: Multnomah Books, 2003), iBooks.

4. Thomas Ice and Timothy Demy, *The Coming Cashless Society* (Eugene, OR: Harvest House, 1996), 50; see also David Jeremiah, *The Coming Economic Armageddon: What Bible Prophecy Warns About the New Global Economy* (New York: Faith Words, 2010), 65.

5. Thomas Ice, "Moving Toward Globalism," article posted at the Pretrib Research Center, www.pre-trib.org.

6. Mark Hitchcock, *The Late Great United States* (Colorado Springs, CO: Multnomah Books, 2009), 122.

7. John F. Walvoord, *Major Bible Prophecies* (Grand Rapids, MI: Zondervan, 2000), iBooks.

Postscript—How Then Shall We Live?

1. John F. Walvoord, *End Times* (Nashville, TN: Word, 1998), 218.

2. Ibid., 219.

3. Erich Sauer, *From Eternity to Eternity* (Grand Rapids, MI: Wm. B. Eerdmans, 1979), 13.

4. J.I. Packer, *Alive to God: Studies in Spirituality,* eds. J.I. Packer and Loren Wilkinson (Downers Grove, IL: InterVarsity Press, 1992), 171.

5. Richard Baxter, cited in *Alive to God,* 167.

Other Great Harvest House Books by Ron Rhodes

BOOKS ABOUT THE BIBLE

40 Days Through Genesis
The Big Book of Bible Answers
Bite-Size Bible® Answers
Bite-Size Bible® Charts
Bite-Size Bible® Definitions
Bite-Size Bible® Handbook
Commonly Misunderstood Bible Verses
The Complete Guide to Bible Translations
Find It Fast in the Bible
The Popular Dictionary of Bible Prophecy
Understanding the Bible from A to Z
What Does the Bible Say About…?

BOOKS ABOUT THE END TIMES

8 Great Debates of Bible Prophecy
40 Days Through Revelation
Cyber Meltdown
The End Times in Chronological Order
Northern Storm Rising
Unmasking the Antichrist

BOOKS ABOUT OTHER IMPORTANT TOPICS

5-Minute Apologetics for Today
1001 Unforgettable Quotes About God, Faith, and the Bible
Answering the Objections of Atheists, Agnostics, and Skeptics
Christianity According to the Bible
The Complete Guide to Christian Denominations
Conversations with Jehovah's Witnesses
Find It Quick Handbook on Cults and New Religions
The Truth Behind Ghosts, Mediums, and Psychic Phenomena
Secret Life of Angels
What Happens After Life?
Why Do Bad Things Happen If God Is Good?
Wonder of Heaven

THE 10 MOST IMPORTANT THINGS SERIES

The 10 Most Important Things You Can Say to a Catholic
The 10 Most Important Things You Can Say to a Jehovah's Witness
The 10 Most Important Things You Can Say to a Mason
The 10 Most Important Things You Can Say to a Mormon
The 10 Things You Need to Know About Islam
The 10 Things You Should Know About the Creation vs. Evolution Debate

QUICK REFERENCE GUIDES

Halloween: What You Need to Know
Islam: What You Need to Know
Jehovah's Witnesses: What You Need to Know

THE REASONING FROM THE SCRIPTURES SERIES

Reasoning from the Scriptures with Catholics
Reasoning from the Scriptures with the Jehovah's Witnesses
Reasoning from the Scriptures with Masons
Reasoning from the Scriptures with the Mormons
Reasoning from the Scriptures with Muslims

LITTLE BOOKS

Little Book About God
Little Book About Heaven
Little Book About the Bible

AVAILABLE ONLY AS EBOOKS

Book of Bible Promises
Coming Oil Storm
Topical Handbook of Bible Prophecy

To learn more about Harvest House books and
to read sample chapters, visit our website:

www.harvesthousepublishers.com

HARVEST HOUSE PUBLISHERS
EUGENE, OREGON